# The Fast Path to Corporate Growth

# The Fast Path to Corporate Growth

*Leveraging Knowledge and Technologies
to New Market Applications*

MARC H. MEYER

OXFORD
UNIVERSITY PRESS
2007

# OXFORD
## UNIVERSITY PRESS

Oxford University Press, Inc., publishes works that further
Oxford University's objective of excellence
in research, scholarship, and education.

Oxford   New York
Auckland   Cape Town   Dar es Salaam   Hong Kong   Karachi
Kuala Lumpur   Madrid   Melbourne   Mexico City   Nairobi
New Delhi   Shanghai   Taipei   Toronto

With offices in
Argentina   Austria   Brazil   Chile   Czech Republic   France   Greece
Guatemala   Hungary   Italy   Japan   Poland   Portugal   Singapore
South Korea   Switzerland   Thailand   Turkey   Ukraine   Vietnam

Published by Oxford University Press, Inc.
198 Madison Avenue, New York, New York 10016

www.oup.com

Oxford is a registered trademark of Oxford University Press

Library of Congress Cataloging-in-Publication Data
Meyer, Marc H.
The fast path to corporate growth : leveraging knowledge and technologies to new
market applications /
Marc H. Meyer
p. cm.
Includes bibliographical references and index.
ISBN 978-0-19-518086-2
1. Success in business.   2. Creative ability in business.   3. New products—
Management.   4. Business planning.   5. Marketing research.   6. Market
segmentation.   7. Corporations—Growth.   I. Title.
HF5386.M564 2007
658.4—dc22          2006022341

1 2 3 4 5 6 7 8 9

Printed in the United States of America
on acid-free paper

*To Olga*

# Acknowledgments

This book is the product of many helping hands. Three in particular deserve special thanks: Mark Anzani, whose steadfast friendship and knowledge of the computer industry lent early momentum to my efforts; Neil Willcocks, who has synthesized user-centered design with technology platforms in ways that few can match; and John Helferich, who has helped me think through the business processes needed for enterprise growth.

Others in industry and academia made important contributions to various chapters. These include Northeastern University colleagues John Friar, Fred Crane, Daniel McCarthy, Mario Maletta, and Dennis Shaughnessy; Al Lehnerd, for many years my mentor and dearest friend; and James Utterback of MIT.

Within industry, my deepest thanks go to George Walsh and Peter Tarrant of IBM; Art St. Cyr, Bill Easdale, and Sage Marie of Honda; The MathWorks' Loren Dean, Peter Webb, and Eugene McGoldrick; Joseph Sawicki of Mentor Graphics; Harry Keegan of Braintree Laboratories. There are many associates at Mars, Incorporated that contributed time and thought to this project. I extend particular thanks to Ralph Jerome, Bob Boushell, Tom Collins, Michael Wilson, and Stewart Townsend. I also wish to thank Harry West of Design Continuum for teaching me much about user-centered design; Kristin Boyle for helping me develop methods for validating prototypes; and James Walter, who showed me how to view new services as modular platforms. Equally important to this effort were Terry Leahy, Martin McDonough, and Jeff Curran who all contributed to the chapters on business model innovation and development.

Special thanks go to my students in Northeastern University's High Tech MBA program who, throughout the years, have helped me refine my methods. For specific examples employed at various parts of this book, I owe special thanks to Chad Haering, Subhabrata Biswas, Nathan Butts, Ofer Michael, and

Kevin Clarke. Teaching this cohort of student-managers has been one of the great honors of my life.

This book is also far better for the writing counsel of Richard Luecke. Appealing to my truest passion, Dick would often say, "Marc, if you can't wrap up that chapter in forty pages, just stop and go fishing." Since parts of this book were written overlooking many fine waters here and abroad, I thank Dick for his sage advice.

I had the further good fortune to work with Oxford University Press editor John Rauschenberg. Truly interested in ideas and their application, John was a true partner—and OUP is an outstanding organization.

Perhaps most important have been the support and "encouragement" I received on the home front. I am sure that many authors have heard words akin to, "Husband, get back up there and finish that book. It's going to be great!" Or "Pops, c'mon, let's take a break and shoot some hoops." Or, "Daddy, you work on the neatest stuff. I love those new M&M's!" The bottom line is this: Olga, Max, and Rosa, your words are the gold of this venture I will remember most and forever cherish.

# Contents

# The Fast Path to Corporate Growth

# Introduction

## *The Fast Path to Corporate Growth*

Growth is the goal of every ambitious business. Growth serves the well-being of the corporation and its shareholders. It provides employees with a dynamic work environment and opportunities for advancement. It provides customers with a stream of new products and services. Growth is what every CEO aims for but usually finds illusive. Many companies that do produce growth eventually find it slipping through their fingers. Indeed, we all know of enterprises that grew on the strength of innovative products or services, gained market leadership, but, for one reason or another, lost their lead and began a steady descent—some into the dustbin of business history. Yesterday's leaders in automaking, minicomputing, and photography come to mind. A comparison of the Fortune 100 of even 25 years ago with the current list will confirm how today's leaders often become tomorrow's laggards—if not losers.

Is stagnation and decline inevitable for companies in mature industries and markets? Must all great companies be bumped aside? Decline happens, but that does not mean that decline is preordained. If a company can create and apply technology to solve real problems at one point in its history, no law of nature dictates that it cannot do so again (and again) in the future. Pessimists should be heartened by the example of Apple, which, thanks to the now ubiquitous iPod, is enjoying a renaissance of growth and shareholder prosperity—and with the same driver at the wheel. The company seemed condemned to a niche market. But by applying its technical capabilities and customer knowledge to other needs—by thinking outside the confines of its existing business and toward the convergence of computing and music—Apple escaped its small niche and created a new and fast-growing business. Rivals in the consumer electronics industry were caught flat-footed.

Business renewal does not happen easily. It requires courage and leadership on the part of executives, focused and creative work by teams of dedicated individuals, and a target market waiting to be served. This book presents a framework and methodology, as well as encouragement, for that important work.

## The Perilous Third Phase

Figure I.1 summarizes the challenge faced by many companies: the three-phase market life cycle. In the first phase, an innovative product (or service) is introduced, usually based on breakthrough technology. Initially, sales are low because the performance of the new technology is not perfected.

In the second phase, sales increase dramatically as price and performance improve, and as customers recognize the utility of the new product. Observing this expanding market, fast-following rivals rush in with products of their own. Some are me-too copies; others represent genuine value improvements. Eventually, however, the market is saturated or better substitutes appear, and the product category enters a phase of stagnation and decline. Profits in this third phase almost always fall faster than unit sales.

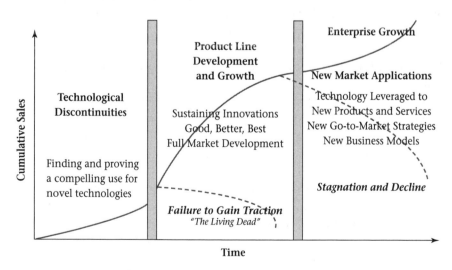

FIGURE I.1  The Challenges of Growth over the Market Life Cycle

This final phase is pivotal in the life of product categories and the companies that provide them. The question is, how can a company get off the downward slope of stagnation and onto the ascending slope of enterprise growth? One way is through acquisition: simply purchase another company that's in either phase one or phase two—perhaps a rival—and ride its coattails through market expansion. Appealing as this solution may be, the track record of acquisitions is discouraging; disappointments outnumber successes. The only sure winners here are the investment bankers who put these deals together, and who reap still more fees when the deals fall apart and are "divested."

## Getting Back to Growth

The innovation literature and industrial practice point to two more promising paths to growth. The first path is the creation of a truly breakthrough innovation—a technological discontinuity. As described so well by James Utterback, breakthrough innovation brings something truly new to the world and represents a distinct departure from existing technologies or forms.[1] The first semiconductor chip fits this description, as do the first inkjet printer, wireless phone technology, the angioplasty heart procedure, and other things we now take for granted. Many of the products that fill our homes and workplaces today—GPS navigation devices, fiber-optic cables, hybrid-powered vehicles, digital imaging, and email—are based on technical breakthroughs. But as every CEO and R&D person knows, projects aimed at developing these breakthroughs are risky and expensive and may not produce revenues for 10 or 12 years, if at all. Those projects that succeed put their companies onto a rapidly rising growth path. But many fall short of technical goals or miss the mark with customers. This is not to say that every technology-based company shouldn't have breakthrough projects in its portfolio; it simply means that they will not stop the downward slope of sales and profits in a timely way. Companies caught in the declining phase of the market life cycle need relief in *two to three years*.

The second path to enterprise growth—and a well-worn path at that—is incremental innovation. This form of innovation improves on or branches from an existing technology or product design. It is close to a company's core business and serves markets and customers the company already understands. The products and services that result from incremental innovation generally require less time and money to develop than do their more radical kin. They are less risky because they are based on proven technologies and are directed to customers already familiar to the company. In many instances, they can be manufactured on a company's existing production line and distributed by the sales force through the distribution channels the company has already developed and refined.

This approach is innovation at the margin, improving something that already exists and enjoys a ready market: a cell phone with a digital imaging feature, a PC with a faster processor, a new version of office application software with more bells and whistles. All are incremental innovations, and to the extent that they address real user needs, they can stem or reverse the downward tide of sales. Brand extensions and product derivatives aim to do the same. As I and Alvin Lehnerd describe in *The Power of Product Platforms*,[2] the challenge here is to create next-generation architectures for these established product lines, architectures that share product and process platforms to reduce cost of goods and time to market. Although this work is less incremental in nature—the development of new architecture, subsystem technologies, and manufacturing processes—it is still aimed at better serving *current users and uses*.

So which path to growth should a company take? The quick answer would be "both." Every well-balanced R&D portfolio contains a mix of incremental and discontinuous projects. If well done, incremental innovation can give a boost to revenues and profits in the short run. The breakthrough innovation route may hold great promise for the future, but many companies cannot wait a decade or more to reap the benefits. They need new revenues right away.

Fortunately, there is a third, less understood path to growth. I call it *new market applications*. That path is the subject of the chapters that follow. New market applications are new product lines and services that leverage a company's technical and, in some cases, production capabilities to serve *new users* and *new uses*. Instead of trying to squeeze new sales out of existing customers with a "new and improved" version of an old product, a new market application focuses a company's talents on an unexploited market segment.

Successful new market applications have the virtue of getting a company onto the growth curve without the high risk, costs, and long development cycles associated with breakthrough innovations. Although the improvement and application of company technology is an essential part of this strategy, a new market application does *not* rely on a technological breakthrough. Projects that do are best left in R&D.

Success here requires management to consider a range of potential market applications—new products or services for new users and new uses. Management can then look at these potential applications through the lenses of *adjacency* and profit potential, as articulated by Chris Zook.[3] Some targets may be clearly adjacent to the current business. For example, a telecommunications company might create a stream of new value added services that leverage its fiber and wireless infrastructures. Other new target applications might be ventures to define and capture a new, emerging market space.[4] For example, a traditional confectionary manufacturer might venture into the bold new world of healthful, nutritious—and higher priced—snacks. Either approach can work, depending on the situation. Some of the firms I studied broke out of their doldrums with bold moves into new market applications, and then exploited their advantage with adjacent developments; others companies prospered my moving aggressively forward markets rich with new, closely related opportunities. Either way, successful companies were all able to leverage their core skills and technology into new product lines and services, making the quest for growth not only exciting but *achievable*.

The best feature of this strategy is that it *gets results quickly* within the context of overall corporate growth. That is why the title of this book is *The Fast Path to Corporate Growth*. In most of the cases described in these chapters, new market applications were launched roughly two to three years after conception; many were profitable within one year of launch. Better still, many new market applications are capable of constituting a *new business*—not just a product line extension.

## What It Takes to Succeed

What does it take to successfully develop and launch new market applications? My studies indicate that innovation is required in three dimensions: marketing, technology, and the business model (figure I.2).

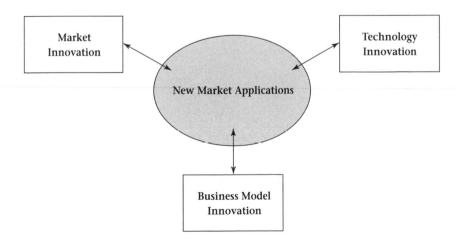

FIGURE I.2 Three Dimensions of Innovation in New Market Applications Development

— *Marketing innovation.* Innovation begins here with market segmentation to identify new target users and users to which a company can leverage its technology. The innovation then extends to user research that embeds the development team in the world of potential new customers. Traditional quantitative methods of market research are secondary; they are no substitute for walking in the shoes of target customers.

— *Technology innovation.* Innovation in this dimension concentrates on two levels. The first is transforming knowledge of users' needs and frustrations into new concepts and then turning these concepts into specific product and service designs. The second level is achieving implementation of those designs wisely. This means adapting working technologies to new applications through a strategy of modularity in architecture and the development of shared subsystems that can be leveraged across those applications. In this way, the shared technologies become enabling platforms for enterprise growth.

— *Business model innovation.* A business model describes how a company makes money. New product lines and services targeting new users or uses offer the opportunity to replace old margin-poor business models with better, margin-rich approaches. Shackling a new market application to an old business model may limit if not destroy its transformational potential.

There is, of course, an important human element to new market applications. These initiatives are driven by teams of employees from R&D, marketing, and other functions who aren't afraid to reach out to customers, observe them in their natural environments, and rapidly develop and test new solutions that meet their needs and remedy their frustrations. Successful new market applications also need executive sponsors who won't try to force square pegs into round holes. If a promising new product line needs a different approach to distribution or pricing or is better suited to outsourced manufacturing than to the company's own production lines, these executives must support what's best for the new product line. More about this later.

## What's Ahead?

This book describes a framework for growth through new market applications. That framework—a series of activities—is explained in chapter 2. Chapters 3 through 11 explain those activities and provide extended examples from exceptional companies. Principal among these are Honda, with its development of the now-popular Element SUV, and Mars, which has launched new candy and pet food products. Many chapters contain templates readers can use in their own projects. Chapters 12 and 13 address the people side of new market applications. These provide plainspoken advice on what executives and innovation team leaders must do to execute the steps of new market applications development.

## The Research Sample

The framework described in this book was synthesized from detailed research with more than two dozen companies over the past decade. These companies represent a broad range of industries, and each has created new product and service lines that have sold successfully to new users and for new uses relative to their traditional offerings. The experiences of these companies are stunningly similar in their planning and execution, organization, and business processes. They include IBM, the world's largest computer company; Honda, one of the most successful and fastest growing automobile manufacturers; Mars, the world's largest confectionery and pet food manufacturer; The MathWorks, a market leader in mathematical computing; EMC, the leader in storage systems; Charles River Laboratories, the world's largest pharmaceutical services company; Mentor Graphics, a respected software company in semiconductor design and testing; and one of the country's largest suppliers of agriculture products. Service companies were well represented in the study group. They included the largest U.S. life reinsurer, the leader in custodial services for the mutual fund industry, and a leading U.S. provider of health care products, systems, and services. One could not have a better group of companies from which to learn methods for achieving internal, organic enterprise growth. In a number of instances, my work with these companies had less to do with survey research and case writing than with working directly with teams to develop new and exciting product and service concepts. These companies provide plenty of examples of how other enterprises can get on a more rapid path to growth—as either an alternative or complement to acquisitions.

Now, you are about to share this journey. Before we launch into the details of our management framework for corporate growth, however, we have a story—a true story of an industry leader that found itself in decline. In the early 1990s, this company's core business was imploding. With sales dropping and losses mounting, something had to be done—and quickly. In this company's reemergence to greatness lie the foundations of the concepts and methods for the rest of the book.

Read on.

## Notes

1. James Utterback, *Mastering the Dynamics of Innovation* (Boston: Harvard Business School Press, 1994).

2. Marc H. Meyer and Alvin Lehnerd, *The Power of Product Platforms* (New York: Free Press, 1997).

3. Chris Zook, *Beyond the Core: Expand Your Market without Abandoning Your Roots* (Boston: Harvard Business School Press, 2004).

4. W. Chan Kim and Renee Mauborgne, *Blue Ocean Strategy* (Boston: Harvard Business School Press, 2005).

# CHAPTER ONE

# IBM Rises from the Ashes

There are few examples of reshaping a withering traditional enterprise as dramatic as IBM's renewal of its mainframe computer business. It is perhaps the greatest industrial turnaround story in American business during the 1990s. Also, it clearly shows the differences between reinvigorating an existing product to better serve *current users and uses* and extending that product line to capture *new users and new uses*.

To make this happen, IBM had to:

1. better segment its markets and research the needs of users in those markets;
2. more effectively translate that understanding into compelling new product designs powered by new technologies; and
3. redefine and then continuously enhance its core business model.

These three areas of innovation are the focus of successive sections of this book and are challenges faced by every corporation, large or small, in the journey toward internally generated growth.

IBM's turnaround is an amazing story of how a management team was able to integrate innovations in all three dimensions, first to save its core business in transactions processing and then to leverage new technology to new market applications. These new applications focused on Web-centric, on-demand computing across major industry vertical markets.[1]

## Dark Days at IBM

The early 1990s were dark days for IBM's mainframe division, the computer giant's traditional powerhouse. The company had completely missed or ignored the client-server technology boom of the mid-1980s, and by the early 1990s, its traditional batch mainframe was sinking. Centralized mainframes controlled in the "glass house" DP shops of big corporations were being replaced with servers decentralized throughout major corporate customers. The engineers who had worked for so many years in IBM's storied research centers saw their careers coming to an abrupt end. They felt adrift in the sea of technological change.

IBM's R&D centers had been the hallowed ground of computing innovation. The Poughkeepsie center had been the heart and soul of mainframes, developing most of its hardware and operating systems technology (essentially multiple virtual storage, or MVS). The Boeblingen Development Laboratory in Germany had been working on mid-range mainframes (IBM S/390 class machines for small business or office environments).[2] Endicott, New York, had developed the mainframe service processor, and certain corporate staff functions were based in another facility in Somers, New York.

First launched in the late 1950s, IBM's mainframes, operating systems, and databases had become the cornerstones of data processing for the world's large corporations. In his classic *The Mythical Man Month*, Frederick Brooks described the development of OS360, which during the 1960s was a pioneering as well as proprietary operating system software.[3] This work, as well as advances in hardware, encryption, and storage, produced a great tradition of innovation in IBM. The mainframe became the king of computing, and throughout the 1970s and 1980s, the engineers who worked in mainframe development centers had every right to feel like kingmakers. Over the next 40 years, technological advances and the sweat of thousands of engineers led to successive generations of increasingly powerful million-dollar-plus machines.

Technological advances in computing over the following decades were breathtaking. By 1995, the effective price per million instructions per second (MIPS) was only 1 percent of what it had been at the launch of the System 360 in 1964. IBM's earliest mainframes were priced at about $256 million per MIPS in the late 1950s; by 1970, about $2 million per MIPS; by 1980, $350,000 per MIPS; by 1990, $100,000 per MIPS; and by 1995, less than $20,000 per MIPS. By the turn of the millennium, the approximate cost per MIPS in a high-end mainframe—IBM's z900 (a recent mainframe)—had tumbled to $2,500. From $256 million to $2,500 per MIPS: a 100,000 times improvement in price performance.

By the late 1980s, IBM's S/390 division accounted for more than $10 billion in annual revenue, and more than 30,000 employees were working on the product line in one way or another. The division was, in its own right, one of the largest manufacturing companies in the country. Everyone within IBM felt that S/390 division remained the heart and soul of the corporation. As it fared, so did the rest of "Big Blue." But by the late 1980s, chinks had begun to appear in IBM's armor in the mainframe business and the corporation as a whole. Large customers were asking for features that the company could not provide in its mainframe products, such as Internet- and intranet-style networking and applications software for online business and collaboration. By the early 1990s, the chinks in IBM's armor had become cracks—cracks that grew into fissures.

Perhaps complacency had set in; the S/390 division might have been too dominant for too long. What is clear in hindsight is that IBM's organization, processes, and approaches to new product development were focused too much on incremental innovation for existing product line architectures. The majority of its resources were allocated to sustaining current product lines. Risk taking had given way to risk avoidance.

For IBM, the move from traditional batch mainframe computing to client server computing and then to distributed peer-to-peer Web-based computing for e-business seemed an insurmountable hurdle. Writing in *Business Week*, John Verity summed up the situation:

> There was a stern John F. Akers telling Wall Street analysts and reporters of a plan: shed 25,000 employees, cut $1 billion from product development budgets, cut $1 billion from administrative expenses, and take a $6 billion charge against 1992 fourth-quarter earnings to cover the terminations and asset sales.[4]

And a few months later, Verity wrote again:

> No question, 1992 was a disaster for IBM . . . the biggest net loss in American corporate history, a 50 percent plunge in its share price, and a hail of criticism that led IBM's directors on January 26 to seek a replacement for Chairman and CEO John F. Akers. Nearly lost in the headlines, however, was a particularly alarming revelation: IBM, it seems, has even lost its touch in mainframe processors and storage systems—a $50 billion worldwide industry that it has dominated for 25 years. While overall sales of such equipment grew by an anemic 2 percent in 1992, analysts figure that IBM's mainframe processor revenues dropped 10 percent to 15 percent in 1992, to about $7.5 billion. At the same time, mainframe rival Amdahl Corp. posted a 48 percent revenue gain. Unisys

Corp., the No. 2 mainframer, reported that its mainframe sales jumped more than 10 percent over 1991. Clearly, the mainframe is not dead. What is dead, though, is revenue growth from the old-style machines, such as IBM's current System/390.[5]

Major technological discontinuities were sweeping across industry, directly challenging IBM's traditional approach to computing. Mainframes had traditionally run the transactions-processing applications in large corporations. For users to get data from them onto their PCs, the PCs were made to emulate mainframe terminals, and then "screen scraping" programs grabbed the data for the user's spreadsheet or some other PC-based application. Client server computing offered a much more elegant and flexible solution for sharing programs and data between large and small computers. Programs and data could be seamlessly downloaded from central computers onto any other computer on a local area network and then run on those computers. By the early 1990s, Fortune 500 companies were adopting Unix- and Windows-based client server solutions wholesale, directly threatening the traditional mainframe solution. Independent software companies such as SAP and Oracle offered client server applications that covered nearly all major operating functions across the enterprise.

There was also a strong trend away from customer applications software to off-the-shelf packages. IBM, again, was not moving with the trend. As a result, these packages were being developed largely for Unix and Windows environments. Data communication between sites was also changing from IBM's proprietary networking standard to Internet addresses: "IP" (Internet protocol) was destroying "SNP" (IBM's proprietary systems network protocol).

IBM's sales force covered up for its aging technology. Its sales force and account management methods are probably the best ever developed in the computing industry. IBM's top salespeople literally became part of their customers' decision-making processes with respect to computers, software, and networking. As the 1980s gave way to a new decade, however, even the world's best sales force could not stem the tide. Customers' needs were changing, and IBM was not responding.

The bread-and-butter customer for the S/390 division was the large, global bank, trading house, insurance company, retailer, or manufacturer. But their needs and organization structures were changing rapidly. These customers were seeking reduced overheads, faster production cycle times, and partnerships with other corporations. These business demands called for distributed computing capable of more closely integrating and synchronizing operations on a global scale, including client-server ERP (enterprise resource planning) systems. Customers also needed an array of Web solutions and office productivity applications within a highly secure environment.

Managers at IBM were not oblivious to these changes. For years, however, they failed to marshal the collective energy and resources needed to address them head-on. And so the company began a long slide toward the abyss.

How deep was the abyss? In 1990, approximately 30,000 IBM employees were working in some way on the development of the hardware, software, and peripheral systems associated with mainframes. Reported net earnings were approximately $6 billion. A year later, the company reported a small net loss. In 1992, the loss approached $7 billion. By 1993, losses exceeded $8 billion! IBM's losses were as large or larger than the annual revenues of many other computer manufacturers. These problems were felt most strongly in the S/390 division, the home of mainframe, where the top thousand S/390 customers accounted for nearly 70 percent of the division's $11 billion revenue.

## Hit from Above and from Below

IBM had two major traditional competitors, Amdahl and Hitachi, during the years of crisis. These rivals began offering features not found in IBM products. While Amdahl never beat IBM at the MIPS game, it consistently sold similar class machines for 20 percent less. Its market share hovered between 4 percent and 7 percent. Hitachi, on the other hand, was working hard on beating IBM at the bipolar large-scale uniprocessor game, just as IBM was abandoning its own bipolar technology for the first generation of mainframes based on CMOS microprocessors.

To hold a logical state (on-off) within a bipolar logic circuit, current is always running through the circuit. Within a CMOS circuit, a burst of current is needed to switch the logical state, but the state is maintained by a much smaller current. This has an enormous impact on power consumption. It also affects size. The continuous current in a bipolar requires circuitry large enough to handle the heat generated. Circuits that were too small would literally fry. At a chip level, a bipolar requires far more energy than CMOS, so these machines required water-cooling systems in addition to the traditional air-cooling from fans. These water-cooling systems were elaborate mechanical developments with a copper piston positioned on the back of each chip, held in place with a retaining housing, and cooled by chilled water flowing through a cold plate.

The analogy might be one house with very powerful lights always left on, day and night, versus a similar house with equal lights controlled by motion sensors, illuminating only when someone walks into a room and then turning off when the person exits. The catch was that while IBM's first CMOS machines were a lot more energy- and space-efficient, they were also a lot slower than the latest versions of the older bipolar chip architecture. And given its huge deficits, IBM did not have enough R&D money to develop both architectures in parallel until CMOS gained the performance advantage.

Hitachi's decision to make a "killer" bipolar machine had a predictable consequence: The next version of Hitachi's bipolar mainframe was even faster than its or IBM's predecessors, and it was at first considerably faster than IBM's first generation of new CMOS-based mainframes.

In 1993, Hitachi introduced the Skyline bipolar microprocessor in its mainframes. These new machines had literally twice the computing speed of IBM's own bipolar mainframes. IBM's large customers—airlines, financial services firms, and retailers—began buying Hitachi's computers for machine-intensive applications. Within several years, Hitachi had taken 9 percent of market share, reducing IBM's share to the mid-70 percent range. This translated into almost a billion dollars of new annual revenue for Hitachi, and a billion dollars less for IBM! That was a billion dollars forfeited to a competitor coming into the market with a better "high end" solution, albeit one based on an aging architecture.

As IBM was being attacked from an expected source, a new set of entrants were gaining even more ground. This was technology from "the low end," multiprocessor versions of RISC-based workstations packaged into small mainframes called "servers." These were running client server operating systems software, which at that time was some version of Unix. Today, that software is Linux, and it is the foundation of open systems computing. It was only a matter of time before these "small" machines would grow to become more powerful mid-sized machines. By the end of the 1990s, Sun Microsystems was offering a RISC-based machine (the UE-10,000), regarded by many as the fastest mainframe on the market for commercial applications. Sun, and other competitors such as Hewlett Packard, had beefed up their machines to achieve mainframe-like throughput.

Even the traditional mainframe had multiuser access to applications and could therefore be called a server. However, the mainframe environment was generally a closed one, living in its own glass house, and not well suited for heterogeneous computing environments. The new breed of servers offered by Sun, Hewlett Packard, and many others was far more suitable to the client-server architecture that raged through industry during the late 1980s and 1990s. Unix, and later Linux, was the key. These computing environments are naturally suited for the peer-to-peer intranet and Internet environments that mushroomed in the late 1990s and are dominant today.

These new machines were also far more scalable than traditional mainframes. A DP manager could start small and then cluster new systems within a distributed processing environment. By the year 2000, a Sun SPARC-Solaris workstation could be purchased for less than $5,000; its high-end UE-10,000 came in at about $1 million. An entry-level mainframe from IBM, in contrast, cost about

$250,000, and its high-end machines cost several million dollars. While less powerful in terms of throughput than IBM's biggest mainframes, these Unix-based machines nonetheless provided significant functionality at a fraction of the price.

Hit from above, savaged from below, IBM had to rearchitect not only its mainframes but also its entire approach to designing, engineering, and manufacturing its products.

By IBM's own estimate, some 80 percent of e-business computing procurements by large corporations in the period 1997–2000 were servers from Sun, storage systems from EMC, networking routers from Cisco, and database software from Oracle. IBM was largely missing in action.[6] Collectively, these companies were staking claims to different segments of the e-business world, and their sales were growing. In 1993, Sun Microsystems reported $4.7 billion in revenue, Compaq $7.1 billion, and Hewlett Packard $20.3 billion. By 2000, Sun had tripled its revenues to $15.7 billion, and Compaq was running at a $38.5 billion clip (it was soon to be acquired by Hewlett Packard), and Hewlett Packard itself reported year-end sales at $48.7 billion.

These competitors were not IBM's only worry; it had to face the reality that there was a new breed of CIO in its core market. Web-focused, e-business aware, this new CIO didn't demonstrate the vendor loyalty that characterized his or her predecessor. The DP people being hired out of college by the Fortune 1000 knew C, HTML, and Java. Schools were not even teaching traditional mainframe computing infrastructure and COBOL programming anymore! The "career customers" who would buy equipment and software only from IBM were disappearing.

These developments spelled disaster for IBM. It still had a strong share of traditional markets but was being attacked by mainframe competitors from one direction and by Unix server manufacturers from another. Worse, it hadn't seriously joined the industry-wide race for development of a new e-business infrastructure. Its once commanding 90 percent market share for all server applications had plummeted to 40 percent. Staff morale was terrible and layoffs were in full swing. By 1995, IBM was developing new mainframe computers and operating systems software with *one third* of the staff it had in 1990.

## Mandate from the Top

Change at IBM started at the top. For decades, IBM had promoted career employees up through the ranks, even to the CEO level. Faced with what many thought was the prospect of bankruptcy, the board agreed that it was time for a change. They brought in an outsider, Louis Gerstner, to run the company.

Gerstner's challenge was massive: IBM was focused largely on slow-growing markets. It was also slow in bringing new products online. An internal study had shown that the average cycle time for developing a new mainframe model from start of R&D to launch was six years![7]

Gerstner demanded and drove change within the traditional bureaucracy. Under his command, IBM adopted a "live by the sword, die by the sword" approach to technological innovation. Small changes in products, organization, and culture would not work. Everything had to change, *without frightening the installed customer base*. Under the new regime, the guiding principle was to make the company's computer designs obsolete with better ones in increasingly shorter time cycles and then *to leverage those designs into new market applications* (which IBM came to call "e-business"). Combined with consulting, systems integration, and hosting services, new hardware and software solutions for these new e-business applications would grow entirely new streams of revenue and restore the company to profitability.

IBM's traditional home base, mainframe computing, became the focal point for change. Four key executives made it happen. First was Nick Donofrio, the division's senior executive; he made the decision to make CMOS pervasive throughout the architecture. Working directly with him was Linda Sanford, who implemented multifunctional team-based philosophies throughout the organization and made sure that new systems were delivered under incredible budget and time pressures. The Donofrio-Sanford team took the S/390 division from its old architecture (known internally as the H series) to its first new architecture, the G series. Dave Carlucci took over the division at the end of 1997 and drove tough decisions regarding open systems server architecture and extending the mainframe brand beyond its traditional online transactions processing (OLTP) roots and into the e-business domain. The result was a second new architecture, the zSeries. Last, there was Sam Palmisano, who became head of the overall server division, which by 2000 included the mainframe group. Palmisano championed Linux and made it both a technical and business reality for IBM. He subsequently became CEO of the corporation and was its chairman at the time of this writing.

### Innovation in the Market Dimension

Target market strategy and a rich understanding of customer needs are the first steps in internal, organic enterprise growth. IBM had to change how it viewed its customers. This started with how it segmented its target markets; that segmentation would reveal specific solutions for different customer groups.

| | Current Markets | | | New Markets<br>New Users |
|---|---|---|---|---|
| | 390 | Unix | Cost | Web, Data mining |
| 250 > MIPS | Traditional DP ↕ | | | ↑ |
| 30–250 MIPS | | | | IBM was not focused on these applications. |
| 0–30 MIPS | | | | ↓ |

FIGURE 1.1 IBM's Traditional Market Segmentation

In the mainframe division, segmentation had been strictly product focused, as shown in figure 1.1, as opposed to a truly customer-focused segmentation. Customer groups are inferred in the figure but not directly stated. In fact, a single customer might possibly use all of the products shown in the figure. This segmentation approach also encouraged product development silos, with one IBM division making large systems, another making mid-sized systems, another making small systems, and each making or licensing their own particular software. Integration between these different systems occurred largely at the customer site.

You can see the focus of the old S/390 group: large computers delivering more than several hundred MIPS. Although there was a category for *new stuff,* shown on the right-hand side of that figure (titled "Web, Data Mining, etc."), that category was seen largely as software applications and peripheral to division's core business. The S/390 division was all about engineering and selling "big iron." This view of emerging client-server and Web applications as peripheral to the core business virtually assured that S/390 engineers would not focus on e-business requirements when developing next-generation machines. In fact, the division's market segmentation grid from the early 1990s could be expressed as a single segment cell: high-volume online transactions processing.

A customer-focused, integrated approach would have shown the migration of customer needs toward client-server computing first and then distributed Web-based computing next. These needs would have then driven more rapid change and integration of IBM's hardware and software products. This was precisely the innovation in market segmentation and user needs research that occurred in IBM during the mid-1990s.

At the time, the S/390 division had no internal marketing staff. Management relied instead on consulting firms. The consultants tried a method that was highly sophisticated and considered state of the art. It differentiated between types of buyer behavior. More than 20 different decision-making categories were identified. Unfortunately, the division's engineers found this behavioral approach confusing. For example, two different types of decision-making behaviors could demand exactly the same type of machine, with the same type of operating systems, database, and data communications software.

IBM then decided to pursue what now seems like an obvious approach: segmentation by industry verticals and company size. The new market segmentation framework is shown in figure 1.2. The division assigned its own product development team to the job of understanding user needs. This team, and the executives sponsoring it, soon learned that users in different industries had different priorities for features such as scalability, heterogeneous environments, and security. Customers within these vertical markets also had different needs, based on their size, in terms of throughput requirements, cost constraints, and

**Market-Driven: Industry Group, Company Size, Incorporating Emerging Markets**

|  | Financial | Distribution | Mft | Telecom | Life Sciences | Etc. |
|---|---|---|---|---|---|---|
| **Fortune 1000** |  |  |  |  |  |  |
| **Medium** |  |  |  |  |  |  |
| **Small** |  |  |  |  |  |  |

IBM focused its user research on the needs/problems for different size customers in each segment, looking at:

> Reliability of equipment
> Scalability of system (spikes in transaction volumes)
> Compression of data (for faster distributed computing)
> Security requirements (cryptography)
> Software needed for e-business and CRM applications

FIGURE 1.2  IBM's Market Segmentation for Server Technology

the type and structure of complementary services to be provided. IBM set about getting its facts straight on each of these issues.

The vertical market approach also allowed IBM to get very specific about the needs of emerging customer groups, such as life sciences. In the old environment, a mainframe was a mainframe. In the new environment, IBM aimed to sell specifically tailored solutions to different customer groups. It no longer assumed that a pharmaceutical company was like a financial services firm, or a brokerage, or a manufacturer.

More important, the segmentation framework included small and medium-sized enterprises—not strictly industry giants. This encouraged IBM engineers to begin thinking about common architectures that could be scaled to accommodate the full range, from small servers to very large servers. The new market segmentation recognized that customers no longer viewed different-sized computers as different universes. This changed the language used within IBM. Instead of talking about mainframes, minicomputers, and workstations, people used the term "server." Using the same descriptor for different models had a powerful effect: engineers—like their peers at Sun, Dell, and Compaq—began thinking about a common, scalable architecture across the entire spectrum.

IBM's market research proceeded along very specific dimensions of user needs, some of which are shown in figure 1.2. The company wanted to know precisely how customers thought about equipment reliability, how they viewed the dimensions of scalability, and how they thought about data and program security. For example, a large brokerage considered scalability as handling without interruption a 15X spike in standard usage on its online transactions processing systems. Just as important, IBM wanted to know how users in different vertical markets thought about mining data about their customers' purchases and how large corporations shared information with their suppliers and channel partners. The answers to these questions became the design drivers that guided the performance parameters of many of the hardware and software subsystems developed for the next generation of large-scale computers.

## Innovation in the Technology Dimension

Technological innovation was IBM's next fundamental dimension for renewal and growth, and product line architecture was the point of the spear.

A product line architecture is simply defined as the major subsystems and the interfaces between those subsystems that are common to all the specific products or models within that generation of the product line. Good architecture, which is modular and scalable, provides the flexibility needed to meet ever-higher levels of performance and to run new types of applications. Poor architecture is limiting. IBM's old mainframe architecture cornered it into the box of online transactions processing (OLTP). IBM's new architecture runs ever-higher loads of OLTP and, at the same time, has separate, dedicated resources for zipping through Linux and Java applications. That's scalability and flexibility all in a single, robust architecture.

Within IBM, product line architectures are referred to as *reference architectures*, where numerous specific models adhere to the major subsystem stated in the architecture, as well as the interfaces between these subsystems. Subsystems that are made common across multiple products—and better, multiple product lines—are the true product platforms. Many corporations make the mistake of seeing their product line architectures as product platforms, because their customers view platforms that way. However, this often leads such firms to try to force-fit a solution into a new market application for which it was never designed and for which it is not really suitable. For example, in IBM, a microprocessor is considered a product platform that can be leveraged across the distinct architectures of mainframes, mid-range servers, and workstations, just as Honda leverages a common engine across a passenger car and an SUV.

## The H Series Mainframe

During the 1990s, IBM shifted through three distinct product line architectures; prior to this, the company's product line architectures tended to last a decade or more. IBM entered the 1990s with a mainframe architecture call the H series, which was based on a 31-bit bipolar microprocessor.[8] Bipolar circuitry was at its core, making H series machines very large, energy intensive, and hard to cool. (Technophiles will relish the detailed description of IBM's technology strategies, mainframe architectures, and subsystem evolution in the appendix.)

IBM's mainframes were large, a thousand square feet large. Figure 1.3 shows an old picture of the glass house with a large mainframe and external storage devices that included disks and tapes for backup. Today, the same picture might show one single four- by eight-foot cabinet containing a System z computer delivering more than ten times the MIPS capacity and also a similarly sized cabinet containing a multiterabyte disk storage system!

These old mainframes had to be delivered on a large tractor-trailer truck. The frames were forklifted into the facility. A team of six to eight people put the frames together and connected the cables, power supplies, and necessary plumbing. The facility had to have a raised floor to accommodate the plumbing. A testament to IBM's field engineering capabilities, a massive water-cooled machine was up and running in one or two days.

FIGURE 1.3 Inside the Glass House: Series Bipolar Processor Mainframe Computers, Circa 1990–1994 (IBM. Reproduced with permission.)

The last derivative product of the H series, the H6, contained up to ten 60 MIPS processors within one system's physical package, and it delivered 450 MIPS. This "old" mainframe was a phenomenal piece of electronic and mechanical engineering. High-voltage electronics were in immediate proximity to copper pipes filled with chilled water to dissipate heat. Cables, as opposed to electronic buses, connected the processors, memory, and I/O channels.

### The G Series: The CMOS Mainframes

By 1993, with the H series as its major hardware offering, IBM's losses reached $8 billion in a single year. Within the S/390 division, the writing was on the wall. IBM's investment in bipolar semiconductor fabrication was enormous, but the only engineers using these chips were in the S/390 group itself. Management also knew that bipolar technology could not keep pace with customers' performance requirements. The technology roadmaps were very clear. IBM was advancing its own bipolar processor speed by 18 percent per year in the early 1990s, whereas CMOS speed was surging ahead at 50 percent gains per year. Mainframes themselves would have to double in power every several years to keep pace with customer demands—so IBM believed. Soon, a bipolar mainframe would have to fill a small house! In an age where hardware budgets were forecast to level, if not decline, that path was not tenable.

In 1993, two very different design plans were floating around the S/390 division. One plan was to build a new mainframe that would provide all the power (450 MIPS) of the H6 but do so with CMOS technology. Staff in Poughkeepsie, the traditional hearth and home of mainframe engineering, championed this plan.

The alternative plan was to make a CMOS mainframe that was substantially less powerful, but for which development would be far less risky. The first CMOS machine would be followed quickly by upgrades to increase throughput. A design group in IBM's lab in Boeblingen, Germany proposed this plan. The German lab had already been working on CMOS microprocessors for smaller IBM machines.

IBM's senior management went with the German plan. It urgently needed a new architecture, and it liked the Germans' CMOS experience. Somewhat shocked, the Poughkeepsie engineers found themselves having to implement the European design.

Toward the end of 1994, after an incredibly intensive two-year effort, IBM released its first CMOS-based mainframe. This new machine—the G series—aimed to stem loss of market share to Hitachi and Amdahl—but it took almost four years of constant improvements to do so. This was a great technological step forward, setting the stage for future developments. However, IBM was still serving *current users and current uses*, that is, large corporations performing on-line transactions processing.

The first product, the G1, was only a tenth the size of the last H6 and used 13 percent of the electricity. It used an electronic bus instead of cables, and fans instead of pipes for cooling. These benefits translated into a much lower total cost of ownership for customers.

Figure 1.4 graphs the performance of the new G machines versus the old H series (as well as the subsequent zSeries). Note that the 450 MIPs in the H6 versus the 100 MIPS in G1. The new machine was four times slower than the last model of the old architecture!

Consider the fortitude needed during this transition period. At 100 MIPS, the new G series would be much slower than the H6. Several years of hard work would be needed before the new CMOS machines would catch up to their bipolar predecessors. At the same time, Hitachi was expected to introduce its Skyline bipolar machine, whose speed was anticipated to eclipse IBM's current H6. IBM would lose a billion dollars of revenue a year to this last of the giant bipolar mainframes. Management had to convince engineers and marketers alike that this fundamental architectural change was necessary and could no longer be delayed.

Another engineering team—outside both the Poughkeepsie and Boeblingen labs—came up with a way to beat the 100 MIPS problem: tightly couple and share loads across separate G computers. This coupling technology, called Sysplex, went a long way toward preserving the installed base during the transition from H to G. Sysplex allowed customers to attach G series machines

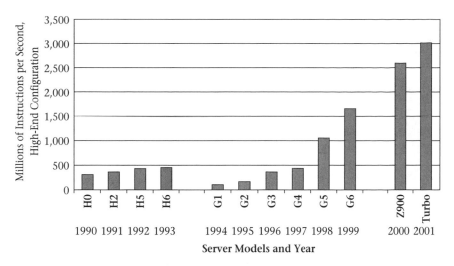

FIGURE 1.4  Three Generations of IBM Mainframe Performance: From H to G to Z

to existing installed H machines to increase capacity without discarding all prior investments. A customer could achieve the power of an old H6 with four coupled G1s.

Despite the risks and pressure, senior management persisted with the CMOS mainframe design. At the time, there was no way that management could have fully anticipated its success. Had G development been seriously delayed, or Sysplex not worked, IBM would have lost many customers. Thus, G series development was a "bet the company" move. Fortunately, the G series architecture had a clear path to add more processors and cache memory. Subsequent models offered accelerating performance.

The G3 (released two years later in 1996) provided even greater benefits: a 95 percent reduction in power, a 98 percent reduction in cooling capacity, and a 90 percent reduction in floor space relative to the old H6. *And* it was as fast as any H machine made by IBM. By the time G4 hit the market, the tide had turned. The system was as powerful as anything in H and offered a much lower total cost of ownership. It had more microprocessor buses, more banks of shared data, and substantially greater capacity to read and write data to networks and storage devices. The G5 that followed in 1998 was twice as fast as the H6, putting both Amdahl and Hitachi under severe competitive pressure IBM pursued its advantage. By 2001, Hitachi and Amdahl exited the mainframe business altogether. IBM was now positioned to take on its other set of competitors, producers of Unix-based servers, and extend its technology to the new market applications of Web-based e-business.

Many readers may ask, "Why didn't the transition to CMOS occur ten years earlier? It was already at least a decade old, and many other companies were using it. IBM itself was using CMOS in other smaller computers. Why was the G series so long in coming?" The answer lies in the design of IBM's organization and its processes. The story of the organizational changes that management made during this time frame is well told in Gerstner's own words and those of a few others.[9]

## The Third Generation: The zSeries
## and E-Business Applications

Having regained its footing in the core business of online transactions processing, IBM was still losing share in the larger server market because it was not adequately addressing client server and more distributed Internet computing. The price of high-end hardware also continued to be a pressing issue. By 1998, for example, the price of IBM's large servers ranged from $250,000 to $3 million per machine. Sun's, by comparison, ranged from $50,000 to $1 million per machine. Also, growth rates for machines over $1 million were in the single digits; growth rates for machines under $50,000 were in the double digits. Additionally, Sun's most powerful computer, the UE-10,000 was fast, reliable, and open to applications and software development tools from the Unix world.

In 1995, the year of the G2, Linda Sanford—a ranking executive in the S/390 division—chartered a team to put together a business plan to compete in the e-business space. IBM would continue to develop successive G series models for the next five years, but in parallel, it would develop a much more powerful architecture: the zSeries.

*Parallel development of next-generation architectures is essential if a company wants to have powerful new solutions available before its current ones "run out of gas." Having been caught at great disadvantage once, IBM's senior management was determined not to let this happen again.*

Sanford assembled a multifunctional task force of mid-level managers from across IBM, including Europe, and asked them to create the growth plan for IBM's server business. These individuals were thought leaders in their respective fields. None had yet achieved executive rank; an executive on that task force might have clung too closely to dated approaches. The team was named ES2000 (for enterprise systems in the year 2000).

In just three months (spring 1995), the team created a new vision for IBM's future that included a new product line of hardware and software, as well as a new business model for the company. The plan synthesized user needs and competitive changes, new hardware and software architectures, channels, branding, and organizational strategies into a unified whole—and then set forth the investment required to achieve a set of projected financial results. In many ways, IBM has been executing the ES2000 plan ever since.

Carlucci and Sanford did more than champion the next-generation solution for e-business computing; they nurtured and empowered the next generation of IBM's executive leaders. Most these mid-level managers went on to executive positions throughout the company.

The ES2000 team came up with the letter "z" to suggest a new dimension of computing. The x and y dimensions in the old world were performance and price; this new dimension symbolized dynamic management and coordination of all subsystems in the computing architecture. The subsystem that would deliver dynamic management within the "z" architecture was called the intelligent resource director. This was a reincarnation of a capability that had been left behind with the H Series on account of time pressures but that the team wanted to bring back into the zSeries. This feature, *multipoint switching*, is an important part of the secret sauce of today's machines.

As successive G series machines were being developed, IBM engineers fondly recalled earlier approaches to achieving scalability. "Let's bring back the multipoint switching of the H," they concluded. This was initially done for the G5 and extended to the G6, the last of the G series line. However, in the new zSeries, the data flows were substantially larger, making the microcode implementation of multipoint switching much more complex. That implementation became known as the Intelligent Resource Director.

Development of the Intelligent Resource Director ranks as one of the computer industry's largest CMOS design efforts. It dynamically moves capacity between partitions in microprocessor-addressable memory and channels (for I/O to storage devices and networks). It allows, for example, a brokerage firm to achieve that 15X peak performance over standard utilization without interruption.

The intelligent resource director and many other highly innovative subsystem innovations came to market in the year 2000 as the z900. All microprocessors used in the zSeries were newly designed 64-bit, RISC-based CMOS chips—called Blueflame. The 31-bit microprocessors of the G series could access only two gigabytes of random access memory. Blueflames could access as much memory as IBM chose to place in the box. The combination of the Blueflame and Intelligent Resource Director innovations created a powerhouse machine. In striking contrast to the earlier H to G transition, a standard z900 systems configuration delivered 2,600 MIPS, which was a *1,000 MIPS faster* than the last machine in the G series.

IBM also sought to make its mark in the software domain by leveraging its mainframe technologies to new users and uses. IBM had been working its way toward "open systems" by providing a Unix emulator within OS/390. However, the new Web commerce applications needed more than just the Unix operating system: The language of these applications was Java components, TCP/IP, and Web programming languages such as HTML and XML. These were foreign to the traditional mainframe world but became the rage in the second half of the 1990s. Fortune 400 accounts were spending heavily on e-business and developing these applications on *other manufacturers'* machines, networks, and programming environments.

To combat this, IBM executives took the bold step of introducing Linux as a native operating system on the G6 in 1999. Even though IBM had tremendous Unix expertise in its Austin, Texas, workstation division, there were simply too many versions of Unix available during the late 1990s to allow true cross-machine software portability. Fortune 400 IT managers worried about version control, applications compatibility, and security.

Linux was new. It also offered an opportunity to achieve excellence in an arena not yet dominated by competitors.[10] At the same time, IBM wanted to prevent the fracturing of Linux that had hurt Unix; it did this by supporting the open standard/open source status of Linux in every way possible.

IBM's German lab had been working in stealth mode to make Linux run on the new Blueflame microprocessor. When managers of that lab made their work known, IBM executives on both sides of the ocean were excited. IBM had a working version of Linux available for its new Blueflame microprocessor. The timing could not have been better.

Dave Carlucci insisted that the entire company—not just the mainframe division—commit itself to supporting and featuring Linux across all its servers. The zSeries was launched with both native Linux and IBM's proprietary operating system called zOS to run traditional applications, such as decade-old COBOL programs.

Once the first zSeries machine—the z900—was launched, development continued to accelerate. IBM introduced the z900 Turbo in 2001 and, with it, broke the 3,000 MIPS barrier. In spring 2001, within only a year of the first zSeries introduction, the z900 was given the "best hardware platform" award at Linux World. Who would have guessed in 1995 that a mainframe would walk away with a major open systems prize?

zSeries has since been renamed System z, and it has been an incredible success. By 2004, it achieved 9,000 MIPS with a 32 co-processor configuration in the zSeries 990. Reflecting a "better, best" product strategy, IBM also introduced at the same time the zSeries 890, a 1,360 MIPS four-processor machine for less computing-intensive applications. To more than a few observers, the 890 was a "Sun killer." zSeries machines were also equipped with special application assist processors, specifically designed to efficiently run the Linux operating system

and Java applications while still running core zOS applications on general processing engines.

By 2005, a number of important trends were in full force. Corporations
wanted to migrate their financial, manufacturing, customer management, and
internal communications systems to an intranet/Internet foundation. IT managers were also consolidating data, systems, and processes on "mainframe
servers." Mining dispersed databases for better customer and product insights
became another top priority. And secure access and data protection were as
important as anything else. These all played to IBM's strengths.

## Business Model Innovation

In addition to market and technology innovation, IBM made important
changes in its business model. As we shall see in later chapters, a business model
is more than financial numbers. A business model is not what you do; it's how
you make money doing what you do.

The ES2000 team proposed a radically different approach to IBM's business
model for software. Up to that point, IBM had garnered substantial revenue
from licensing its proprietary operating systems to customers. With Linux,
IBM made a 180-degree turn. It made the unconventional yet essential decision to use third parties to sell and support Linux, the cornerstone of its foray
into open systems computing. IBM would no longer make money on the sale
of the operating system. Rather, it would make money on the development
and licensing of software created to run on that operating system. Further, it
would foster the development of as many third-party Linux tools and applications as possible. To do this, the company had to help software vendors rather
than compete with them.

IBM selected independent companies to distribute and support Linux for its
new zSeries machines. These included RedHat, Suse, and TurboLinux. It then
handed its software development tools over to Linux and either acquired or
developed many more. It also applauded when Sybase, SAP, and Oracle did
Linux ports for their own products. By the end of 2002, there were some 2,000
off-the-shelf commercial software products available for Linux.

The ES2000 team also saw that IBM would have to invest heavily in im-
proving software development and integration tools for its new mainframes.
Today, this is called "middleware." IBM became one of the market leaders in
Java-based middleware (with its Websphere, Information Management, and
Tivoli storage management offerings). Getting to this point required a her-
culean effort.

New business models need to be supported with forceful marketing and branding. Gerstner, coming from Nabisco, understood this and asked the company's Internet Division to form a team similar to ES2000 to assess IBM's product positioning and branding. Three very powerful ideas emerged from the marketing team's work. First, e-business would help IBM's customers increase efficiencies, shorten cycle times, and lower costs in their operations and supply chains. Second, the Web would build a closer connection between companies and their customers, strengthening customer loyalty, and extend market reach to new customers. Third, intranets developed within companies would help them make their own employees more effective and productive. This, in turn, would improve new product development, service deployment, and sales. The marketing team took these core benefits to the next level by translating each benefit into tangible systems and services requirements for all other divisions across IBM. It also created a single, unified promotional message around e-business. Gerstner was prepared to place $1 billion on the table to communicate the new e-business brand.

IBM then made the very unconventional decision to *not* copyright the term "e-business." IBM hoped that other companies would use the term "e-business" in their own marketing, lending credibility to a new concept in which IBM would strive to be a leader in both product and in image. Within five years, Hewlett Packard's brand became "e-services," Compaq's "non-stop e-business," and Oracle's "the engine of e-business." EDS created its new e-business solutions unit, and even Microsoft started touting "the Business Internet." The snowball effect was far greater than IBM could have predicted. Within three years of the e-business brand launch, the company found itself having to differentiate. In 2000, IBM launched "e-business infrastructure™" and allocated another $300 million to this campaign. That brand campaign has continued to evolve and was recently enhanced to focus on "e-business on demand." Then, IBM extended its on-demand brand to "hosting on demand" for application servers, "capacity on demand" (blade servers), and "information on demand" (database access), all reflecting IBM's Web services architecture.

This business model innovation transformed IBM from a company that made most of its money selling "big iron" to one that would provide complete solutions for customers: hardware, middleware, and services that would wrap around the operating systems and end-user applications made by independent companies. Approximately half of the company's revenue during the zSeries epoch came from professional services.

The combined effects of market innovation, technology innovation, and fundamental changes to IBM's business model transformed a company that was on its deathbed into one of the fastest growing and most profitable technology companies in the world. E-business continues to reveal new users and new uses. From a low point in 1993 of $8.1 billion in losses on about $63 billion in revenues, IBM closed out 2005 with more than $91 billion in revenues and $8 billion *in profits*. Like the phoenix, IBM emerged from the ashes.

## Take Courage from IBM's Example

What can we learn from IBM's successful turnaround and growth? Perhaps the most important lesson is that a company with good people and good technology doesn't have to go on an acquisition binge in order to grow. It can grow from within—by leveraging its capabilities to new users and uses. Another lesson is that good people and technology are insufficient. A growth-seeking enterprise needs a strategy for leveraging its technologies into new market applications. It also must invest in R&D. IBM would not have pulled back from the brink without the core technology work done in Germany and the systems developed in Poughkeepsie.

A powerful marketing strategy that creates excitement for new product lines and services is also a must. Gerstner understood the power of marketing and branding; e-business and On Demand have helped fuel IBM's resurgence.

Finally, senior management must be committed to growth, willing to structure the organization to better pursue it, and not be afraid to empower teams and *share their risks*. Executives must have "skin in the game."

It would be naive to generalize this much from a single case. But IBM is not unique. Other companies have found the path to internally generate growth through similar marketing, technology, and business model innovations. You'll meet some of them in the chapters that follow. But first, let's turn to a framework you can use—a practical roadmap—for getting on the fast path to growth.

### Notes

1. I wrote this chapter with the valued help of Mark Anzani, an executive of IBM. It draws on the work we did (with George Walsh, another executive with IBM) for an article in *Research Technology Management*, which is the journal of the Industrial Research Institute. Peter Tarrant, an executive leading IBM's branding initiatives during the turnaround, was another invaluable source of information. See: Marc H. Meyer, Mark Anzani, and George Walsh, "Innovation and Enterprise Growth: How IBM Develops Next Generation Product Lines," *Research Technology Management*, July–August 2005, 34–44.

2. IBM, MVS, VTAM, DB2, S/390, AS/400, RS6000, zSeries, and System z are registered trademarks of IBM. Solaris and Java are trademarks of Sun Microsystems.

3. Frederick Brooks, *The Mythical Man Month, Anniversary Edition: Essays on Software Development* (Reading, MA: Addison-Wesley, 1995). Also see Carliss Y. Baldwin and Kim B. Clark, *Design Rules*, Volume 1 (Cambridge: MIT Press, 2000).

4. John Verity and Stephanie Forest, "Does IBM Get It Now?" *BusinessWeek*, December 28, 1992.

5. John Verity, "Guess What: IBM Is Losing Out in Mainframes, Too," *Business-Week*, February 8, 1993.

6. By the turn of the millennium, IBM would be competing head to head with Sun, supplying drives to EMC, and competing with it on storage systems. IBM had also sold portions of its networking division to Cisco and was working in partnership with Cisco for the mainframe business.

7. Marc H. Meyer and Paul Mugge, "Make Platform Innovation Drive Business Growth," *Research Technology Management*, January–February 2001, 25–39.

8. Customers would know products based on that architecture as the 9021 family.

9. Louis Gerstner, *Who Says Elephants Can't Dance?* (New York: Harper Collins, 2003); Marc H. Meyer, Mark Anzani, and George Walsh, "Organizational Change for Enterprise Growth," *Research Technology Management*, November–December 2005, 48–56.

10. Linux was initially created by Linus Torvalds, then a student at the University of Helsinki in Finland. He had an interest in Minix, a small UNIX system, and decided to develop a system that exceeded the Minix standards. He began his work in 1991, when he released version 0.02. He kept improving the system and released 1.0 in 1994, just as IBM was working on its first CMOS mainframe. By the end of 2000, Linux had had almost several dozen major kernel releases.

# CHAPTER TWO

# A Framework for Action

*A business process for new market applications with three
phases for each project—Growth strategy formation as an
ongoing process for the business unit—User-centered design,
product and platform development, scale and ramp up as
three phases—for each team—Time horizons.*

The IBM experience described in the previous chapter poses an important
question: Must a corporation undergo a near-death experience to realign attitudes, organization, and processes with systematic innovation and enterprise growth? My study indicates that a close encounter with the grim reaper
is not a necessary precursor to internally generated growth. As long as people
are diligent in seeking ideas for products and services to serve new uses and
users, growth is possible without having to stare into the jaws of business
oblivion.

Ideas are essential for growth, but even great ideas are insufficient for success. Few of the companies studied for this book were short of ideas. What
many lacked was an effective framework, or process, for developing those
ideas into viable businesses. The traditional processes used to develop incremental products and product line extensions did not suffice when new market applications were the goal. When managers think about growth, too
many—particularly in technology-intensive industries—think narrowly
about new technology. A new technology, however, does not necessarily make
for a good product, nor does a good product necessarily make for a good business. Successful organic growth is about creating a profitable business that
leverages a firm's core technology to new market applications. Profitability is

enhanced when these new applications share common product and process platforms.

Enterprise growth also requires as much market innovation as technological innovation. The very definition of the new market application means that the corporation must learn about the needs, preferences, and frustrations of potential customers and how they currently use products and services. And that learning must be done fast as well as effectively; in the companies I studied, often the most learning took place as the new product line was being test-marketed on *real* users. Much less was learned from traditional types of market studies prior to launch.

Growth through the development of new market applications may also require a firm to embrace innovation in its core business model. The new product or service line may require or allow a fundamental change in how a firm prices its offerings, the channels it uses to reach users, and whatever forms of recurring revenue from services or product add-ons it might enjoy. That means that in addition to user research, product prototypes, and user tests of those prototypes, an innovation team developing a new market application must also build (and sell) a tightly integrated business plan to senior management.

Many of the companies studied for this book have been leaders in their traditional markets, and each has been adept at incremental improvements to core product lines. However, all have found that leveraging current technologies to new users, for new purposes, and even through new channels is a harder nut to crack. Yet, all want to do it. Consider the recent pledge of George Buckley, the chief executive of 3M, to shift the "psychology" of the company toward opportunities that "leverage 3M's technology and development skills into even greater sustainable growth."[1] In effect, the CEO is taking the company back to its roots, for 3M is well known for its prowess in creating new technology and leveraging it into thousands of products for many new market applications.

It is rare that I encounter a company without ideas for growth or enterprising individuals struggling to make those ideas realities. What most desire and need, however, is an effective process for planning, prototyping, prioritizing, and scaling up new product lines and services. No doubt, existing organizational hierarchies and business norms can create formidable barriers to internal enterprise growth. The companies in my research that overcame these barriers did so through teamwork, creativity, diligence, and executive support. These companies also worked differently. Their success is the foundation for the business process presented in this chapter—a management framework specifically designed for the rapid and effective development of new market applications: the fast path to corporate growth.

## The Framework

The following pages describe a business process whose goal is to reach a rapid test market for new market applications, and if that test market warrants continuance, to scale the business to seize market advantage. The fast path to growth is a business process with a central framework. As presented here, it has specific "templates" for each part of the framework that readers can apply to their own efforts. The remaining chapters of this book explain these templates and illustrate them with examples from many different industries.

The underlying philosophy of this framework is *rapid launch and learn, aggressive ramp and scale.* "Ramp" refers to higher volume manufacturing or service deployment, and "scale" refers to fuller distribution and other forms of market penetration. Figure 2.1 captures this simple yet powerful two-phase concept.[2] You can see that one phase of the process is labeled "prove the business"—which in this case is to not only build a new product line or service to market test but also develop a business plan for marketing, producing, and making money that is validated in the market test. With that validation, the company can more safely invest in scaling up the new business.

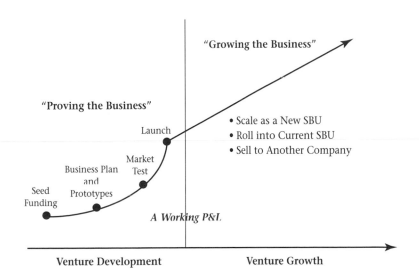

FIGURE 2.1 The Trajectory for Business Ventures:
Prove the Business, Then Scale It

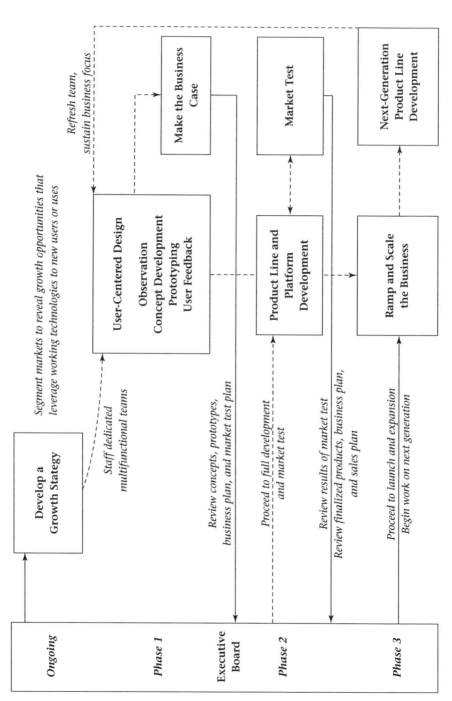

FIGURE 2.2 Framework for Developing, Testing, and Scaling New Market Applications

Teams that work within this framework do far more than develop new product lines or services. They are business innovation teams—not just product development teams—creating new businesses with new streams of revenue.

The framework shown in figure 2.2 is also a roadmap to the remaining chapters of the book. It has three distinct phases for each development effort, preceded by an initial activity to identify new market application opportunities. Each phase leads to the next and then circles back to begin anew. Unlike more traditional business processes for product development, the "launch" is hardly the end; in some ways, it is just the beginning.

## Develop a Growth Strategy

Growth strategy development is the foundation for all that follows. Without a clear, focused corporate growth strategy, developments will be opportunistic, ad hoc, and subject to the whims of turf holders. This activity is continuous and, if successful, will spawn multiple new market applications. For example, IBM's e-business growth strategy led to new hardware products, new software products (proprietary and Linux based), and the creation of consulting, systems integration, and hosting or outsourcing as new services. Both initiatives, however, were part of a strategy that aimed for dominance in the new e-business applications being embraced by corporate users.

Strategy can be expressed in many ways. Among the companies studied, the simplest and most powerful expressions of growth strategy were couched in terms of solutions for particular target users and specific target uses. This way of expressing strategy is not new. It was first described by Derek Abell in *Defining the Business* but remains vital today because of its power and simplicity.[3] Corporate planners and consultants, in contrast, have made growth strategy obtuse, overly complex, and difficult to operationalize. For our purposes here, the specific purpose of strategic planning is to identify a handful of highly promising projects that are both technically feasible and commercially attractive, that focus on new users or new uses, and that can support new and profitable product lines or services.

To be effective, a growth strategy must be specific in terms of its target markets and the emphasis of its products and/or services for those markets in terms of form and function and in terms of position on the price-performance spectrum. Looking ahead to some of the companies profiled later in this book, concrete growth strategies might be to:

— create a new sports utility vehicle suited to the first-time young male car buyer, when previously the company's products had focused on families and young single women;

— sell premium marine products for powerboats when in the past the company has served only sailboats;

— leverage the mathematical modeling and simulation tools developed for engineers into premium quantitative modeling and analysis tools for financial services and biotech companies;

— develop new pet food products that appeal to a dog's inner instincts and command a price equal to that of leading premium brands, when in the past the company focused primarily on "value" segments;

— leverage a company's traditional excellence in making tasty snack foods into the burgeoning arena of health and wellness;

— move the corporation from breeding research model rats and mice to full-service drug development and testing services.

As statements of strategy, these are clear and powerful to anyone with some knowledge of industry. Clarity of strategy gives innovation teams clarity of purpose and a direct path out of the "fuzzy front end."

No strategy is complete without a clear target market objective. Where in the wide market of current and potential customers should the company set its sights? Market segmentation provides an answer. As an element of strategy, market segmentation points the way by subdividing the universe of customers into identifiable groups and revealing business opportunities. This is the first step toward targeting the group or groups for which the company is ideally suited to leverage it technology and know-how. Among the firms studied, market segmentation always revealed at least two or three tangible, pragmatic growth opportunities. As described by W. Chan Kim and Renee Mauborgne in *Blue Ocean Strategy*, most firms were able to find "white spaces," or gaps between existing solutions in various markets.[4] I call this "segmenting markets for growth." Chapter 3 reveals the methods used by the companies I studied to identify opportunities for new product line and service development.

Once growth opportunities are identified, prioritization is the next order of business. "Focusing on two or three growth projects," said one executive, "is more likely to produce a new business for us than throwing two dozen balls up in the air and seeing which ones actually land well." We will see how, for example, The MathWorks, a software company committed to internally generated growth, focused first on leveraging its software to modeling derivatives in the financial services industry. Once it gained traction with lead customers, the company went after systems biology applications—an entirely different set of new customers. Similarly, as Honda's light truck division was launching a new SUV for young men, it putting the finishing touches on a new pickup truck (the Ridgeline).

Forming and articulating a growth strategy is the bedrock of all subsequent activity. It cuts across multiple new market applications development efforts within a business unit and needs to be a continuous process. This is why it is labeled as "ongoing" in figure 2.2. Once teams are formed to tackle opportunities that emerge from this strategic market segmentation, they, too, may want to make finer cuts on that part of the segmentation that applies directly to their own specific project.

Strategy formulation requires constant vigilance with respect to users and their product, system, and service uses. It also requires ongoing attention to competitors, technology suppliers or partners, and regulators. That vigilance should uncover two or three important new market applications opportunities every year. The executives who "own" strategies need to be particularly alert. At IBM, for example, executives on portfolio management teams—people who make new product and technology investment decisions—spend much of their time visiting lead customers. They keep their radar tuned to emerging needs, competitive threats, and potential technology partners. One of the senior executives who helped with the first chapter of this book—an R&D executive—allocates more than a third of his time to visiting customers.

## Phase 1: User-Centered Design and the Business Case

We will now look at three distinct phases for *each* new market application development, which, if successful, will lead to a new product line or service that will drive new revenues and profits to the corporation.

Phase 1 of the management framework entails two parallel activities: *user-centered design* and *making the business case*.

### User-Centered Design

User-centered design combines four activities: (1) observing user behaviors, (2) translating those observations into product and service concepts, (3) creating prototypes based on those concepts, and (4) having users interact with and provide feedback on these prototypes. Chapters 4 and 5 focus on the concepts and methods of user-centered design. The purpose of these four activities is to develop design drivers—not just for single products but for entire product lines. A company can make money on a great new product, but it can make a fortune on a successful new product line.

Users can be understood at different levels: at a conscious level, where users can readily articulate their needs, and at a deeper level, where they cannot. Fortunately, that deeper level can be penetrated through close observation of the user in his or her environment and by exposing potential customers to prototypes.

In *The Power of Product Platforms*, Al Lehnerd and I referred to the revelations of that deeper level as *latent needs*. Satisfying just one latent need with each generation of a new market application sets the stage for a winning business.[5] This approach to design is very different from traditional approaches that delve quickly into feature-cost matrices and that are focused largely on "doing what we already do, but doing it better." Such innovation may well lie in the product, in the packaging of the product, or even in how the product is merchandized.

Prototyping and user tests help companies uncover latent needs. As noted by Steven Wheelwright and Kim Clark, managers too often treat prototyping narrowly, as a technical tool for finding technical solutions. It is capable of much more.[6] Prototyping and user testing provide insights for product strategy (good, better, best offerings) and marketing strategy (optimal channels and communications). The prototyping process itself, if implemented holistically, helps validate the business plan, which is developed in parallel with user-centered design.

### Make the Business Case

Phase 1 of the management framework also encompasses the development of business plans for new market applications. We have all seen many business plans. The best plans focus on target markets and solutions and integrate specific strategies for marketing, product or service development, and manufacturing and/or fulfillment. Solid business plans also explain how the product line or service generates revenues and profits, as well as the investments required to grow the business over time. The great challenge in business planning for new market applications comes when the most attractive and logical business model for the effort differs from the company's traditional business model. When that happens, executives and staff may be tempted to compromise the new product to *fit the corporate mold*: "Let's change the design so we can manufacture it on our existing equipment." "It will be easier to distribute if we use our existing channels and sale force." Such changes can do irreparable harm to a winning product or service concept. The new users might prefer a different channel, new uses may warrant a much higher price (compared with the company's core products), or the company's manufacturing assets may not be well suited to a low-volume, more complex product offering.

In traditional new product development processes, senior executives review and approve or reject prototypes and business plans in separate stages, typically separated by many months. In the process advocated here, user-centered design and business planning are done in parallel and must be approved as a single package. One without the other leaves too much at risk. A change in packaging can totally change conversion costs, a channel decision can prove totally unsuitable for a product prototype, and a change in target market may make a product concept totally unfitting for its intended use. Product and plan must go hand in hand, both within an innovation team and within senior management. Chapters 9 and 11 examine how the companies I studied approached business model innovation and then the specific techniques employed for projecting profit and loss, as well as capital needs.

During this phase, the team should also develop a focused plan for market-testing the product—an activity that comes in the next phase of the framework. This might be a beta-site program for a software or services company, where several lead customers work with the new offering for two or three months before general release. Or it might be a special agreement with a retailer to have a dozen or more stores market-test the new product for three months in return for exclusivity the year after. Either way, market-testing is an essential part of rapid "launch and learn," and a team must tell management what it plans to do.

## Phase 2: Product Line/Platform Development and Market Test

Phase 2 of the management process also has two key activities—*product and platform development* and *market test*. Once the first is sufficiently under way, the second can be run in parallel to save time.

### Product and Platform Development

Once they get the green light from executives, teams must "productize" their concepts, developing not only the necessary form, function, and optional features of a product but also the product's packaging. Go-to-market offerings or stock-keeping units (SKUs) must be defined, packaged, and priced. The production processes required for product, package, and services must also be defined and implemented.

A prototype is not a product. Unfortunately, managers without technical experience often try to force innovation teams to quickly make prototypes commercial products without serious investments in product architecture and in product or process platforms. As expressed by Alan Cooper, "prototypes are experiments made to be thrown out, but few of them ever are . . . a manager looks at the running prototype and says, "Why can't we just use this?""[7] This product may in fact be launched faster, but it never really works or soon breaks down under stressful use.

In the successful companies I studied, innovation teams used their prototypes to aggressively focus on specific user needs and desires but then regrouped to design a robust architecture and all of its component parts—be it for hardware, software, food, or drugs.

A product line for a new or existing market application rarely succeeds on the back of a single product or service. A company that approaches each product or service as a one-off is unlikely to make the profits it deserves or move its various offerings to market in a timely manner. Success is more likely when a product line offers a range of features, performance levels, and prices. Numerous successes across consumer, industrial, and service industries show that creating *good, better, and best* offerings often helps a company provide users with choice and expand the market for its product line or service. Further, the new market application might require a company to develop a combination of products and services, hardware as well as software, or allow for add-ons or plug-ins developed by business partners.

Developing a closely related set of products or services—as opposed to a single product or service—presents certain challenges to an innovation team in terms of engineering cost, manufactured cost, and time to market. However, these challenges can be minimized when the range of solutions shares a common architecture. That architecture, in turn, utilizes both common subsystems and common manufacturing assets or service delivery mechanisms. Sharing a product subsystem or manufacturing process across different products produces a true "product platform." The design of product platforms and a "good, better, best" product strategy is the focus of chapter 7. Specific activities to identify intellectual property created in a new market application—and how best to protect that intellectual property either through patents or via preservation as a trade secret—are also an essential element in this phase of the framework.

Using an existing manufacturing asset to produce a new product line can be the most powerful platform of all in terms of saving money and time. In the forthcoming chapter on Mars, Incorporated, for example, we will see how that company manufactured a chocolate-rich, heart-healthy bar for adults on the same line used to produce snacks for kids. In this regard, the successful manufacturers studied for this book made a practice of improving the concurrent engineering for their new products. This means designing a new product for efficient manufacture as well as for user function. Concurrent engineering, in one way or another, was an empowering concept across all industries I studied. For software teams, it meant designing core infrastructure and services to provide remote diagnostics, to facilitate Web-based customer support, and to support unanticipated future plug-in enhancements or add-ons. For service innovation teams, full-scale deployment typically meant integration into established business administration and customer support systems and processes.

### Market Test

A focused test market is another important Phase 2 activity. Executives should expect to receive a detailed market test plan soon after approving the business plan for the new product line or service. For some teams studied, this was no small matter, involving as much detail if not more than the business plan itself!

Few corporations allocate funds for a new market application without market validation. A market test that measures customer response can provide the needed assurance. Among some of the companies studied, regional test markets were used to reveal the extent of user demand. Others tested new uses within their current customers. Yet others enlisted the services of third-party market research companies to perform rapid market tests. Regardless of the method used, management must see that real customers in the new target market space will pay real money for the new product line or service.

Some managers studied saw these rapid test markets as more effective replacements for traditional survey research that their companies had traditionally used to test-market acceptance for new products.

A properly executed test market also gives the innovation team an opportunity to debug its new offering, its delivery, and how the benefits of the new product line or service are communicated to intended users. Further, among the companies I studied, many produced the volumes needed for test markets on specifically designated "pilot plant" facilities, others used external comanufacturers, and yet others produced needed volumes on the graveyard shifts of their regular production lines.

The market test also gives the team important opportunities to learn what it needs to know to develop and refine a specific go-to-market launch plan that includes channel selection, communications messages, and sales force training. In some companies' studied, the launch plan was a subset of the business plan; in other cases, it was a separate document reviewed specifically with the corporation's marketing and sales departments. The team also needs to update its business plan and the financial projections in that plan as a result of its market testing. The results of the market test, together with samples of the improved product or service, a revised business plan, and the sales launch plan, become the package for executive review. Here, executives decide if they wish to allocate more substantial resources to succeed in next phase of our framework.

## Phase 3: Ramp and Scale and
## Next-Generation R&D

In the third phase of the management framework, the corporation reaps the rewards of its experimentation. It includes the scale and ramp of manufacturing and distribution; it also includes as a parallel activity the initiation of next-generation R&D based on what's been learned in the market.

### Ramp and Scale

The new market application now enters a critical period. The team must ramp and scale the business. Any first-mover advantage may be short-lived if the company fails to exploit its early lead through aggressive marketing, distribution, and, in many instances, investments to achieve higher volume manufacturing to meet accelerating demand.

Typically, a new computer, a new piece of software, or even a new drug sells slowly at first and gains momentum only in following years as advertising and word of mouth have a cumulative effect. In these cases, modest first-year sales make it difficult to justify the high cost of manufacturing investments. Scale up, then, becomes a great financial challenge—and risk—unless the corporation has flexible manufacturing plants that can be shared across several newly launched product lines. In a few other cases, such as the automobile and chip manufacturers studied, a company must be ready to accommodate high-volume sales right away. This makes concurrent engineering—the design for manufacturing and parallel testing of new tooling while some product components are still being designed—essential during product line and platform development.

A word of caution: Many companies studied used contract manufacturer for new product lines in order to get to market quickly. These supply agreements are themselves often an experiment. Some teams founds that after a six months to a year after launch, it was the contract manufacturers who were making most of the money on the new product line. Switching to a new supplier proved difficult for several teams because the supplier itself had helped design key parts of the new product, and therefore, owned certain intellectual property. They were stuck; and their products doomed. A team must plan for such contingencies, either to bring manufacturing in-house at some point in time, or to have more flexible partnerships with key suppliers. Otherwise, wonderful products can soon become business failures.

It is also at this point that executives make the critical decisions with respect to *who* should continue to manage the new product line or service and *where* the new business should reside and report within the corporation.

---

**Practical Criteria for Launching New Projects**

Most companies have more opportunities than resources. The business executives with whom I worked in developing this book suggested the following criteria for new market applications:

— Projects should leverage company technology—either product or process.
— Projects should target either new target users relative to core business or new uses for products or services by current users. Projects operating within this framework should not be incremental product development activities that current business units should be doing already. Using this fast path process to siphon resources from business and R&D managers in these groups for work that they should already be performing will only cause resentment and create barriers for reintegration later on.
— An experienced full-time market professional and a full-time technical person should be assigned to every project at the beginning. Consumer product or consumer durables manufacturers might find that they also need a manufacturing or supply professional right from the beginning as a full-time team member. Executives can then determine future staffing needs as the project proceeds forward.
— No more than two or three projects should be launched in any given year, even within a $1 billion-plus business unit. In addition to the new product line or service itself, a new market application may require creation of a new brand, a new channel, or even a new business model. The sage advice that it is best to do a few things well applies even more to new product line and service development.

---

### Next-Generation Product Line or Service Development

Development of the new application's next generation ideally begins in this same phase of the framework. Whether the focus is on extending the new product line or on leapfrogging its architecture with something better, follow-on R&D must be planned and funded.

Unfortunately, many companies create brilliant new product concepts, launch them, and then fail to become real forces in the marketplace because of a lack of this important follow-through. Established competitors see these initial offerings and say, "Hey, that's a great idea. Let's copy it and use our dominant sales forces to recapture the market." As noted by Richard Foster, unless the new entrant keeps fast-following competitors like these on their heels with continuous innovation and exciting marketing, it may find itself muscled aside.[8] No framework for managing product or service innovation should allow that to happen. In our framework, next-generation product line or service development is an essential activity, pursued in parallel with ramp and scale.

## Time Horizons for New Market Applications Development

A business process for new market applications development must be both simple and powerful. For these applications, the best way forward is getting to market quickly and learning from that experience. That cannot be accomplished when teams are encumbered by excessive steps, checklists, and bureaucracy. As argued by Gary Hamel and C. K. Prahalad, executives should sponsor low-cost, fast-paced market incursions designed to bring the target quickly into view and redefine success metrics in ways that encourage managers to create new products and services outside the company's core business, that is, to take risks.[9]

How long should it take to get through this new process—from raw idea to launch? Every situation, of course, is different. But here are some estimates.

Although corporations are always in the process of defining strategy, it is safe to assume that the type of growth strategy required here is much more specific and requires a new, dedicated effort of market and competitive research. Many corporations embark on expensive, year-long endeavors to define growth strategy, but readers should recall IBM's experience with its ES2000 team in 1995, which developed a robust growth strategy *in three months* that proved a guiding post for the decade to follow. Chapter 3 will present simple yet powerful methods focused on segmented markets for growth. Once markets are segmented in this way, a management team should revisit and refresh its segmentation on a regular and continuous basis.

Phase 1, user-centered design and business plan development, should take no more than six to nine months, even for complex systems. The result of this phase is a prototype, not a final product ready for market. Another deliverable is a cohesive business plan.

Phase 2 aims to produce detailed product and process development and a focused market test. Product line and process development may take upward of 12 to 18 months (although the software companies I studied always seemed to shoot for less than six-month development cycles). A proper test market

requires at least two to three months. Toward the end of Phase 2, initial production assets must be ordered and installed, and lead times—while varying
between industries—normally require about a year. Even nonmanufacturers
require time for code or new services to ripen.

Phase 1 and Phase 2 together bring us to about 18 to 36 months from start
to the initial launch of a new market application. Phase 3 then proceeds in a
continuous manner, where next-generation R&D works on a similarly aggressive time line.

Obviously, these numbers are intended as a general yardstick and vary by
industry. This pace may seem aggressive for the amount of work that must be
done, but many of the companies I studied achieved it. Of course, the pace
may vary. For capital-intensive industries, bringing a new plant on line requires more than a year. A development cycle of four years or less is considered highly ambitious for the automobile industry. A drug discovery firm prepares itself for a much longer haul, with various phases of animal and human
tests. Nonetheless, even here, the early drug discovery phase can be dramatically shortened by applying known effects of particular chemistries to new
medical applications. *Rapid launch and learn is a mindset that is portable across
industries.*

The chapters that follow explain the details of this framework for new market
applications development and how you can apply it to your business. Each
piece of the framework is grounded in experience and research. Each is based
on commonsense concepts and illustrated with examples from a broad set of
products, systems, and services. And each chapter presents its own set of specific planning tools that embrace concepts and methods focused on that particular part of the overall framework. Think of these as *templates* the reader
can apply to his or her own new product line or service development effort—
ranging from market segmentation, to product and technology planning, to
business modeling, to project management. Under the heading of Reader Exercises, the methods chapters challenge readers to apply each chapter's templates
to their own projects—all in the effort to transform raw ideas into real business
developments.

## Notes

1. Doug Cameron, "3M Chief Plans to Release Areas of Trapped Growth," *Financial
Times*, April 22, 2006, 7.
2. I developed this figure with my colleague and friend John Helferich—then the
senior R&D executive for a major corporation—as we contemplated the struggles companies often encounter in turning good product ideas into good businesses.

3. Derek Abell, *Defining the Business* (Upper Saddle River, NJ: Prentice Hall, 1980). Abell dimensionalized growth in terms of core technologies (what today are often called platforms), as well as target users and their uses of products and services.

4. W. Chan Kim and Renee Mauborgne, *Blue Ocean Strategy: How to Create Uncontested Market Space and Make Competition Irrelevant* (Boston: Harvard Business School Publishing, 2005).

5. Marc H. Meyer and Alvin Lehnerd, *The Power of Product Platforms* (New York: Free Press, 1997), 18–19.

6. Steven Wheelwright and Kim Clark, *Revolutionizing New Product Development* (New York: Free Press, 1992). This book is best known for the authors' descriptions of aggregate project planning for balancing R&D portfolios and for their comparison of lightweight versus heavyweight teams. However, the reader might wish to take a close look at chapter 10 on prototype test cycles.

7. Alan Cooper, *The Inmates Are Running the Asylum: Why High-Tech Products Drive Us Crazy and How to Restore the Sanity* (Indianapolis: Sams, 2004).

8. Richard Foster, *Innovation: The Attacker's Advantage* (London: Macmillan Books, 1986).

9. Gary Hamel and C. K. Prahalad, "The Core Competence of the Corporation," *Harvard Business Review*, 69(4): 81–92.

# CHAPTER THREE

# Segmenting Markets for Growth

*Defining new users and uses in a market segmentation grid—*
*Developing a product strategy with design foci—Defining*
*good, better, best for a new market application—Using*
*a segmentation grid to reveal changing industry*
*demographics—Techniques for segmenting markets—*
*Examples from marine and construction products,*
*pharmaceuticals, and software—New value*
*propositions for new target users—*
*Reader exercises.*

Up in the executive suite, corporate planners fill thick binders with five-year strategic plans, supporting budgets, implementation steps, and performance milestones.[1] Why are these not sufficient to fuel internally generated enterprise growth? Observers such as Russell Ackoff have argued that formal corporate strategic planning has limited utility for true growth. By the time the formal strategic plan is finished, he argues, the firm's competitive environment has changed and made the plan obsolete. For growth-seeking companies with sound technologies and executives who aim to create new streams of revenue within two or three years, strategy need not be so complicated.

As an alternative, Ackoff argued for strategic planning systems that focus on "what designers would like to have *right* now, not at some future date. Therefore, the environment in which the system would have to operate need not be forecasted; it is the current environment."[2]

Ackoff's advice provides a pragmatic approach to new product line or service development. Management can identify a few clear market targets and then quickly construct what Ackoff called an "idealized design" of the solution that uses the best available component elements to quickly produce something that can be market-tested. An idealized design uses best-of-breed components or subsystems that exist *today*, not in the future. Of course, target market opportunities must be found *first*. Companies use many different methods for framing such targets. The simplest and most powerful way to frame these targets are in terms of users and product or service uses, and market segmentation is the key for understanding the differences between them.

Market segmentation is the first step in new market applications development (see the box highlighted in figure 3.1). Different customer groups have distinct needs and unique tolerances for price. They may exhibit distinct buying behaviors. We refer to distinct customer groups as market segments. Market segmentation defines these segments in ways *that are useful* for product and service development, branding and communications. If management defines its segments solely in terms of existing customers, new customer applications will appear only by chance. If, on the other hand, a company's market segmentation also shows new customers and new product uses, the company will have positioned itself for growth.

Market segments are always changing, particularly in dynamic industries. New user groups emerge over time, and existing user groups change their buying and usage behaviors. Consequently, market segmentation must be ongoing to have a sustained impact on enterprise growth.

Market segmentation should involve as much innovative thinking and as much research as any other aspect of the business. Each new segment will have a unique set of customer requirements, channel requirements, and price constraints, as well as different margin, volume, and profitability characteristics. The story of IBM's turnaround in chapter 1 illustrates what can be accomplished when innovation in marketing is on a par with innovation on the technological front. That company's success derived from its new view of target markets and the needs of users within those markets. The assumption that batch mainframe computing was *the* target segment was as limiting as any of IBM's aging technologies. Replacing that product-bound assumption with a customer-focused view of the world was the first step in its long journey back to profitability and market power. IBM's ES2000 team crisply defined compelling user needs and competitive positioning. That made it possible for IBM's developers to translate customer needs into a new generation of hardware, software, and service solutions.

When users represent a new, unfamiliar customer target, *nothing* should be taken for granted. Nor should the company rely solely on consultants, its advertising agencies, or independent market researchers for its customer information. New market insights can be transferred only through people; consequently, a company's own managers and staff must directly participate in

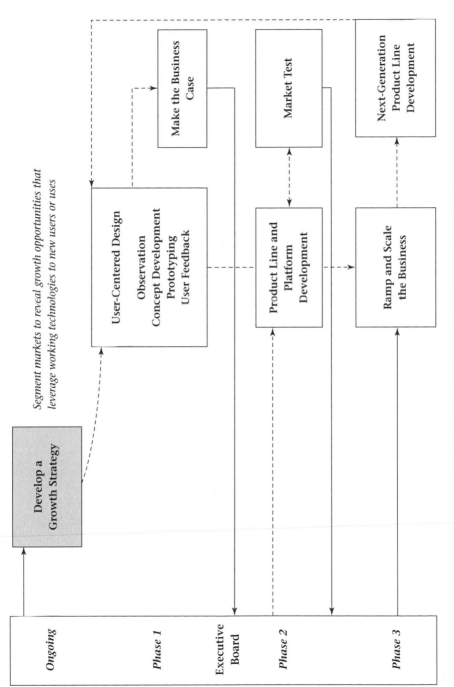

FIGURE 3.1 Develop a Growth Strategy: Segment Markets for Growth

market and user studies. Consultants provide fresh perspective, the experiences of other firms, and reports. Their insights can help a company expand its thinking. However, these insights must be translated into actual products and services to generate growth, and sooner or later, that will require the work of internal management and staff.

The best way to understand market segmentation is, like most things, to understand its fundamental principles and observe those principles at work in different examples. The examples offered here run the gamut from physical assembled products, to software and systems, to biotechnology, and to services.

## A Template to Segment Markets for Growth

Market segmentation employs a combination of *users* and *uses*, according to Derek Abell, author of *Defining the Business*.[3] Abell believes that growth is achieved by developing and leveraging technology platforms to new users and new uses. Figure 3.2, the market segmentation template, is a generic template of Abell's approach and is best thought of as a grid showing users and uses. This approach helps executives and teams think through the various targets available to the corporation. Growth-oriented segmentation aims to reveal new potential targets, not reformulate the timeworn market strategies that the firm has been pursuing. At the same time, not all potential users or uses should be placed within a market segmentation grid, but rather only those for which the company has a reasonable chance to leverage its skills and capabilities in the form of new products and services. This makes the growth strategy pragmatic and achievable.

For a software company such as Microsoft, users range from home desktop users to computer gamers, to corporate desktop users, to corporate IT shops. Uses range from operating systems to programming, to personal productivity, to networking, to database and data mining, to gaming. Microsoft's growth strategy has been to leverage a set of software platforms (operating systems, middleware or software development tools, and applications) to a series of new uses with a customer base that began with home users and then expanded into corporations large and small. Similarly, as we'll see in a later chapter, Honda has leveraged its engine technologies across different types of consumers for uses that include transportation, leisure, and home care. Cars, all-terrain vehicles, powerboats, and lawnmowers are just a few of the products that use Honda engines.

A pharmaceutical company can also think about market applications in terms of users and uses; in this case, the users are patients with certain types of

| | Traditional Users | | | New Users | |
| --- | --- | --- | --- | --- | --- |
| | Segment A | Segment B | Segment C | Segment D | Segment E |
| **Use/Application 3** | | | | | |
| Product/Service | | | | | |
| Market Size | | | | | |
| Market Growth | | | | | |
| Leading Players/Share | | | | | |
| **Use/Application 2** | | | | | |
| Product/Service | | | | | |
| Market Size | | | | | |
| Market Growth | | | | | |
| Leading Players/Share | | | | | |
| **Use/Application 1** | | | | | |
| Product/Service | | | | | |
| Market Size | | | | | |
| Market Growth | | | | | |
| Leading Players/Share | | | | | |

FIGURE 3.2 The Market Segmentation Template: Identify Users and Uses (Marc H. Meyer)

diseases, and the uses are prevention, diagnosis, and therapy. By expanding its range of market applications, this type of segmentation can wean pharmaceutical companies from the risky "blockbuster" drug strategy that so many of them now pursue.

The market segmentation template can also direct the growth of service companies. Commercial banks, for example, generally categorize their users as consumers and businesses, each representing a range of uses: lending, investments, and cash management. Large banks have broadened the range to include mortgages, mutual funds, and life insurance—all tailored to these different users and their uses. Specific financial products marketed to the "younger" 20-to-30 year olds are becoming increasingly popular.

The point is that some new products happen by accident, but the majority of product lines are well-planned, well-executed forays into new market applications. Management picks a target and organizes a team to implement a product, production, and marketing strategy to attack it. That target must be on the corporation's strategy map; otherwise, it is unlikely to receive adequate R&D, production, and distribution resources. "Market innovation" in enterprise growth starts by adding these new targets to strategy, and resegmenting markets to achieve this important first step.

### Applying the Template: A Food Products Example

Let us consider the hypothetical example of a food manufacturer that over the decades has largely focused on making snack food products for young children. Those snack foods are generally purchased by mothers buying for the household. Even though this strategy has produced substantial revenues—say, billions of dollars—it may still be considered a "segmentation of one," namely, fun food for kids. Within this single box, marketers might try to understand different behaviors (uses) in terms of children's needs to satisfy hunger, to have fun eating their food, or to share snacks with friends. However, because the consumer is generally the same—a kid—the vast majority of R&D has focused on incremental improvements to existing products with slight changes to flavoring and packaging.

Now, let us say that senior management wants real growth. To get it, management begins to segment its potential target markets by something as simple yet profound as different ages of consumers. Once "age" is made a dimension of segmentation, new insights appear. Figure 3.3 shows the result and the product strategy that might emerge from this exercise. The age of the user is on the

**A Product Strategy Map**

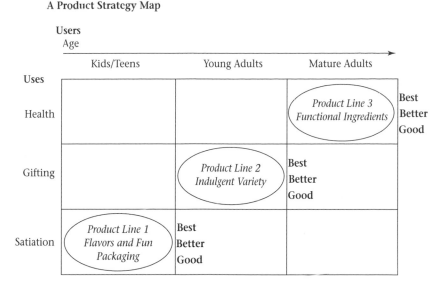

FIGURE 3.3  A Product Market Strategy Template
(Based on a Market Segmentation Template)

horizontal axis; on the vertical axis are three very basic uses: hunger (satiation), social occasions (gifting), and personal goal (health). Today, the adult-health segmentation cell gets food developers in many corporations highly energized to create new snacks and meals with special nutritional attributes. Gifting is another hot spot for innovation.

Used in this way, the market segmentation grid becomes a product strategy map to operationalize growth. The three ovals in the figure represent, in theory, three very different design emphases, each tuned to a particular region of the segmentation grid. One might be a flavorful, fun recipe for children and teens; another might represent premium gifts for young adults; and the third, snacks that provide vitamins and other healthful ingredients desired by health-conscious adults.

Within each of these prospective product lines, management might then consider "good," "better," and "best" offerings. For a food company, these variations typically take the forms of different SKUs (stock-keeping units) that appear on the store shelf. The differences between good, better, and best need not be limited to the type and quality of ingredients. Packaging can also provide considerable functionality, either by preserving food freshness or by providing more convenient preparation. Microwavable food preparation, for example, is a packaging innovation that might be seen as "better" relative to traditional forms of preparation; it is more convenient. Computer companies likewise offer good, better, and best choices, often defined in terms of capacity, network attachments, and software. With each new mainframe model, for example, IBM has several dozen specific offerings on its sale sheet, each with more microprocessors and I/O channels.

Good, better, and best categories provide a multiyear roadmap for new product or service development. For example, good might appear in Year 1, better in Year 2, and best in Year 3. The definition of these three tiers of performance is also often related to the cost to produce and the price charged to the user. A solid roadmap helps the innovation team figure out where to focus first and where to focus down the road. In some instances, only good and better are definable at the present time; in others, all three grades are clearly understood. Some companies might find that only two tiers make sense for a new market application; others might demand four or even five (such as premium and super premium).

It may sound obvious that "good" should be a team's initial development target, with greater levels of power and sophistication coming later. For example, senior management at IBM decided to get to market quickly with a 100 MIPS version of its new CMOS architecture (the G1) rather than wait several more years to launch a much better 500 MIPS machine. This seemingly simple decision was one of the most controversial during the company's period of crisis. Engineers in Poughkeepsie wanted to make the G4 right away. This divide is not unusual. Product developers want to shoot for the moon by putting their very "best" foot forward with every project. However, striving for the best as an initial launch strategy has serious pitfalls:

— "Best" may take years to develop. In the meantime, a competitor can introduce a "good" version, develop the brand, and become the market leader.
— Not all customers need the best, nor will they pay for it.
— What constitutes best for a new market application isn't always known at the outset. A more prudent approach is to work toward a rapid launch and then learn from lead users what better and best might be.

Starting with the good for the first test market and subsequent commercial release has clear benefits. Technical success is more likely, and that success translates into a healthy team climate and a sense of accomplishment. This first release provides a robust and scalable architecture that can later accommodate higher levels of performance and plug-in features once the needs of users are better understood. The innovation team should get to work on the better version just as the good product enters the scale and ramp phase. This activity set is shown clearly as a parallel activity in the last phase of the growth management framework (figure 3.1).

Each region of the product strategy map helps focus the attention and work of innovation teams. For example, among Honda's passenger cars, the Civic has a different market focus than the Accord, and the Accord has different focus than the Acura. A market segmentation grid not only helps to identify new opportunities for growth but also helps to establish the boundaries between different product lines within the corporation's overall product strategy. Those boundaries help to determine how each product line should evolve, be positioned, and be branded.

Trying to capture a growth-focused product strategy on a single page, as in figure 3.3, also has important communications benefits. Putting product strategy on one page gives executives a framework that is both simple and inclusive, and one to which they can add their own insights. Prioritization of targets becomes clearer. Marketers understand how to shape their messages and channels. Developers not only have a customer focus for each respective initiative but also understand how that focus differs from other new product lines or services. Perhaps more important, the framework helps developers understand that they cannot work on a dozen different strategies *at the same time*. Only three or four major product line strategies can reasonably fit on a market segmentation grid turned *product strategy map*, which is probably the most that most business units, even billion-dollar ones, should try to achieve at any given time.

## Breaking Out into New Markets: A Marine Winches Case

To illustrate the idea of adding new targets for growth, consider an assembled product—a winch—manufactured by a company in our study. In the nautical world, a winch is used for hauling in the "sheets" (ropes) attached to sails. The company had a solid but slow-growing business and a large share of the sailboat market. During the mid-1990s, growth-hungry new management came aboard. To accelerate revenue growth, it formed a team to design a new line of winches with a replaceable internal motor. This design eliminated exposure to saltwater and rain. The replacement motor also could be easily installed by the boat owner. This design opened up an aftermarket of retail dealers. At the same time, the project team took a hard look at the materials and manufacturing processes the company was using to produce its winches and found that it could reduce its cost of goods through more efficient processes. After considerable effort, it was able to leverage the new winch architecture into smaller craft. This effort

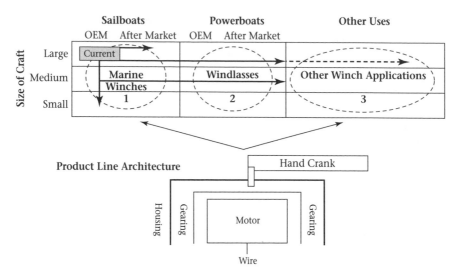

FIGURE 3.4 Leveraging a Winch Architecture to New Market Applications

is shown in the first circle in figure 3.4, labeled "Marine Winches." The figure reveals the company's entire growth strategy on a single page. The high-level architecture of the product line is also shown at the bottom.

The team also opened up an entirely new market: It designed a new external interface that allowed its motorized winches to be mounted sideways, producing a "windlass" capable of pulling up primarily powerboat anchors. This windlass used the same modular architecture as the winch, complete with replaceable motors. In figure 3.4, the second circle is labeled "Windlasses." This was a new market application for the company. Because there are many more powerboats in the world than sailboats, it greatly expanded potential sales. Further, the new product strategy allowed the company to break into the major distribution channels in North American market, channels geared toward high-volume components with replacement parts.

The company also considered how it might leverage its technology outside its traditional marine applications. Helicopters and lumber haulers, for example, also used windlasses. These were merely two of many new market applications management explored.

Over the course of a year, this once sleepy manufacturer became more market focused and customer driven. Its product managers and engineers, now formed into specific teams and working toward very specific new product launches, were, in the words of one observer, "having great fun." The addition of new markets had an incredibly powerful effect on the entire corporation.

## Identifying Growth Opportunities in the Context of Industry Demographics

The market segmentation framework can be used to reveal major industry trends and, within these, attractive growth opportunities. We show this in figure 3.5, the market facing a manufacturer of construction products. This particular grid contains three major segments: new home construction, home repair, and light industrial and commercial building construction. Each of these was perceived as a different world by an innovation team assembled by the manufacturer's vice president of R&D to expand beyond the company's core market of high-end products for new residential construction. Differences between segments went well beyond product features. The distribution channels were different, as were the sizes of average purchases and the installation. Support services also varied widely between segments. Nested within these major segments were subsegments with unique characteristics. For example, the new home construction segment contained subsegments of custom homebuilders and volume builders. The home repair segment included do-it-yourselfers and professional tradesmen.

As the team began to populate its grid with unit sales, subsegment market share, niche leaders, and so forth, it became apparent that new product sales in the subsegment in which the company was competing were either flat or declining. Sales in its highest volume subsegment—premium custom home new construction—were declining at 4 percent per year! That meant that no matter how hard R&D worked, its new products would be in for some rough sledding. In fact, the company's sales had been mostly flat over the previous five years, even though total industry sales had been growing at a healthy rate. Management knew it had to expand into current and new market areas, such as commercial construction. The company had focused most of its R&D resources on its traditional markets, and new markets, such as the aftermarket and the commercial segments, were left to chance. That would change as management directed substantial resources toward new market opportunities. Management's goal was to create revenue streams from new products that would leverage components, materials, and processes from the "old business."

A consulting team had been hired to define a new growth strategy. It left the company a hundred-page report, a number of acquisition targets, and several dozen internally focused strategies. R&D had no idea how to implement those strategies in a coherent way. With support from the president, the R&D director pulled together a multifunctional team: Its goal was to operationalize strategy into an internal development plan. The market segmentation grid

# Market Segmentation Data by Volume

| | | New Construction | | | Repair and Maintenance | | | Commercial | | | |
|---|---|---|---|---|---|---|---|---|---|---|---|
| | | Custom | High Volume Noncustom | Low Volume | Full Service | Self Repair | Specialty | Retail | Hospitals | Rental | Industrial |
| **Super Premium** | Units (millions) | 0.6 | 0.2 | 0.2 | 1.1 | 0 | 0.2 | 2.1 | 3.3 | 1.4 | 0.7 |
| | Annual Growth | Unknown | Unknown | Unknown | Unknown | Unknown | Unknown | 1% | 3% | 5% | 3% |
| | Firm A Units | 0 | 0 | 0 | 0 | 0 | 0 | 0.2 | 0.2 | 0.2 | 0.2 |
| | Market Leader | Fragmented | Fragmented | Fragmented | Firm C | Fragmented | Fragmented | Firms K, L | Firms K, L | Firm K | Firm L |
| **Premium** | Units (millions) | 1.5 | 0.5 | 0.4 | 3.5 | 1.8 | 0.8 | 5.8 | 6.0 | 2.5 | 1.4 |
| | Annual Growth | 4% | Flat | Flat | Flat | Flat | Flat | 1% | 3% | 5% | 3% |
| | Firm A Units | 1.3 | .3 | .0 | 1.1 | .4 | Unknown | .03 | .12 | .08 | .004 |
| | Market Leader | Firm A | Firm A | Firm A | Firm A | Firm A | Firm G | Firms K, L | Firms K, L | Firm G | Firms K, L |
| **Upper Mid Band** | Units (millions) | 0.6 | 0.1 | 0.3 | 2 | 1.3 | 1.1 | | | | |
| | Annual Growth | 4% | 19% | Flat | 3% | Flat | 1% | | | | |
| | Firm A Units | .1 | .2 | .2 | .05 | 0 | .05 | | | | |
| | Market Leader | Firm B | Firms A, B | Firms A, B | Firm B | Firm B | Firm B | | | | |
| **Lower Mid Band** | Units (millions) | 1.1 | 1.2 | 0.5 | 4 | 2.6 | 2.1 | | | | |
| | Annual Growth | 2% | 8% | 4% | Flat | -1% | 4% | | | | |
| | Firm A Units | 0 | 0 | 0 | 0 | 0 | 0 | | | | |
| | Market Leader | Firm D | Firm E, Firm D | Firm D | Unknown | Firm F | Firm F | | | | |
| **Price** | Units (millions) | 1.9 | 5.8 | 1.9 | 8.6 | 5.5 | 6.2 | 6.5 | 2.1 | 1.6 | 2 |
| | Annual Growth | -1% | -3% | -1% | Unknown | Unknown | Unknown | 1% | 3% | 5% | 3% |
| | Firm A Units | 0 | 0 | 0 | 0 | 0 | 0 | 0 | 0 | 0 | 0 |
| | Market Leader | Firm H | Firm H | Firm H | Firm H, Firm J | Firm H, Firm J | Firm H, Firm J, Alenco | Fragmented | Fragmented | Fragmented | Fragmented |

Current Targets

Common Material and Component Platforms

FIGURE 3.5  A Market Segmentation Example with Three Stages of Growth (figure 3.5) was the first step in that plan. It indicated three phases of a single focused growth strategy.

Step 1 of the strategy was to revisit the core product line architecture for each of the company's major product lines. Over time, materials, components, and processes had proliferated as new SKUs were added. This "platform" project resulted in dramatically fewer components and streamlined manufacturing processes. These allowed the firm, for the time, to effectively compete with the lower cost competitors that had been stealing sales in the upper mid-band tier shown in figure 3.5. While the cost of goods was being dramatically reduced, team members ventured for the first time into the field to observe homebuilders, both custom and high volume. Their aim was to better understand usage, installation, and support requirements. Their user research led to product lines that were less expensive to manufacture and more functional for users. That project took the better part of several years to complete, but the new products took the market by storm.

Step 2 of the strategy was to aim for the burgeoning home repair market. Products developed in Step 1 found a natural home in this segment as well, but new marketing programs and channel development were needed to forge a connection. Once again, the innovation team worked alongside users—do-it-yourselfers—to understand how best to fine-tune the company's offerings for this massive market. Step 3 of the strategy was to then adapt product line architecture and user research methods to architects and builders of light industrial and commercial structures.

## Digging Deeper Can Lead to Segmentation Insights

The companies I observed had several highly effective approaches to market segmentation. There is no single right way to segment markets for growth. Each company must determine the best approach, given its circumstances.

How does your company approach segmentation? Perhaps it doesn't really believe in it. I once heard the vice president of marketing at a data storage provider state, "Storage is storage. Banks, the government, drug companies— they all have the same priorities and they all need the same thing." In his view, solutions development and marketing for specific user groups was expensive and unnecessary. This type of undifferentiated "segment of one" mentality can be limiting and dangerous. In contrast, leaders in storage systems, such as EMC, have worked hard to develop marketing programs, product packages, and services specifically tuned to different industries, based on the reality that the needs of CIOs are different. This particular marketing VP needed to advance his thinking.

An innovation team chartered by the CEO took the marketing VP on a road trip to visit lead customers in various vertical markets, hoping to broaden his perspective on solutions development. These markets (for storage) included banking, insurance, pharmaceutical companies, health care, and government. After a month of intensive visits, the VP became a believer in the differences between users and the importance of customer segmentation. His notion of a monolithic market changed. Even within customer organizations, CIOs, computing managers, and technical staff had different needs that had not been fully recognized or exploited with storage software. At one level were traditional users of the company's software: systems administrators who wanted to know what data resided where. At a higher level were the managers of computer departments. They wanted to know the volumes of data created, accessed, and moved during production shifts. Storage information, when aggregated, could help the computing center manager make decisions on computing assets and consolidate data on servers with extra capacity. Last, the team found specific needs among customer CIOs who could use storage information to "charge back" their own user departments for disk utilization. These three specific uses appear as rows on the left side of figure 3.6, which shows the segmentation used to guide the company's new product development. Different industry groups are arrayed across the top. The first are the same type of industry verticals that we saw IBM using in the previous chapter. Next are companies that outsource the storage and management of data. These storage service providers, charging on a pay-as-you-go basis, include IBM, Hewlett Packard, EMC, Sun Microsystems, and Electronic Data Systems. The company made modifications to its software to allow these outsourced storage providers to create separate accounts for their own customers.

The last customer group shown in figure 3.6 identifies third-party software and storage hardware manufacturers. Eager to "sense" the files and data residing on any type of computer or device attached to a network, the software firm polished its own data I/O software routines and aggressively marketed them as a "software development kit" to these hardware manufacturers. It also provided additional data access and report writing features to systems integrators.

Thus, from its initial, undifferentiated market view—a "segment of one"—this firm developed a more nuanced understanding of users and uses. Thanks to that more sophisticated understanding, it identified many specific product opportunities. Segmentation for growth transformed this company's approach to product development and led to a series of innovations that resulted in the company's being acquired for more than $400 million. The once recalcitrant VP of marketing was a happy man!

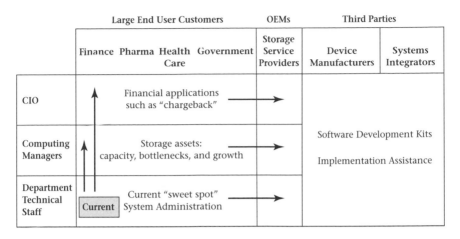

FIGURE 3.6 Segmentation by User Level and Industry

## Applying Segmentation to Parallel Product Line Developments

Segmentation can be based on any number of user or use factors: demographics (age or income), behaviors (skiers), occupation (computer programmers), and so forth. Let's turn to another company from my field studies to see how two factors—gender and medical condition—can be used to initiate parallel development activities. The company in question specializes in the application of a particular molecule to different medical problems, one largely afflicting men, another largely afflicting women, and yet another found in both genders. Its product market strategy is shown in figure 3.7.

We usually think of pharmaceutical companies as large, publicly traded, and heavily capitalized enterprises. The company described here is much different. It is privately held and was started on the founder's personal savings in 1982. It has funded its R&D, including clinical trials for six new drugs, entirely with earnings. This is truly impressive in an industry where cycle times for *each* new drug development are at present in excess of 12 years and the cost is in excess of $800 million per drug.

This founder recognized the power of product platforms years earlier, when he was a manager in the shaving systems division of Gillette. In that company, successive generations of increasingly better blade designs were leveraged into razors packaged and marketed specifically for different market segments: men on one hand (Mach) and women on the other (Venus). When he left Gillette, he knew that his likelihood of success would improve if he could apply that

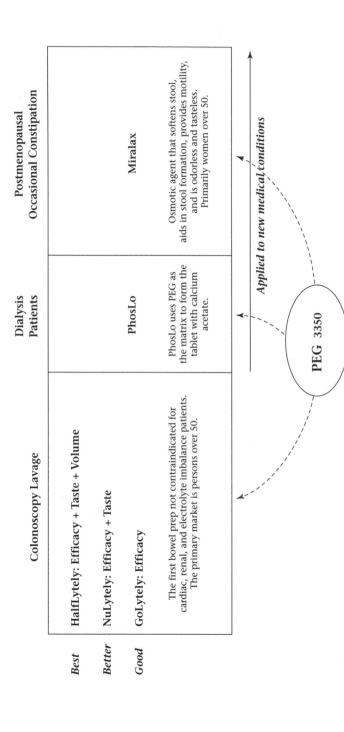

FIGURE 3.7 Leveraging a Compound to New Medical Applications

principle to his new business. In this case, the "blade" would be a particular for-mulation of polyethylene glycol (PEG 3350 by molecular weight) that would be applied to a series of related medical applications for different segments of the population. Figure 3.7 is the firm's product strategy map.

The company's first market application of PEG 3350 was a new "lavage," a bowel cleanser used to prepare patients for colorectal examinations. Early "preps" hurt some patients with certain medical conditions by draining essen-tial electrolytes from their bloodstreams. That loss of electrolytes could lead to heart failure and other severe problems. The PEG 3350 plus electrolytes used by this company did its work without affecting the patient's blood chemistry. PEG had itself been used for years as a compound to increase the bioavailabil-ity of other drugs. This company's founder had teamed up with physicians to explore new applications for it.

The company's first product was called GoLYTELY, a brand name that sug-gests the preservation of patient electrolytes. The product, a powder mixed with water, is actually PEG 3350 combined with electrolytes. GoLYTELY quickly became the preferred solution for colonoscopy preps.

Any reader who has used GoLYTLEY can appreciate why the company ad-dressed the drink's palatability in its "better" version. That effort led to U.S. Food and Drug Administration (FDA) approval for NuLYTELY, which comes in different flavors (such as orange.) For the company's next development, the "best," it received FDA approval in 2005 for a half-dose version of NuLYTELY called HalfLytely. It provides the same efficacy with only half the amount of oral solution. Today, the company's lavages are U.S. market leaders; if you are over 50 and receive good medical care, chances are that you either are or will be a user!

During the development of its first lavage, the company began a parallel drug development, seeking to leverage PEG 3350 as a platform into several new market applications. The first of these was a phosphate binder for patients suffering end-stage renal disease so that the phosphate could be more effec-tively removed from the blood. The practice up to that point was to give pa-tients calcium carbonate, which would bind with phosphates. The phosphates would then pass with the patients' stools. Unfortunately, this calcium would also be absorbed into the blood, which could lead to serious medical problems for some patients.

A physician working with the company determined that PEG 3350 would work as a tablet matrix when mixed in very small amounts with calcium ac-etate. With several children actually on dialysis, this physician had great in-centive to find a better solution. Using calcium acetate to bind phosphate lessens the absorption of calcium into the blood by about half. Thus was born PhosLo, which has become an important new therapy for dialysis patients.

PhosLo has only one direct competitor. At the time of this writing, there are some 280,000 dialysis patients in the United States alone.

While GoLYTLEY and PhosLo proceeded through development, the company was exploring other new market applications for PEG 3350. As the founder remarked, every successful company has its own particular focus, and his company's focus is the human bowel! Consequently, postmenopausal constipation, a frequent condition in women, seemed a promising target. Available laxatives at the time sometimes produced unwanted effects, such as diarrhea or nausea. A formulation of PEG 3350 that would act in a much gentler and more effective way was created, tested, and approved by the FDA. Branded as Miralax, the product was formulated so that the user could stir a tablespoon of the powder into her coffee, tea, or orange juice. PEG causes water to be retained in the stool, allowing for better stool formation and regular passage through the intestine. Miralax became the first new FDA-approved, doctor-prescribed laxative to hit the market in 24 years!

## Different Market Applications Can Have Different Value Propositions

We can define a value proposition as the amount of money a target customer is willing to pay for the perceived benefits of a product or service. A firm may find that target users place a substantially higher—or lesser—value on its new market application relative to traditional users, even though the product lines or services themselves are based on common core technology. The growth of Mentor Graphics into three distinct market applications presents a dramatic example. Its applications are the design, the verification, and the manufacturing of integrated circuits.

Founded in 1981 by three former Tektronix managers, Mentor Graphics had by 1995 become a market leader in computer-aided engineering (CAE). Quality assurance engineers at computer companies, electronics manufacturers, and automotive parts suppliers, among others, were using Mentor Graphics software to assure that integrated circuits would function as designed. Putting a flawed design into production is costly. Nonrecoverable engineering charges for an integrated circuit (IC) mask set, for example, can easily hit $2 million.

Despite solid revenues and earnings, Mentor Graphics management wanted to grow by addressing new users and uses. Toward that end, the company launched two new product lines after several years of intensive development. One headed into an "upstream" segment of the chip value chain, and the other, downstream. First, let's head upstream. Having targeted quality assurance engineers up to this point (referred to as tapeout engineers in this application), management decided to build software products for the actual chip designers. By providing simulation and diagnostic tools in the chip designing software, Mentor Graphics could help its customers catch problems earlier in the design cycle. This would save everyone considerable time and expense.

The second strategic move saw Mentor Graphics venture from its home base of chip design to another segment: chip fabrication. The new target users in this segment were manufacturing engineers working in the production process. These engineers faced a big problem. As the number of transistors crammed into a fixed area of silicon continued to double every 18 months (Moore's Law), the equipment used to manufacture circuits could not keep up.[4] So, Mentor Graphics developed a new capability called optical proximity correction (OPC), which takes the intended design and distorts it in a way that compensates for the limitations of the manufacturing equipment. This enabled ever finer grained circuit designs to be cleanly produced on silicon wafers. OPC made it possible for manufacturers to continue using—and amortizing—their massive capital investments.[5]

Mentor Graphics realized that each of its new product lines served a different set of users: the chip designer, the chip tester, and the manufacturing engineer working in chip-wafer fabrication plants. Also, the number of users in each category is very different. For every 10 chip designers in a computer or electronics company, there might be a single quality assurance engineer, and there are far fewer chip engineers working in fabrication plants than there are designers or quality assurance engineers in the industry. The value of catching problems by each type of user was also different, which led to a fundamentally different pricing structure for each of the three applications.

As shown in figure 3.8, as Mentor Graphics worked down its industry value chain, the price it could charge to license its software (on a per seat or user basis) increased substantially, while the number of prospective users went down. Yet, the value proposition changed from a relative scale of $10,000 per user, to $100,000, to $1,000,000 for each of the three audiences.

Mentor Graphics was rewarded handsomely by its customers for these and other innovations, and its revenues grew elevenfold from 1997 to 2005. If management had not seen the differences in perceived value for its three market applications, that outcome would have been far different.

Few products are as unrelated as food, marine winches, construction products, software, and laxatives (although many users might find it difficult to find *any* difference between the last two). Yet, from the perspective of market innovation

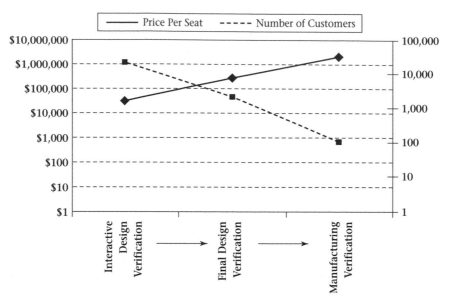

FIGURE 3.8 Different Value Propositions for Users
in Three Different Market Applications
(Relative Scale)

and segmenting markets for growth, the companies described in this chapter seem to be close cousins, and their innovations were based on similar thinking and orientations. In each instance, management understood that it had to pursue parallel product developments using shared *platform* technology. To succeed, each had to explore new and current *users and uses*. This may seem simple enough, yet most companies don't operate this way. Instead, 99 percent of their staff and resources are instead focused on—in the choice words of one executive—"just polishing the marbles." They see their markets as undifferentiated and monolithic and fail to perceive unmet needs in particular segments, be they current segments or new.

## Reader Exercises

The exercises for this chapter involve segmentation and developing a segmentation-based product strategy.

**Exercise 1** Of the several segmentation techniques offered in this chapter, which one makes the most sense for your company? Try your hand at creating a market segmentation grid for your company with figure 3.2 as a model. Be sure to identify new users and uses in addition to the existing ones; otherwise, your product strategy will focus on nothing more than improving existing product lines. Observe these cautions as you develop your market segmentation grid:

— Avoid segmenting markets by your company's current products. Saying that mainframe computers users were a distinct market and minicomputer users another distinct market—while perhaps reasonable during the 1970s and 1980s—is precisely what led to IBM's lack of integrated solutions, in which different types of customers might use all of its different types of computers and software. Your business will begin to grow only when management views markets in terms of users and uses.
— Avoid geography as a primary segmentation criterion. It often leads to different product lines and manufacturing processes for different regions or countries, each with its own architecture, underlying platforms, and components.
— Define one dimension of the two-dimension grid in terms of users, and the other dimension in terms of uses. Three dimensions, while arguably useful, are hard to work with and understand. Most managers do not explicitly think about strategy in three dimensions. So stick with two. They will be easier to explain to executives and team members.

**Exercise 2** Draw circles on your segmentation framework to create a product strategy map, using figure 3.3 as a template. Try to show the design focus of specific product lines, both current and new, that your company can develop. By design focus, I refer to the essential theme, features, and price performance characteristic of these product lines. If the design foci for these different product lines look identical, either your segmentation is incorrect or you are not thinking deeply enough about the different needs of different target users and product users. The result of this particular activity is one "deliverable" that you might consider showing to your colleagues. Don't show this result to peers in your own functional area alone. Enterprise growth is inherently multifunctional. Start breaking down those barriers by showing your work to like-minded, growth-focused executives and managers whom you would like to have on your team.

**Exercise 3** After you are reasonably satisfied with your segmentation grid and the product line strategies that emerge from it, begin gathering industry data for different cells or regions on the grid. This will help you and management to prioritize initiatives and develop the market analysis, competitive analysis, and pro forma financial projections required by your business plan. New market applications should target market segments that show strong levels of growth.

Marketing specialists correctly suggest that the differences between segments must be measurable and meaningful. That means that you must have concrete data for the different regions on your grid. Figure 3.4 is a good example of such data. These data might include:

— Current sales by segment
— Annual growth rates
— Your market share
— Competitors and their market shares

Putting all these together on a single page provides a rich picture of the market and the competitive landscape. Beyond this, write up a set of bullet points on the lead competitor in the market segment you aim to capture. Who is currently the "lead dog" in the new target market, and to what extent does that company compete on more than product alone? Also, what are the marketing requirements for success? Clearly, most successful new entrants combine powerful marketing with exciting new products or services, be it in the form of a great direct sales force, a powerful brand, or a dynamic promotional campaign. Consider the powerful communications programs used by Bose for its Wave music systems, or by Apple for its iPod/iTunes.

Once you have identified your product line strategies on the segmentation grid, start thinking about the feature or features with which you will lead—in terms of business planning, product development, and marketing. Create a sketch of how the product should look, or list the features that the product or service should provide. A subsequent chapter will provide a simple yet powerful method for more fully developing these new product concepts. But start thinking now about the specific theme or focus that will drive design for the product line you wish to create. Also, think beyond technology to the market elements that will drive your success: price, distribution, promotion, and positioning in the minds of customers.

Once you have completed these activities to your satisfaction, start talking with colleagues in different functions about the product line strategy that you have formulated. In some instances, you may wish to speak first to a sponsoring executive; in others, you may pursue a bottoms-up approach to change. In reality, to make a major strategic change, you will need both approaches. The templates presented in this chapter for the initial (and ongoing) market segmentation activity provide a simple yet powerful currency for initiating that dialogue. Those discussions should produce a set of action steps, some of which will highlight the need for new, insightful customer research. We turn to that topic next.

## Notes

1. A number of seminal books and articles have guided traditional strategy formulation over the years. Some of my favorite classics are Peter Lorange and Richard Vancil, *Strategic Planning Systems* (Englewood Cliffs, NJ: Prentice Hall, 1977); Michael Porter, *Competitive Strategy: Techniques for Analyzing Industries and Competitors* (New York: Free Press, 1998); and Henry Mintzberg, *The Rise and Fall of Strategic Planning* (New York: Prentice Hall, 1994).

2. Russell Ackoff, *Designing the Corporate Future*, (New York: Wiley, 1981), 105.

3. Derek F. Abell, *Defining the Business* (Upper Saddle River, NJ: Prentice Hall, 1980).

4. As I write this chapter, Intel and IBM have both announced incredible breakthroughs in transistor design, achieving 70-nanometer (0.07-micron) elements, and are expected to get transistor elements down to less than half that width in the next several years. IBM, for example, announced in February 2006 that its scientists had used ultraviolet light to create 30-nanometer circuits. This will allow chips to have more processing power and to also use less electricity. In January 2007, Intel achieved a breakthrough in energy consumption through the use of high-K dielectric materials in chips.

5. Developments continued within each of the three product lines in the years that followed, leading to important new functional capabilities: better interactive tools for chip designers, yield analysis (chips on an area of silicon) for final design verification, and more advanced manufacturing verification for the process engineers. To best see the scope of these developments, the reader can visit the company's Web site.

CHAPTER FOUR

# Understanding User Needs

*User-centered design—Diving deep for latent needs—*
*Developing use case scenarios—Develop a clear picture of the*
*user—Differentiating between different types of users—*
*Observing users under conditions of leisure and stress—The*
*emotional side of learning and new product adoption—*
*Developing learning models—Testing ideas with*
*users—Reader exercises.*

Segmenting markets for growth should provide one or more clear targets to which a company can extend its core technologies and other business assets. Those targets, going back to our definition of a new market application, are some combination of new users or new product or service uses relative to the company's existing customers and applications. The next step is to define user needs within those target markets. The focus of that activity is shown in the shaded box in figure 4.1.

To define user needs, a company must first learn all it can about the frustrations, behaviors, and preferences of target users. *Absolutely all it can!* Doing so requires the innovation team to go beyond the market studies, consultant reports, and the 20-question surveys usually associated with incremental product developments.

Instead, an innovation team must physically and cognitively step into the world of users—where the team can experience their environment directly. This type of activity—often called *ethnography*—is the best way to truly understand the needs and frustrations of potential customers. That understanding will lead the team to the combination of product form and function that appeals and satisfies. As expressed by Don Norman in *The Design of Everyday*

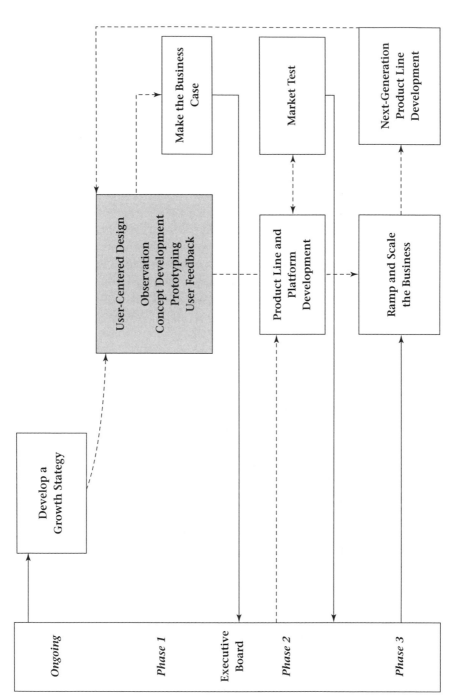

FIGURE 4.1 Focus on User-Centered Design

*Things*, that combination addresses the *total user experience*.[1] Further, as Dorothy Leonard stated so well, innovation teams that fail to step into the user's world can create costly failures and sour senior management's appetite for innovation.[2] And as we will see later, this work must continue after the new product or service is launched. After the launch, a team has even greater opportunities to learn about user needs and wants—opportunities it must exploit as it plans the next generation of its new products or services.

While a new market application may be *new* to the innovating company, target users are often served by existing solutions that must be displaced by a superior offering. That superiority must be based on more than cost. Clayton Christensen argued in *The Innovator's Dilemma* that new product lines that have a disruptive impact on an established market typically provide better functionality *in addition* to cost advantages.[3] Determining the focus and purpose of that functionality requires insight; the leveraging of current platforms and technologies can reduce costs.

## User-Centered Design as a Guiding Philosophy

User-centered design links the needs, goals, and aspirations of target users to the design of new products and services. A conceptual model of user-centered design is shown in figure 4.2; the thinking behind it comes from my friend Harry West of Continuum, one of world's leading design firms, and it reflects the design approach of the best innovation teams I have observed over the years.

As shown in figure 4.2, a compelling design reflects two streams of learning: technical learning on the product category side (left side) and deep knowledge of target users and uses (right side). It blends the aspirational with the pragmatic. The aspirational part aims to eliminate the frustrations of users or bring them new levels of delight. The pragmatic side of user-centered design brings a robust architecture, efficient use of materials, and first-rate manufacturing quality.

Each reader knows the power of this approach from personal experience. When I drive my Mazda Miata, it's the synthesis of performance, quality, and cost that brings me pleasure; my son feels the same about the synergy of form, function, and cost in his iPod. These products are each more "special" to one of us than to the other; my son likes my automobile but would rather have a Honda Element, and I view his iPod as a nicely designed appliance. If Mazda tried to make its convertible wonderful for everyone, the concept would be watered down, just as the iPod would look silly in less contemporary packaging designed for older folk. In systems, I feel that same sort of pleasure when I

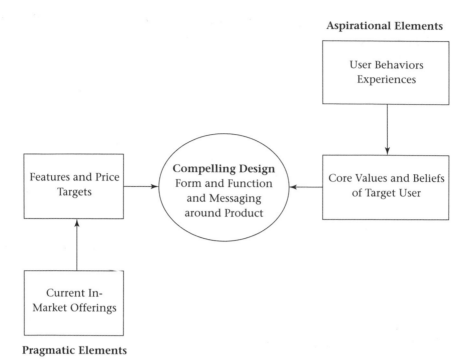

FIGURE 4.2 Integrating the Pragmatic and the Aspirational (Marc H. Meyer, Harry West, Design Continuum. Used with permission.)

use my Microsoft Visio to create diagrams or eBay's Skype to teleconference with colleagues around the world.

An innovation team's responsibility is to build each stream of learning—aspirational and pragmatic—into a powerful body of information and reflect that information in each generation of the new product line or service. To stay true to its vision, a team must first shape that vision, and this requires a deep understanding not only of what will please the target user but also of the technical and financial capabilities and limits of current materials, components, and services that can be used to deliver the solution.

Of the two streams of learning, the aspirational one is the most challenging and the one that technically trained product developers are most likely to shortchange. Most developers start straightaway on writing specifications and benchmarking them against existing solutions. Understanding aspirational desires and translating user behaviors and beliefs into design concepts involves greater uncertainty and explorations of human behaviors for which few technical people have much training.

If we could ask target users what they need and get a direct answer, break-through product development would be easy. Unfortunately, users cannot always articulate what they want and need, so an innovation team must observe how they work, live, and interact in their environments. As Vincent Barabba has written, "Consumers themselves cannot always point the way. Depending on how they are asked to describe their needs, customers rarely venture beyond their current frames of reference. More likely than not, they'll describe incrementally improved versions of current products."[4] The information we need most must be teased out through inquiry and careful observation, belly to belly, eye to eye. A user's sigh, frown of frustration, or smile of satisfaction indicates pain or pleasure with a current solution. These observations must be recorded and then aggregated into a cohesive set of user needs, from which specific design drivers can be formulated.

The pragmatic learning on the left side of the figure, in contrast, is generally less challenging intellectually, but it is equally important. For example, IBM knows precisely the performance and cost parameters for the various microprocessors and electronics that it can package into a new-generation mainframe server. Likewise, the teams that create new car concepts within Honda have access to extensive databases containing cost and other key information for components and materials. In this way, a team gets a quick handle on the costs of various "concepts"—be they for interior (such as seating) or exterior design. The ultimate goal is to bring the two streams of learning together into a compelling design that (1) satisfies the perceived and latent needs of target users and (2) is built on a robust architecture that can be cost-effectively produced and used as a launch pad for other products or services.

It's easy to say, "Yes, we pursue both streams of learning when we create new product lines," but the reality is that time-to-market pressures force the vast majority of development teams to focus overwhelmingly on the left side of the figure. That left-side focus leads to either incremental improvements to current product lines or failed new market applications. If a company is not prepared to invest as heavily in user research as it does in engineering, the strategy of new market applications development will fail.

## Four Key Elements

User-centered design is both a process and a way of thinking. It involves four key elements.

1. *Understanding the user's points of pain and pleasure.* This comes from observing what people do, why they are doing it, and the problems they encounter.

Many of the companies with which I have worked employed multimedia techniques, including videos, to capture and relay the user experience to fellow team members and management. The perceived and latent needs revealed by close observation become the design drivers for new products or services.

2. *Concept creation.* A team must take itself to a place where it can reflect on and analyze its experiences to create a set of potential solutions for users. This place should be designed to reduce distractions: no phone calls, no other meetings. It should be equipped with thinking tools: flipcharts, whiteboards, and displays of data gathered from the field. Samples of existing products and service solutions should be on hand as well. Concept creation is best accomplished when marketing and technology people work together, blending the pragmatic and aspirational sides of figure 4.2. Their brainstorming should produce graphic representations of possible solutions. For physical products, these might be concept sketches; in systems businesses, diagrams of improved workflows indicate the impact of new systems' functionality.

3. *Prototype development.* Prototyping is so easy today that there is no excuse for not doing it. In the software field, new tools allow extremely rapid prototype development. If the intended product is a new snack food, it's off to the company kitchen. If a durable consumer product is the goal, it goes to the model shop. For ever broader ranges of products, CAD and other forms of graphic designs can be electronically sent to 3D modeling firms that literally "print" prototypes in three-dimensional laminates. Services can be prototyped, too, in the experience that the user will receive, the new processes or computer systems needed to deliver the service, or the packaging of the service. Once prototypes are complete, the innovation team must work through each prototype in the context of the user and the competitive information that it has gathered and continues to gather. If the team has done its work well, at least one high-potential concept is likely to emerge.

4. *Validate the prototypes against a broader audience of target users.* The most successful companies studied for this book engaged prospective customers and their own sales forces with prototypes as a means of gathering feedback and validation—usually within a one- to two-month time frame. IBM and the software companies profiled in this book showed their prototypes to lead customers; Honda showed its new car concepts to focus groups of target users; consumer products companies assembled similar focus groups and, in some cases, placed their concepts into empirical "concept screens" with large market research firms. Whatever the method, getting prototypes into tests *fast* is the key to rapid learning. The sage advice to not let the perfect get in the way of the good applies here.

For the companies studied for this book, those that followed the four-step process had high success rates in leveraging their technologies to new market applications. Once they had probed potential customers and developed product concepts, they moved rapidly into one or more rounds of prototyping and corrections based on user feedback. *All companies can do this.* The greatest challenge may be to free talented marketing and technical staff from more mundane activities, to get out of the office and do this work.

Let's return to these four steps and dig a bit deeper.

## Diving Deep for Latent Needs

As stated earlier, the only way to truly understand target customers and their unsatisfied needs is to immerse oneself in their world. One must enter that world unencumbered by personal preferences and any preconceived notions of user needs. *Never assume that what excites you will excite others.* Never make the mistake of thinking that your problem is a problem for them. The goal is to discover what *they* like, what *they* need, what frustrates *them*.

One of the classic examples of this comes from the 1920s, when a young 3M laboratory researcher, Dick Drew, made a visit to an auto body shop near his company's St. Paul, Minnesota, headquarters. Though his mission that day was to test a new formulation of sandpaper—a staple 3M product at the time—Drew encountered a number of frustrated and angry workers who had just spoiled a new paint job by masking one color of the two-color vehicle with a piece of butcher paper, which was held in place with heavy adhesive tape. On removing the tape, they had peeled away part of the new paint job, ruining a day's work. Their frustration cued an insight for Drew, who promptly returned to his lab to begin work on a new, low-adhesive tape product that was eventually launched as "masking" tape. That tape was destined to become a successful product line for 3M and a rich source of revenue over the next 80-some years.[5]

Deep beliefs and feelings often lie just below the conscious level. Thomas Reynolds and Jonathan Gutman recommend an interviewing technique they call "laddering" to surface those beliefs and feelings. Laddering is a process that gets to the root of buying motivations by (1) digging below initial reactions and (2) mapping the linkages between reactions to specific product features, the consequences or benefits of these features, and how these benefits relate to the users' own values.[6]

For example, in a dog food product, a user might respond well to a food that looks like a bone. When asked why the shape of a bone appeals, the user might respond with thoughts on pet enjoyment. Then, when asked why pet enjoyment is important, the owner might indicate that the pet is a valued member of the family, in which case happiness is as important as health.

Deep dives into the user's environment are doubly important when the target customer is notably different than the company's traditional customer. Assuming that the person has the same needs as traditional users is foolhardy, much like failing to appreciate the difference between one type of product or service use and a new one. Market segmentation should identify the different targets in a clear way. User research then fills in each cell in the segmentation grid with the detail needed for effective design. IBM was surprised to learn, for example, that solutions for banks are different than those for the life sciences sector, just as e-business applications that connect manufacturers and suppliers are different from more conventional online transactions processing. As explained in a coming chapter, Honda learned that the needs of young men for personal transportation are very different from those of young women or most middle-aged drivers.

User needs, for the purposes of new product line or service development, span the range from the obvious, to the less obvious, to those needs for which even the user cannot imagine a solution. Let us call the first of these *perceived* needs and those with unimagined solutions *latent* needs. A user can express and articulate a likely solution for a perceived need; the latent need, by contrast, is typically expressed as a frustration for which the user has difficulty imaging a remedy.

To appreciate the difference, consider a piece of software. Software that is error-free and safe from security threats would be considered a perceived need. Software that provides seamless collaboration with colleagues over the Web to work on the same document at the same time might be a latent need. Many professionals working on joint projects want this capability, but they cannot imagine how it would actually work and how they might actually use it.

If a firm is a newcomer to an existing market, it is generally safe to assume that vendors currently serving that market are focusing on *perceived needs*. Their new products usually address some aspect of *performance, price,* and *quality* because users are consistently asking them to provide better performance at a lower price. These same customers want products and services to be even more reliable and consistent. Thus, to differentiate itself from rivals, an innovation team must address both current perceived needs *and* problems or needs for which there are *no effective solutions*. Providing such solutions will delight users and give the newcomer a competitive wedge to displace established suppliers to that market.

To win with a new market application, an innovation team must build into its products or services a resolution to *at least* one latent need. For example, the first software company to release a seamless environment for real-time collaboration on document preparation could be a winner in the next generation of office productivity tools, just as software vendors with speech recognition for certain vertical applications—such as taking physician notes—are on the cusp of mainstream success.

Successfully addressing one latent need per generation of a new product line or service is probably the ultimate answer to sustained growth. If an innovation team can discover a series of latent needs in a target market application, it can then focus development and marketing efforts on those needs, in sequence, over successive product line releases. Doing so will set competitors on their heels when the new market application is launched and keep them there as the product line or service evolves and builds share over time.

How can we uncover needs that customers themselves are unable to articulate? The answer is through intimate and direct observation of target users and buyers. One cannot uncover latent needs by sitting around the office. As spy novelist John le Carré once put it, "A desk is a dangerous place from which to watch the world." Innovation teams must get close to customers and share their experiences. And they must approach this task with humility. As a serial computer intrapraneur in one of the companies I studied commented:

> We have lots of people in this company who think that they are smarter than
> our customers. That sort of arrogance gets us into trouble. None of us is as
> smart as our customers! For new applications, our smartness has to be in trans-
> lating users' needs and frustrations into working solutions. If we do that, we
> will outsell entrenched systems and we can probably get a price premium for
> what we do. This won't happen if we just sit behind the desk and starting cod-
> ing right away.

A word of warning: Marketing departments in the larger companies studied weren't always keen on observational market research. They were more comfortable reading demographic studies and industry studies, executing customer surveys, and so forth. Those are the standard tools of the market research trade. Work was divided between those who did the research and those who used it. Engineers—the research users—were "chained to their desks" or benches and rarely given opportunities to visit and work with customers. It makes little sense having a marketing person observe a customer and then try to describe that customer's frustration to an engineer who has remained in the lab. Because the engineer has a greater sense of technical possibilities, he or she must see and "feel" the user's pain and frustration. Development teams should observe, interact with, and in some instances *become* the new target user. *"Living it" is the best way of "knowing it."* Obviously, this approach imposes costs and inconveniences, but these are justified by the rich information obtained when the people designing products or services dive deep into the experiences of users.

## Revealing Needs through Use Case Scenarios

One way to uncover the perceived and latent needs of target customers is through a use case scenario. A use case scenario describes the entire spectrum of activities that a customer experiences in using a product, system, or service. IT professionals and software developers can think of the use case scenario as the user's workflow or business process. This book contains many examples of companies that developed use case scenarios in one form or another to create interesting new products and services. IBM built an enormous business in systems integration. EMC, a storage systems manufacturer, has set its sights on "cradle-to-grave" management of information: its creation, extraction, archiving, and disk storage. In designing its new SUV, Honda identified and studied how owners would use the vehicle in an active sports mode, a party mode, and a dorm move-in mode—all very different activities than just "driving a car." Thinking about the user's before and after experiences is very important. It is in these adjacent areas that one often finds opportunities to leverage current technology.

Considering the full spectrum of use for a product or service has become a widely accepted practice in certain industries. In the software industry, for example, many consider developing use case scenarios as the best practice for creating a more holistic understanding of the software application prior to writing detailed specifications.[7] Now, let's see how it can help new product line and service development more generally.

Figure 4.3 is a template for developing a user case scenario. The three activity boxes represent the different use phases: before, during, and after. A team must understand each phase at a level of detail that reveals perceived and latent needs. Thus a construction materials manufacturer would pay attention to the architect who is designing the building, to the contractor during installation work, and to the homeowner doing repairs. By diving into these phases, innovators develop a total systems perspective.

For simplicity, the figure indicates only one layer of activity under each phase. In reality, there may be several layers; the researcher must dig down through them to a point where further digging is fruitless. As a rule of thumb, confine your digging to no more than two or three levels. Always remember that a senior executive must be able to follow what you are doing; you don't want to lose that executive in needless detail. Alternatively, if you work in a complex field, such as

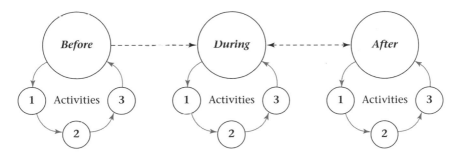

Complete for each activity: the points of pain, the points of pleasure, and competitors doing something particularly well. Also try to note differences between types of users (new, experienced) and conditions of use (stress, no stress).

FIGURE 4.3 Developing the Use Case Scenario

defense systems, your team might develop a summary version of the use case scenario that wraps up the details in a tidy package. Once all use case scenario process steps are constructed, work closely with potential customers to see what is going on within each step of the user's experience. Examine behaviors, beliefs, and needs. Try to identify the following in each process step:

— Points of pain: Points of user pain will most likely lead to specific latent needs. For example, a traveling salesperson's frustration with trying to dial a cell phone and drive at the same time might lead an automotive engineering team to consider a hands-free cell phone and speaker solution integrated into the cab. Of course, points of pain such as high cost can also lead to perceived needs and solutions in the form of less costly materials (plastic instead of wood).

— Points of pleasure. Typically, some solutions currently in a target segment provide clear value. An innovation team must understand features and functions that users find desirable in these solutions and be sure to consider these for their own new concepts. At the extreme, a team may find that the current products in a category leave little to be

desired, and as a result, the team must look elsewhere in the use case scenario to apply the company's skills and assets.
— A team should take note of those specific in-market competitors who do things well, and this attention can even lead to a new set of partners. For example, a competent service provider in the target market space might serve as an excellent business partner for a new product line.

The points of pain and points of pleasure can then be crystallized into a list of specific perceived and latent needs to drive further development.

Figure 4.4 is a simple example of a use case scenario—in this case for diapering. For a number of years, I have asked my students to develop new architectures and applications for diapering as an in-class exercise. (Users include the newborn and the incontinent, as well as hospital and industrial cleanup applications.) The figure shows a composite of the work of MBA teams during a recent class session.[8] The parenting experiences of these students helped them imagine improvements that diaper manufacturers have made or might make to address perceived and latent user needs.

For example, rash prevention emerges as a clear perceived need, and diaper manufacturers have already applied chemistries for this purpose. "Change me" indicators are much sought by first-time parents, particularly my students who are new at it. Then there is the classic latent need—a biodegradable diaper that can be flushed down the toilet after use without harm to the environment. Some students interviewed their parents for this exercise. Some elderly parents have a problem with incontinence, an entirely different diapering need; for them, privacy is a latent need. As one senior citizen put it, "I don't want anyone to see me buying diapers or know that I'm wearing one."

For another example of these same concepts in action, consider the case of military field rations, developed by the U.S. Army Soldier Systems Center in Natick, Massachusetts. Napoleon's remark that "an army moves on its stomach" has inspired generations of food scientists to develop and improve portable and nutritional field rations. In fact, the science of canning is said to have originated with the French army's need to supply Napoleon's forces in the field during the early nineteenth century.

Today, the Natick facility works continuously to improve the field fare of soldiers with meals that are lightweight, convenient, tasty, self-warming, and capable of maintaining health through the rigors of combat. Its current First Strike Ration (FSR) contains two pocket sandwiches (barbequed beef and barbequed chicken), two flavors of HooAH! energy booster bars, two servings of an energy-rich, glucose-optimized beverage mix, a dairy bar, crackers or bread, cheese spread, two sticks of beef jerky, a package of dried fruit, and a modified version of applesauce (Zapplesauce).

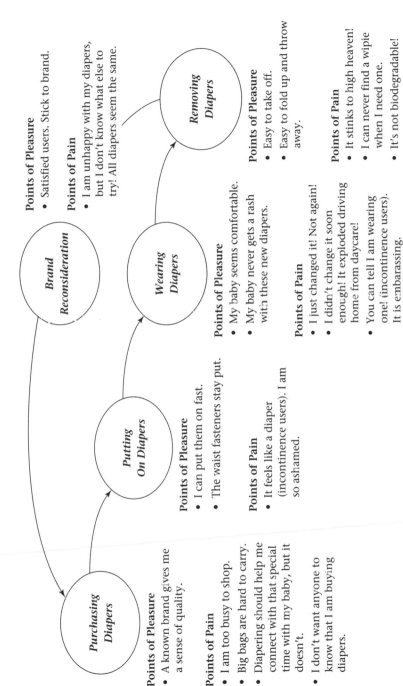

**Brand Reconsideration**

**Points of Pleasure**
- Satisfied users. Stick to brand.

**Points of Pain**
- I am unhappy with my diapers, but I don't know what else to try! All diapers seem the same.

**Removing Diapers**

**Points of Pleasure**
- Easy to take off.
- Easy to fold up and throw away.

**Points of Pain**
- It stinks to high heaven!
- I can never find a wipie when I need one.
- It's not biodegradable!

**Wearing Diapers**

**Points of Pleasure**
- My baby seems comfortable.
- My baby never gets a rash with these new diapers.

**Points of Pain**
- I just changed it! Not again!
- I didn't change it soon enough! It exploded driving home from daycare!
- You can tell I am wearing one! (incontinence users). It is embarassing.

**Putting On Diapers**

**Points of Pleasure**
- I can put them on fast.
- The waist fasteners stay put.

**Points of Pain**
- It feels like a diaper (incontinence users). I am so ashamed.

**Purchasing Diapers**

**Points of Pleasure**
- A known brand gives me a sense of quality.

**Points of Pain**
- I am too busy to shop.
- Big bags are hard to carry.
- Diapering should help me connect with that special time with my baby, but it doesn't.
- I don't want anyone to know that I am buying diapers.

FIGURE 4.4 A Use Case Scenario for Diapers

## Pack

**Points of Pleasure**

- Small, portable.

**Points of Pain**

- Can't take all you want in a field pack.
- Knowing what not to take can be hard.
- Being handed the same MRE meal that you've eaten for five days in a row.
- Carrying a heavy load.

## Consume

**Points of Pleasure**

- Hot food in the field.
- Nutrition, energy, and fortification.

**Points of Pain**

- Variety: eating the same thing day after day.
- Weight loss in the field is common.
- Packages can be hard to open.

## Dispose

**Points of Pain**

- Creates trash that has to be burned, not buried or hauled away.

FIGURE 4.5  Use Case Scenario for Infantry Field Rations (U.S. Army Soldier Systems Center. Reproduced with permission)

---

**Use Case Scenario Technique Comes to Microsoft**

In 2005, Microsoft bought Massachusetts-based Groove Networks, a start-up developer of collaboration software. In the bargain, it got Groove's innovative founder, Ray Ozzie, and named him chief technical officer. In the world of software, Ozzie is a wunderkind, best known for the creation of Lotus Notes and Symphony.

Commenting a year later on what Ozzie brought to his new position at Microsoft, Bill Gates told the *Boston Globe*, "He's bringing to Microsoft his scenario-based approach to the development of software and services. Ray's a world-class engineer, but perhaps most importantly he focuses on what people want to accomplish and then envisions the types of technologies that can make it happen. It's this type of end-to-end thinking, combined with an emphasis on simplicity and clarity, which makes Ray such an asset. . . ."

Note the language used by Gates: Focus on what people want to accomplish. Envisioning technologies that can make it happen. End-to-end (i.e., systems) thinking. Simplicity and clarity. These are code words for user-centered design and use case scenarios.[9]

---

Development of these and other rations recognizes the points of pleasure and pain, with special attention to the soldier's need to pack, consume, and dispose of ration packets (see figure 4.5).

Use case scenarios can also reveal opportunities to *eliminate* costly process steps from services. "Drive-by" meter reading by utility companies using wireless sensors is one example of how analyzing the points of pain and pleasure in use case scenarios can open the eyes of innovators to steps they can eliminate in creating value for users. Prior to drive-by metering, an employee had to stop at every house and, assuming its owner was at home, ask permission to enter and read the gas, water, or electric meter. If the homeowner was away, a card was left at the door, requesting the owner to read the meter and phone the result to the utility company within a day or two. This didn't always happen, and the utility then had to estimate usage for the next billing. That old process—and all its costs and annoyances—was eliminated with wireless technology. In fact, the drive-by step in meter reading is itself ripe for cost-saving innovation by linking homes together in a neighborhood "wireless mesh" for utility management.

## Developing a Crystal Clear Picture of the User

As we have seen, user research requires keen eyes and ears, good listening skills, and an ability to translate behaviors, attitudes, and beliefs into concrete concepts for new products and services. The best way to get started in user research is for the team to spend time with users in their own environments. It might be tempting to meet with lead users in their offices or conference rooms, but it's better to meet them where the wheels meet the road. If the target application is a food product, arrange to meet in the user's kitchen or where the food is served. If the product is a new material, go to the laboratory where lead user engineers are working with various materials. In other words, meet the user in the appropriate environment. If you listen and observe intently, needs and frustrations will become apparent.

Do not begin your first user encounters via focus groups. Group meetings usually fail to provide the intensive interactions that result in concept breakthroughs. They are too removed from the environment of the user and from the points of pain and pleasure. Rather, work one on one with users where they work or live. Save the focus groups for later, when you have sketches or prototypes.

As you observe users in action, encourage them to describe their points of pain and pleasure. Then dig for more "Ladder." If they express positive or negative reactions to products, systems, and services, tease out the reasons behind their reactions. As you develop a use case scenario, record key moments in the user's experience. Many of those moments are best captured in videos, photographs, and voice recording, so have at least two people there: one to create a warm and friendly connection with the user and another to work the camera. Videos or photographs of users in situ can also become important elements of business plan presentations to senior management.

The goal, using captured moments in film or simply the written word, is to create what Alan Cooper has called the "persona" of the target user: his or her driving needs, beliefs, experiences, emotions, and norms, which together become the ultimate arbiters for the product ideas and specific design concepts we will discuss in the next chapter.[10] That persona can be for a machine operator in a factory, a pilot in an airplane, an insurance broker trying to work with an underwriter, a young person driving a car, or even a pet eating its food—to take just a few of the examples from the companies that I studied who found user-centered design to be the essence of successful new product line or service development.

Sage words of advice from Cooper: "If you want to create a product that satisfies a broad audience of users, logic will tell you to make it as broad in its functionality as possible to accommodate the most people. *Logic is wrong.* You will have far greater success by designing for a single person" (p. 124). And further, "The broader the target you aim for, the more certainty you have of missing the bull's eye . . . you can create a bigger success by targeting 10% of your (total) market and working to make them 100% ecstatic." In a later chapter, we will see how important this concept was in Honda's success in designing a new SUV, and how by staying true to the vision captured in the persona of the target user, Honda ironically found itself appealing to a much broader population.

Therefore, an innovation team needs to create a persona for the representative target user—a set of multimedia-rich information surrounding a photograph of one of the lead users encountered in the research, a user who seems to capture the essence of the new market application. Take this back to the shop, hang it on the wall, and surround it with descriptive additions. The persona becomes the focus, the bull's eye for the team's development and marketing efforts.

With use case scenarios and personas in hand, a team can begin to identify perceived and latent needs and how current solutions fail to satisfy them. They should then ask this fundamental question: What single thing could we do to bring a smile to this user's face and make her or his experience special? The answer will help the team find design drivers for a new product line or service. Those, in turn, should lead to sketches and prototypes.

## Differentiating between Types of Users

*Not all users are the same.* Some are technically demanding; others are less so. An innovation team can learn from both. Within a market segment, one cannot assume that all users share the same needs, desires, and frustrations with current solutions. A good approach is to differentiate between lead adopters and successive stages of later adopters. Perhaps best articulated by Geoffrey Moore, the early-stage adopter of an innovation is keen to try new things.[11] These innovative early adopters are willing to experiment, share ideas, and help a company determine ways to best integrate the new product line or service within existing environments. Eric Von Hippel has even suggested that these early users—"lead users" in his terminology—can be the source of new product or service concepts for the company. Proven for certain industrial markets, the lead user as innovator concept also holds up to experience in the systems and software business (where users are constantly prototyping new applications for their own use) as well as in certain consumer markets (new food ideas being an example).[12]

At the same time, to assume that a lead user is representative of later-stage users can be disastrous. The later-stage adopters or laggards, who generally constitute the *majority* of a target market, are often skeptical of new technology. They like the functionality of an electronic device but do not appreciate gadgetry and therefore want simple, clean interfaces and interactions. In some cases, the laggard might even desire a *service* based on a new product rather than the product itself. For example, if it is software, late adopters may want the functionality but would rather run the software elsewhere and merely use it on a Web services basis. Moore's hypothesis is that a company building a new product line or service must make sure that it does not try to sell an early adopter type of solution—with all its complexity—to a market dominated by late-stage adopters.

An innovation team should start off by visiting early adopters, the self-aware users in the target market. Such users may be more knowledgeable of new competitive products and services hitting different parts of the use case scenario than members of the innovation team, at least in the beginning. Early adopters should also be able to direct the innovation team to other users who might have a better handle on experiences and process steps before or after the user's own area of concentration. These contacts are important for completing other areas of the use case scenario.

Then an innovation team must also spend time with users who are not so "smart" and not on the cutting edge of new products and technologies. This latter group may not be as interesting, but it *represents most of the potential revenue* in a target market.

This basic idea took on various subtleties among the companies I studied. One agricultural products firm wanted to better understand recent changes in its customer base. This company had always segmented its markets by "size of farm." That segmentation approach affected product packaging, volume discounts, and some service offerings. Recent performance suggested that a change in the differentiation of user types would lead to more suitable product and services offerings.

The team charged with this inquiry conducted telephone interviews with several dozen "star" salespeople who worked daily with farmers. Ideas on behaviors and buying preferences quickly emerged. Team members then went into the fields, to spend an entire day with farmers as they went about their daily operations. They observed how they used various products, how purchasing decisions were made, crop planting, growing, and harvesting technologies, and the financial challenges faced by these farmers. Strikingly different behaviors and beliefs emerged among what first seemed to be a homogeneous population of farmers. Some were highly sophisticated in their analysis of prior-year performance, decision making, and postharvest sales. These farmers were seen as lead users.

Other farmers followed a less sophisticated regimen. "If it ain't broke, don't fix it," they said. They were late adopters, if not laggards. For others, known as "sundowners," farming was a weekend avocation or a side business. They were interested in new technology but did not have a compelling business reason for trying it. All three types of farmers had distinct needs and preferences with respect to new technology, new products, and new services.

The team applied these insights to create packages of products, services, and pricing for each of these customer types and provided its channel partners with suitably tailored marketing programs.

## Observing Users in Conditions of Leisure and Stress

As suggested by Don Norman, the conditions under which products and services are used should affect their design. Thus, researchers should observe each type of condition carefully, whether the scenario is leisurely or stressful, casual or urgent.[13] Designs intended for stressful situations have to pay special attention to matching the needs of the users—such a fire exit door—and make appropriate actions easy to apply. An innovation team targeting an urgent application must place a premium on efficient, functional design.

For example, a medical device manufacturer studied for this book had two types of products: diagnostic equipment and monitoring devices for intensive care applications. For each application, teams spent substantial amounts of time with end users, cardiologists and radiologists for one application and intensive care nurses for the other. Diagnostic equipment users desired all sorts of mechanisms to "fiddle and diddle" with information, whereas the critical care nurses wanted machines that were simple and direct, easy to attach to patients, and equipped with audible, computer-based alarms. The design drivers for each type of product were heavily influenced by the intensity of the occasion of use—a visit to the radiology lab versus intensive care.

New products or services made for nonstressful situations—such as occasions of leisure or learning—also force designers to adopt a much broader focus beyond pure functionality. Norman describes this as an integrative application within the user's environment. Here, the appearance of the product will have a more pronounced effect on the user, who has more time to appreciate the styling. At the end of the day, innovation teams must seek a balance between form and function. As Norman writes, "Good design means that beauty and usability are in balance," even though the occasion of use may have an important role in determining emphasis within that balance.[14]

## The Emotional Side of Learning and New Product Adoption

As teams dive deep into the user experience, they should heed user emotions and how those emotions respond to both current offerings and prototypes. Emotions in many instances are the portal through which the latent needs of potential customers can be accessed.

Many of the technology and systems companies studied for this book provide products and services with little explicit emotional content, such as data storage systems. Others, however, are in the realm of consumer products, where user emotions matter. Gerald Zaltman has studied the role of emotions in user decision making with respect to trial and repeat usage and how traditional survey research generally fails to capture emotional content.[15] Use case scenarios, particularly points of pain and points of pleasure, help capture that emotion. Some of the consumer product teams I studied went to great lengths to understand, map, and utilize user emotions as they developed new product concepts.

Consider the case of Mars, a food manufacturer we will study closely later in this book. Its pet food division performed user research for a new product line for dogs that looked like a bone but was also a fully nutritious main meal. The team that worked on this project had to consider many different types of users. First were the pets—different breeds, sizes, and ages, each with unique nutritional needs. Then there were the pet owners—men and women—each with different behaviors and needs. The use case study of pet owners revealed a web of emotions, many conflicting, about giving the animal what it might enjoy versus what the owner knew to be most nutritious, about all-natural versus processed, and so forth. (See figure 4.6.) Last, pet food retailers had to be considered as "users," and there were very different types of retailers. Wal-Mart, for instance, is quite different from a grocery chain, and a grocery chain has some needs that a pet specialty store does not share. Each of these three constituencies had to be observed and understood to create an effective solution. The animals' needs would affect nutritional and other health-related decisions, the pet owners' needs would have an impact on packaging and product design, and the needs of retailers would affect merchandising and SKU decisions.

Team members went shopping with these different users. They tagged along as owners fed their pets and took them for walks. When team members reconvened, they synthesized their observations. Specific needs, frustrations, and pleasures associated with shopping, feeding, and playing with dogs were written on Post-It notes, with user comments. Those notes were stuck onto a wall and then consolidated into groups of common emotions. This is shown in figure 4.6, a "path map" of humans' emotions regarding feeding their pets.

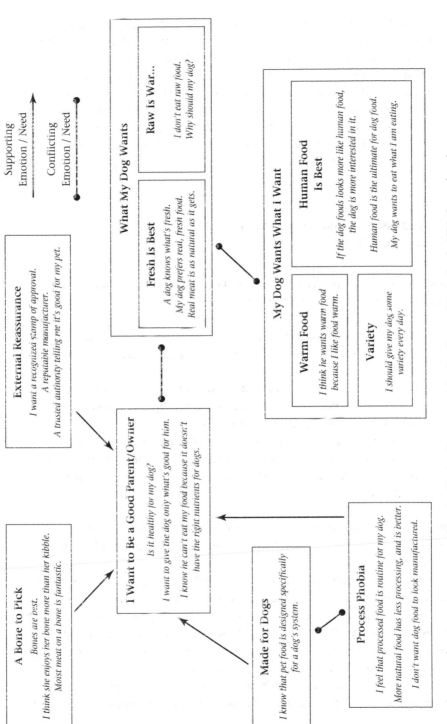

Supporting
Emotion / Need

Conflicting
Emotion / Need

**External Reassurance**

*I want a recognized stamp of approval.*
*A reputable manufacturer.*
*A trusted authority telling me it's good for my pet.*

**What My Dog Wants**

**Fresh Is Best**

*A dog knows what's fresh.*
*My dog prefers real, fresh food.*
*Real meat is as natural as it gets.*

**Raw Is War...**

*I don't eat raw food.*
*Why should my dog?*

**My Dog Wants What I Want**

**Warm Food**

*I think he wants warm food*
*because I like food warm.*

**Variety**

*I should give my dog some*
*variety every day.*

**Human Food**
**Is Best**

*If the dog foods looks more like human food,*
*the dog is more interested in it.*

*Human food is the ultimate for dog food.*

*My dog wants to eat what I am eating.*

**A Bone to Pick**

*Bones are pest.*
*I think she enjoys her bone more than her kibble.*
*Moist meat on a bone is fantastic.*

**I Want to Be a Good Parent/Owner**

*Is it healthy for my dog?*

*I want to give the dog only what's good for him.*

*I know he can't eat my food because it doesn't*
*have the right nutrients for dogs.*

**Made for Dogs**

*I know that pet food is designed specifically*
*for a dog's system.*

**Process Phobia**

*I feel that processed food is routine for my dog.*
*More natural food has less processing, and is better.*
*I don't want dog food to look manufactured.*

FIGURE 4.6 The Conflicting Emotions of the Pet Owner (Masterfoods, USA. Reproduced with permission)

The team had uncovered a rich world of user emotions and conflict. The first conflict should be familiar to any parent of small children: Food that a dog might enjoy most isn't always the most nutritious. There was also a conflict between convenience and taste appeal. The food that was easiest for the pet owner to serve, dry kibble, was less appealing to the pet than canned food. As often happens, within those conflicts was a latent need for a food that dogs would enjoy eating, that would be fully nutritious, and that would be convenient to serve. That latent need became the design driver for a new product that we will encounter in chapter 10.

## Developing a Learning Model for Target Users

Learning is a two-way street in the world of new market applications. An innovation team must ask itself some questions.

— How do potential customers learn about new products or services? Do they respond to general advertising, or do they require trusted sources of information?
— What must users learn to make a decision about trying a new product or service? In addition to the benefits claimed by the innovator, how important is price in the user's overall trial decision?
— Once the decision to try a product or service is made, what else must the user learn to gain maximum value and appreciation from that trial?
— What proof will make the trial of a new product or service a lasting adoption?

A systems approach to the user and the end-to-end experience can reveal answers to these questions, and those answers should guide product development and marketing.

The learning requirements for complex products, such as new software, can be very demanding—so demanding that the learning "problem" may stand between innovators and the new product's adoption, *unless* users' learning needs are anticipated and addressed. When an innovation team asks target users to learn a new way of doing things, they must understand how users try, or decide not to try, new approaches and technologies.

Even for simple products, such as the food, tools, and personal hygiene items studied for this book, understanding the user's learning model can be critically important. As noted earlier, just because a new product line or service represents a new market application for a company, it does not mean that users aren't already using another product. In fact, they typically are, and they typically have plenty of choices. The innovator must therefore understand what it will take to break through the various barriers that prevent users from adopting superior solutions: laziness, fear, switching costs, and/or downstream integration factors.[16] The innovator must also understand what it will take to cut through all the marketing thrown up by competitors.[17] Put all these together, and one has a learning model.

A learning model describes the target user's cognitive process for learning about products, trying them, and choosing those that provide solutions. A well-constructed learning model does more than inform product design; it also reveals user decision making and suggests ideas for marketing communications and customer support.

For example, one of the companies studied wanted to make a new product line for 20- to 30-year-old consumers. Its current products, however, were designed for an older crowd. The company created an innovation team with marketers and engineers, all under the age of 30. The team began a series of ethnographic observations of target users recruited through friends who were still at universities in the Boston and Boulder areas. Team members went shopping with these people and spent time in their homes to observe behaviors. They returned with some clear conclusions. People in this age bracket were distrustful of mass media advertising and preferred to get their information from trusted sources. They were aggressive testers of new products yet would quickly return to old ones if a first trial produced an unsatisfactory result. The new design concepts and marketing programs this team created—with the intention of encouraging trial and adoption—were radically different from those used by the company's existing product lines.

## Test Ideas with Users

The next step is to test and validate the new product or service concept with a larger set of potential users. Focus groups are useful for this purpose and should be formed around different subsegments or user populations within the broader target market.

But what about the formal, survey type of market research that is so common in modern business? When should it come into play? Perhaps never! The technology firms I studied created new concepts, developed them into prototypes,

---

**Make the Sales Force Your Ally**

Target users are not the only people the innovation team should talk to. They should also learn from their company's own salespeople. Unfortunately, in many of the large companies studied, whereas R&D and marketing were often at odds, R&D acted as if sales was not even part of the company.

A good salesperson knows how customers are being underserved by current products, both yours and those of competitors. The good salesperson also understands what frustrates users and how they make purchasing decisions. Sure, a salesperson may not be able to create a knockout solution, but he or she can often recognize a winning idea.

So don't be afraid to show salespeople your prototypes. Get their counsel on developing ideas and marketing programs. Make them part of your larger team. Make them your ally for innovation, and they will help you understand how to communicate the proposition to the sales force, middlemen, and users.

---

worked with users to improve them, and then went into a launch and learn mode. Even consumer product companies known for their extensive empirical market research created new norms focused on testing prototypes with actual user panels, as opposed to placing "concepts" into blind tests with large samples. However, teams developing new product lines with substantial capital investments for manufacturing may be asked to justify their revenue projections with empirical research, and then, you must do it. For the pharmaceutical companies, empirical validation is built into the drug approval process. Each team, however, must decide whether a more rapid launch and learn approach is suited to, and feasible for, its new market applications development. If it is, set aside convention and push hard for in-market experiential learning.

## Reader Exercises

It is now your turn to apply the methods presented in this chapter to a new market application of your choosing. You should already be armed with a preliminary market segmentation grid from the previous chapter, and you should have circled one or several of the regions on the segmentation grid as target candidates. Select the most promising as your main target.

Here are your exercises:

**Exercise 1** Identify a set of individuals or companies that are the target users of your new market application. Consider how to approach these users, using the contacts you have. Ask to spend a day in their work or social environment, whichever is better suited to your product or service idea. Try to set up at least two meetings but not more than five for this first pass.

**Exercise 2** Spend time with these users over the coming weeks. Ask the user's permission to videorecord or take photographs of a few representative scenes pertinent to the product or service concept. Visuals will help you later as you close in on a design concept. A few excellent photographs will also bring your executives into the user's world. Your goal is to develop a clear image of your target user. After each visit, develop the use case scenario. Add in the points of pain and pleasure in the user's own words. Do not worry about format. Surround the visual image of your target user with a montage of Post-It notes or other records of the user's statements.

**Exercise 3** Aggregate your ethnography from these field visits into a robust use case scenario, then develop a list of perceived and latent needs. Try to benchmark these needs against current products and services in the target market. You should be able to identify one or more clear opportunities to create a distinctive product or service that makes something possible that is not possible now and that brings pleasure and satisfaction to the target use that no other current competitor can match.

Now, sketch your product or service concept. If it's software, have someone on your team or a colleague build a quick prototype of a central screen or report. Modern software tools make this easy! These needs, and the potential product or service solutions, become the hypotheses to be validated through further research.

**Exercise 4** Present your findings as a package to colleagues who have not participated in the field research. For that presentation, assemble and integrate your use case scenarios, your list of perceived and latent needs, competitive benchmarks, video clips, sketches, and prototypes as a package of ethnographic, empathic research. You will also need this package to get endorsement from the senior management team. In fact, most executives will be just as interested in your user insights as they will be in financial projections.

After this presentation, sit back, reflect, and decide whether it worthwhile translating these user insights into full concepts and prototypes. It is to that topic that we turn our attention next.

## Notes

1. Donald Norman, *The Design of Everyday Things* (New York: Basic Books, 2002).

2. Dorothy Leonard and Jeffrey Rayport, "Spark Innovation through Empathic Design," *Harvard Business Review*, November–December 1997, 102–13. This remains a fundamentally important article for those seeking to build new market applications.

3. Clayton Christensen, *The Innovator's Dilemma* (Boston: Harvard Business School Press, 1997).

4. Vincent P. Barabba, *Meeting of the Minds* (Boston: Harvard Business School Press, 1995), 49–50.

5. 3M Corporation Web site, www.3m.com/about3M/pioneers/drew2.html.

6. Thomas Reynolds and Jonathan Gutman, "Laddering Theory, Method, Analysis, and Interpretation," *Journal of Advertising Research,* February–March 1988, 11–31. Also see Gerald Zaltman and R. Coulter, "Seeing the Voice of the Customer: Metaphor-Based Advertising Research," *Journal of Advertising Research*, 1995, 35(4): 35–51.

7. Dean Leffingwell and Donald Widrig, *Managing Software Requirements: A Use Case Approach* (New York: Addison Wesley Professional, 2003); Kurt Bittner and Ian Spence, *Use Case Modeling*, (New York: Addison Wesley, 2003).

8. Northeastern University High Technology MBA, Class of 2007, Managing Innovations session on November 5, 2005, with particular acknowledgment to Brad Biswas and Nathan Butts, who, as new parents, led our discussion that day.

9. Robert Weisman, "How Office Got Its Grove," *Boston Globe*, March 13, 2006, E1, E5.

10. Alan Cooper, *The Inmates are Running the Asylum: Why High Tech Products Drive Us Crazy and How to Restore Sanity* (Indianapolis: Sams, 2004), 124.

11. Geoffrey Moore, *Crossing the Chasm: Marketing and Selling Mainstream Customers* (New York: HarperCollins, 2002).

12. Eric Von Hippel, *The Sources of Innovation* (Oxford: Oxford University Press, 1988).

13. Donald A. Norman, "Emotion and Design: Attractive Things Work Better," *Interactions Magazine*, 2002, 9(4): 36–42.

14. Ibid., 42.

15. Gerald Zaltman, "Rethinking Market Research: Putting People Back In," *Journal of Marketing Research*, 1997, 34(4): 424–37.

16. Everett Rogers, *The Diffusion of Innovations*, 4th edition (New York: Free Press, 1995).

17. Marty Neumeier, *The Brand Gap: How to Bridge the Distance between Business Strategy and Design* (Berkeley, CA: New Riders Publishing, 2003).

# CHAPTER FIVE

# Creating Design Concepts, Prototyping, and Validating Design Choices

*Translating needs into design concepts—Total product versus design versus individual subsystems—Food and computer applications—Automobile and service applications— Prototyping and participative user design: a software example—Validating prototypes with conjoint studies, market testing, and prelaunch filters.*

The next step in user-centered design is to translate observed user needs into product or service concepts. This chapter introduces methods for leveraging insights gained from user research into full-fledged, user-tested designs and prototypes.

## Creating Design Concepts

As explained in the previous chapter, use case scenarios are a powerful method for uncovering the perceived and latent needs of target users. From this work, the innovation team can develop a list of potential features and benefits to build into its new product line or service. Most practitioners use that list to propose a product or service concept and illustrate it with sketches or diagrams. This act of creation produces a *design concept*. A design concept is the creative and cost-effective solution that satisfies users' needs—that delivers points of pleasure and removes points of pain. A design concept can be applied to the entire product or service. However, as we will see, many firms find it best to create design concepts for major parts or subsystems of the overall product or service and then aggregate and harmonize these into a pleasing and manu-facturable whole.

Form and function are important elements of a design concept. As Donald Norman has argued so eloquently, good design balances form and function without sacrificing either.[1] People generally want products that have a pleasing appearance *and* a high level of usability. *Simplicity* is increasingly become more important as designers struggle to unify form and function; many actually now see simplicity as a way to achieve greater functionality for the user. *Elegant* design combines a clean exterior with a high level of usability.

Design elegance must be achieved at all levels, not just on the surface. Over-all appearance—and touch and feel—is important, but it is just one of several subsystems through with customer needs may be addressed. Further, each level has its own requirements for elegance. For example, in an automobile, el-egance in exterior styling is critical, but so is elegance in passenger compart-ment styling, the power train, and so forth. Each of these subsystems plays an important part in the overall architecture of the vehicle. You cannot have a great automobile if any one subsystem is "clunky" or subpar. The same applies to services. For example, there is nothing clunky about the user's experience with Amazon. We can easily find titles, read reviews and ratings, see related ti-tles, and have Amazon keep our payment and shipping information to expe-dite our purchases. It is a simple yet powerful shopping portal.

## Linking Needs and Subsystems

In Ikujiru Nonaka's theory of organizational learning and knowledge creation, tacit knowledge is transformed into explicit knowledge.[2] In the context of new product line and service development, that tacit knowledge is the team's un-derstanding of the target user's beliefs, values, and needs—both articulated and unarticulated. An engineering specification for the product to be made (or of the computer system needed to enable a new service) is the end point ex-pression of explicit knowledge. Getting from A (a team's tacit knowledge of user needs) to B (the engineering specification) is the challenge. For Nonaka, multifunctional teams are a primary means for making this transition; they bring to bear the diversity in thinking needed for new concept creation.

The most successful companies studied mastered the transition from tacit understandings to explicit expression. They did this by connecting user needs with one or more subsystems of the product or service. Once that connection is identified, a subsystem design concept for serving that need can be created. Linking needs to design concepts for subsystem innovation helps resolve internal debate over which features should be designed into a particular subsystem.

But what is a subsystem? A subsystem is a part or set of parts that collectively provide a particular functionality within the total product or service. For example, the disposable diaper has many different components. A smaller set of major subsystems includes the absorbent core, the cuffs, and the fastening subsystem. These provide the major elements of functionality in the diaper: the core, absorbing the unmentionables; the cuffs, keeping the unmentionables contained; and the fasteners, keeping the diaper on the body. Within each of these major subsystems are subsidiary subsystems, such the external barrier and the internal barrier surrounding the absorbent core. These, too, have specific materials and chemicals, or parts. Subsystems, as well as the parts within subsystems, are typically connected through engineered interfaces, which in this case are chemical bindings between the various layers.

The combination of the major subsystems and interfaces constitutes the *architecture* of the product or service. And because we are talking about a line or series of related products or services, the architecture is really a *product line or service architecture*. In a later chapter, we will examine how to maximize the utility of an architecture—to create *platforms*—for rapid and efficient generation of products and services. For now, however, we merely need to know that few products are monolithic; they have subsystems and connections between those subsystems called interfaces.

Figure 5.1 describes general approach for linking user needs to design concepts and, in turn, to subsystem innovation. The increasing modularity of products and services lends itself to greater flexibility in designing solutions to meet specific user needs. In the figure, the compelling user needs are shown on the left, arrayed in no particular order. The middle is a series of design concepts created to serve each compelling user need. The major subsystems of the product line architecture are on the right side. The arrows in the figure represent a mapping of needs to design concepts to specific subsystem innovations. Although the relationship may be one need to one design concept to one subsystem, that's the exception. Most needs can be served by more than one design concept.

Every development team in my study found more than one way to address perceived or latent user needs. They accomplished this by drilling down through layers of systems and subsystems, and connecting each to a need. For example, "taste" could be addressed through a recipe, "easy open" through packaging, "ease of use" through the user interface, "durability" through the product frame, "economy" through component design and/or materials, and so on. The overall product design, then, is a composite of many specific subsystem design concepts.

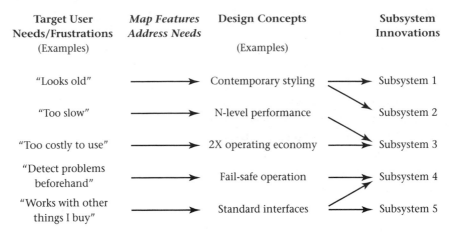

FIGURE 5.1  Mapping User Needs to Design Concepts to Subsystem Innovations

## Two Applications: Food and Computers

Let's see how figure 5.1 applies to a product line developed by Mars, a company whose work will be described in greater detail in chapter 9. Mars launched a new energy bar to the market in 2004. It was actually a product *line* with four varieties. The overall product concept for this new line may be summarized as "an energy bar that tastes good!" The company performed a number of concept tests with consumer panels to validate the attractiveness of this concept. Great idea. But how could the customer's need for high energy and good taste be translated into a design concept?

If you were part of the energy bar's development team and were tasked to implement this concept, you wouldn't rush to final design. Instead, you would ask, "What does that concept really mean and how do we translate it into various parts of the product?" Those parts might include the bar's ingredients, its packaging material and packaging graphics, and even the display of different varieties on store shelves (i.e., how will it stand out from the competition).

The innovation team focused on the recipe and size of the bar, creating a design concept that provided 10 grams of protein with less than 3 grams of fat. The recipe in this design would also have a superior taste based on peanut and other nut flavors already well understood and highly refined for the Mars Snickers candy bar. As for the packaging subsystem, the design concept aimed to convey high energy and great taste all at once. This concept was executed by printing distinctive colors and graphics on the bar's wrapping. Other members of the innovation team focused on "shelf leadership" through store placement and merchandising strategies. In the end, the product was a success, in no small part because the team stayed true to very specific design concepts for three major subsystems—product, packaging, and merchandising—and balancing them against pragmatic considerations of cost and shelf life.

Concept design is no less important for "high tech" products. For example, IBM's new mainframe server concepts, while incredibly complex, can be reduced to a few major subsystems. Each addresses a clear need, but when combined, they deliver an even greater synergistic punch to serve and satisfy users. Its parallel processing architecture allows banks of microprocessors to scale pure processor power for high-volume users (Need #1); high throughput I/O channels provide the capability to access ever larger amounts of data (Need #2); special-purpose processors provide more efficient execution of Linux and Java applications (Need #3); and the core operating system (zOS) and encryption chips provide robust, multilevel security (Need #4). These four needs are not executed amorphously. Rather, they are baked into specific parts of the overall design and provide impact that is clear and decisive.

In IBM's case, the compelling user needs that would appear on the left side of figure 5.1 include processing power, data capacity, application flexibility, and security. Some are perceived needs, and others are latent. IBM's systems designers conceived of specific design concepts to address each of these needs. Multipoint switching—described in chapter 1—was the concept for achieving unmatched scalability in processing power. Special processor designs for Linux and Java, running in parallel with standard zSeries microprocessors, provided users with application flexibility. By putting these two design concepts together and merging them with other subsystems concepts for achieving high-bandwidth I/O and systems security, IBM produced a killer machine. And yes, the company gave its computers a sleek and powerful look, very different from the behemoths of yesteryear.

Both Mars and IBM worked hard to understand users' perceived and latent needs. They then moved to create design concepts for specific subsystems that would serve those needs. Finally, each company built its subsystems and overall solutions within the strict confines of a predetermined and rigorously enforced architecture. The result for Mars was an energy bar product with growing sales; for IBM, the result was a best-selling mainframe server. These were not serendipitous outcomes; they resulted from user-centered designs and balanced product architectures.

### Why Simple Is Best

The template in figure 5.1 follows the established literature on "voice of the customer" concepts and methods, but seeks a simpler approach. The voice of the customer method stems from the quality functional design (QFD) literature, where the "house of quality" links customer needs to specific engineering measures of product performance.[3] A team's engineering objectives are then often benchmarked against competitors on a feature-by-feature basis.

In practice, many of the product developers in the companies I studied struggled with the escalating complexity of creating and maintaining such design matrices. The prioritization of numerous user needs, matched against multiple customer sets, proved cumbersome and often ineffective. For example, as described by Abbie Griffin and John Hauser, discussions with customers usually identify 200 to 400 customer needs,[4] which are then placed into need hierarchies. Half a dozen user needs entail substantial complexity. Imagine working with dozens, or hundreds! Then consider the difficulty of managing a needs hierarchy and its associated design implementation matrix in a dynamic market where users and needs are changing rapidly. Then, there is always the risk that when a method requires "empiricization," an attribute that cannot be empirically measured—such as appearance or ease of use—is often left as an afterthought. Figure 5.1 offers a simpler, more intuitive approach.

## Driving Form User Needs to Design Concepts to Subsystem Innovation

The product development work of Honda Motor Company provides an example of how design concepts can be translated into product features that users cherish. An earlier generation of the Accord product line, which came to market in the late 1990s, brings the template shown in figure 5.1 to life.

Key customer need drivers were integrated into Honda's concept development for this Accord. All were based on user research. For the market segments targeted by the Accord team, users looked for these qualities:

— A clean environment
— Passenger safety
— High performance
— Fuel economy
— Ample interior space for both passengers and cargo
— Sporty styling and handling

These user needs became drivers for the new Accord's concept design. Honda also added its own requirements: It wanted its new vehicle to (1) enhance Honda's reputation for providing great value (i.e., benefits relative to price) and (2) surpass users' expectations of value. Figure 5.2 captures those user and

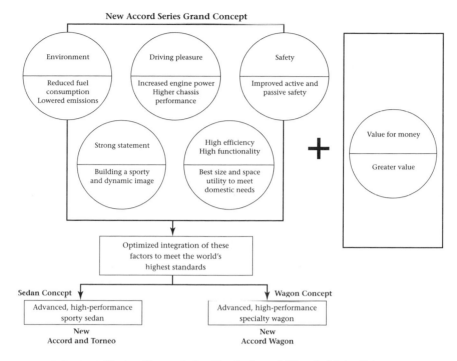

FIGURE 5.2 Design Concepts for Honda Accord (Honda Motor Company. Reproduced with permission)

corporate values. Together they formed the grand concept for the Accord vehicle platform.

The Accord team had to translate those high-level values into more specific product themes and then into specific design strategies for all major subsystems in the product line architecture. Some of the major Accord subsystems included:

— The exterior styling
— The interior styling and fixtures, such as seating
— The power train, which included the engine, the transmission, and the exhaust system
— The chassis, including frame, suspension, and braking systems

Figure 5.3 indicates how those key subsystems were translated into specific design concepts. Let's walk through a few examples. The sporty design requirement (see "Strong statement" in figure 5.2) was implemented in specific exterior

| Theme ⟶ | Concept ⟶ | Technology ⟶ |
|---|---|---|
| Driving pleasure | • Engine: combine high power and lower fuel consumption<br>• Transmission: improved shift feel<br>• Suspension: high stability and passenger comfort<br>• Steering: dramatically improved control and road feel<br>• 4WD system: combine tenacity and lighthearted ride<br>• Body: dynamic performance and safety, with quiteness | • 2.0 liter DCHC VTEC engine<br>• Directly controlled 4 speed automatic with S-matic<br>• 5-link double wishbone rear suspension<br>• New EPS (electronic power steering) and VGR (variable steering gear ratio)<br>• Dual-pump real time 4WD<br>• Rigid, quiet body |
| Environment | • Low fuel consumption and higher power output<br>• Low emissions reduced exhaust gas emissions<br>• Further progress in utilization of resources and recycling | • 1.8 liter VTEC engine<br>• 2.0 liter VTEC LEV (Low emissions) engine<br>• All versions clear standards in force<br>• Switch to polypropylene plastics<br>• Reduced weight |
| Safety | • Active safety: improvement in basic functions (driving, turning, stopping)<br>• Thorough pursuit of stability in vehicle behavior<br>• Passive safety: meeting world standards for impact safety functions | • VSA (Vehicle stability assist)<br>• ABS standard in all models<br>• Navigation system with wandering alert device<br>• HID headlights<br>• Body designed for safety for impact from any direction<br>• Driver and passenger front SRS airbags as standard equipment<br>• Direct clamp ELR seat belts with load limiter |
| Strong statement | • Exterior: advanced, dynamic image<br>• Interior: fashionable, sporty image | Exterior<br>• Advanced styling giving foretaste of performance<br>• Forward cabin and long tail for wedge shape design<br>Interior<br>• Sporty cockpit<br>• Deluxe finishing |
| High efficiency<br>High functionality | • Packaging: practical size and spacious interior<br>• Accessories: full complement of features for increased performance and comfort | Packaging<br>• Compact (5 number) design<br>• Thoughtful details to make driving easier<br>• Generous interior space<br>• Accessible, roomy trunk space<br>Interior<br>• New generation Honda Navigation System<br>• BOSE sound system<br>• Numerous amenities and ample storage space |

FIGURE 5.3  Translating User Needs to Design Concepts to Subsystem Innovations for the Honda Accord (Honda Motor Company. Reproduced with permission)

and interior concepts. For the exterior, Honda developed a wedge-shape design with a forward positioned cabin, a long tail, and a sharply defined view of the car from the rear. A sporty cockpit was deemed essential to achieve a sporty image for the interior styling. Its components had to be freshly developed.

Driving performance, another important user need, would be achieved through a number of key subsystems. Look carefully at figure 5.3 in the row titled "Driving pleasure," and you will see that Honda's team developed specific concepts for the power train and the chassis. Note the clear differences between the second column and the third, where design concepts are the goals, and technologies are specific means for achieving those goals. The row titled "Environment" is equally interesting; it cuts across both engine technology and new composite materials used to reduce weight (and yield higher fuel efficiency).

Together, figures 5.2 and 5.3 indicate how this company translated what it learned about user needs into specific product developments. Take a few minutes to study these figures and reflect on their application to your own situation.

User-centered design made it possible for Honda to simultaneously develop two new Accord sedans and one station wagon, all based on common platforms. That architecture was sufficiently robust to accommodate vehicles with slightly different physical dimensions built for different geographic regions. It accommodated a front-wheel drive North American Accord sedan and coupe, a Japanese Accord sedan and wagon, both with four-wheel drive capability, and a front-drive European Accord sedan.

At the time, the estimated development budget for the new Accord and its five models was more than $500 million (in 1998 dollars), including tooling at three plants.[5] Given the magnitude of that investment, it was obviously essential to get the product concept correct.

Honda has followed this approach in subsequent model changes. By any measure, that approach succeeded, and it continues to succeed. In 2006, for example, the Accord was rated best in class for the $20,000–$25,000 passenger car category by *Consumer Reports*.

## A Service Application of the Method

Honda's successful method of moving from user needs to design concepts to product features works equally well for services businesses. I observed this in one of the companies in my research base—a workers' compensation insurer. In that industry, companies have pursued profitability and market success by using computers to reduce costs and to catch cheaters making false injury claims. The firm I studied pursued a different approach.[6]

This insurer, a spin-off from a managed care health insurer, aimed to apply classic managed care approaches to workers' compensation. The traditional philosophy of managed care is that better health leads to reduced life cycle costs. As applied to workers' comp, this insurer decided to focus on *injury prevention*. The company felt if prevention could be understood and systematized, claims could be substantially reduced.

Armed with that vision, an innovation team—which included an operations executive, a nurse, a workplace injury consultant, and a claims adjudicator—visited customers, observed employees at work, spoke with people who had been injured, conferred with facilities managers, and worked with finance departments on plans that would reward workplace injury prevention. The design concepts that emerged were then translated into procedures, policies, computer systems, and actual insurance contracts, once again following the template shown in figure 5.1. The subsystem innovations that emerged were

— *Injury prevention.* To prevent injuries, the company developed and implemented a "total injury prevention process" tailored to each targeted market. This program initiated practices that would substantially reduce worksite injuries. Compliance with these practices was built into the insurer's contracts with its employer customers.

— *Accident reporting.* Each company used a combination of reporting processes and computer technology to quickly move injured workers into treatment. These processes were also built into the insurance contracts.

— *Treatment and return.* This subsystem focused on the full recovery of injured workers and their rapid return to work. The treatment subsystem itself had two major components: a medical delivery network (physicians and therapists) and case managers who helped shape workers' treatment plans. For the former, the company developed a network of several thousand physicians who specialized in the types of injuries suffered by its clients; these physicians were familiar with return-to-work issues. Each injured employee was directed to the most appropriate medical provider for care. The company also hired case managers, often former nurses, to speed recovery and return to work by arranging proper therapy and by monitoring conformance.

— *Claims management.* This involved the adjudication of injury claims. Here, the company trained claims adjusters and equipped them with computer technology. Here, the company just tried to use existing best practices in the industry.

These concepts and the programs developed to achieve them are shown in figure 5.4. This insurer's innovation team looked at how competing insurers

| Subsystem | The Problem | Traditional Approach | This Insurer's Approach |
|---|---|---|---|
| Injury Prevention | Inadequate safety guidelines; 85% workplace injuries due to workplace hazards. | Random Workplace checking for basic compliance, but not so much so as to increase the insurer's expenses. *Injuries due to hazards constitute 85% of injuries.* | **Total Injury Prevention Process.** Loss control consultants, assigned to a group of companies, work intensively with top management to identify hazards, set shared goals to fix them, apply prepackaged programs. *Injuries due to hazards drop to about 10%.* |
| Management Systems and Training | Accidents are not reported rapidly. Injured persons go untreated or see the wrong physician. Problems that might be corrected quickly are left to worsen. | Insurers see rapid accident reporting as increasing claims expense, or at least increasing their own working capital requirements. | **Rapid Reporting.** This lessens overall claims expense. Procedures ensure that injured workers are assigned a physician and a case worker within 24 hours. |
| Medical Delivery System | Injured persons often see doctors who do not know best how to treat them. This increases disabled rates and lengthens return to work periods. | To "save costs," insurers will refer injured workers to any physician that is part of discount network. *Injured claims are 90% of total claims.* | **Managed Physicians Network.** Developed a network (now about 2000 doctors) of primary occupational physicians who are paid on services contracts and measured on medical outcomes. *Injured worker claims are about 10% of total claims.* |
| Case Management | Injured workers are left at home to fend for themselves. | Injured workers are not assigned a case manager for weeks. | **Back to Health Case Management.** A nurse, responsible for a panel of companies, is assigned to an injured worker within 24 hours of injury to establish return to work plans and oversee care. |
| Claims Management | Claims are paid late. Workman's comp in also known for significant levels of fraudulent claims activity. | Claims are paid as late as possible to reduce claims expense. Claims are also funneled through functional departments—getting delayed in the shuffle. | Claims managers obtain medical diagnosis and return to work plans, and have responsibility for specific employers and for fraudulent tendencies. Unresolved claims are tracked to try to keep them at a minimum. |
| Performance Measurement | Employers measure only final outcomes, by which time it is too late to affect those final outcomes. | Most insurers only measure the loss ratio (claims to premium dollars) and the average claim dollar amount. | **Shared Performance Rewards.** Management tracks a whole series of activity measures and outcomes measures for service teams, physicians, and partners. |

FIGURE 5.4  An Insurer's Translation of User Needs to Design Concepts to Service Innovations
(Marc H. Meyer)

addressed each of these subsystems. The team then designed programs and processes that would either bring each subsystem to parity with competitors or, better, surpass them.

This new way of thinking about workplace injury was widely adopted by thousands of the insurer's client companies, with impressive results. The average client reduced its workers' compensation costs by more than 25 percent, and 95 percent of all client companies experienced cost savings. Employers also litigated 60 percent fewer claims. More important, the average claim dropped to about a third less than the industry average. The application of managed care as a design concept, coupled with subsystem innovation, gave traditional industry leaders not only a surprise but also a new business model to follow.

## Building Prototypes and Getting User Feedback

The next step in the new market applications development process is to rapidly build prototypes and use them to obtain intimate user feedback. A basic rationale for prototyping comes from Stefan Thomke, who cites a leading industrial design firm's use of cheap, rough prototypes and its willingness to "fail often to succeed sooner" as ways to quickly eliminate suboptimal solutions and close in on designs that do the job for users.[7] Another rationale is that a good prototype makes concept sketches and business plans *come alive* for senior executives.

The prototyping process is straightforward. An innovation team works in its own model shop, on its computers, or hires an outside design firm to put together a series of potential solutions that link user needs to design concepts to subsystem expression. The team then shows its prototypes to target users, observes their reactions, *listens carefully* to their ideas for improvement, and quickly reflects those ideas in improved prototypes.

To take advantage of rapid prototyping, a firm must invest in mechanisms that assure access to willing users and prospective customers. IBM has built computing centers in which developers, marketers, and lead users convene to test and evaluate new solutions. Honda creates new model prototypes and demonstrates them to panels of users, often in the users' own environment. In the Mars pet products division, user panels are both four-footers (dogs and cats) and their two-footed owners. In some cases, testing is done in the company's facilities; in others, prototypes are sent to the owner's home.

Every prototype represents an experiment, and every failure provides an opportunity to learn and improve. These prototypes are not fully architected, stable production systems or fully usable products or services. That comes later. My work with companies has shown that successive improvements through a series of prototypes and user feedback help refine a product or service concept better than anything that can be accomplished through impersonal surveys or virtual descriptions. "Hands-on" wins over questionnaires and virtual reality every time.

## The Prototyping Process in a Software Company

For an example of prototyping and iterative development, consider The Math-Works, a market leader in computational software. It was founded in 1984 in the belief that desktop computers, not centralized servers, would become viable platforms for numerical computation. That vision is now a reality; desktop computers are the primary tools for mathematical modeling in corporations and research and educational institutions. The million-plus users of The MathWorks are creating an incredibly rich variety of mathematical models and simulations with its languages and toolkits.

The technological core of this company's products is MATLAB, a powerful language for performing complex numerical calculations and modeling. Its serves as a platform for a family of computational toolkits, each tuned to specific markets. MATLAB is ideal for working with large data sets. It allows users to solve many technical computing problems, especially problems with matrix and vector formulations, in a fraction of the time it would take to write a program in a noninteractive language such as C or FORTRAN. These applications take the form of complex data analyses, visualizations, and system design tools for the engineering and scientific communities. Controls and digital signal processing systems are traditional applications for the company, and these have taken root in key industries such as automotive and aero engineering.

Just before the turn of the millennium, senior management determined that the company would grow by leveraging its technologies to new market applications. One of those new market applications was to create real-time data acquisition tools that would allow MATLAB to function directly on, or in conjunction with, instrumentation and devices. These new toolkits have proven to be very popular with instrumentation manufacturers and integrators. Management then decided to target the financial services industry, which was outside the company's traditional focus on automobile, airplane, and instrumentation manufacturers. The financial industry was especially attractive. It had large data sets, heavy computation needs, and a need to analyze new flows of data streaming into mathematical models because of changing market conditions.

Financial services were not totally unknown territory to The MathWorks. Several years earlier, it had developed a software application for traders and portfolio managers. That product contained prepackaged solutions for asset allocation, risk management, financial instrument pricing, and portfolio analysis. That product did not sell well, for several reasons: The MathWorks software developers lacked deep knowledge in finance and risk management, and the sales force had few direct connections to the industry. More important, the leading firms needed more than canned programs. They wanted a set of flexible, interactive tools that could be used to build models based on proprietary domain expertise and customer understanding.

Rather than abandon this potentially lucrative market, the company's CEO made a fresh start; he decided to pursue both a different design concept and a different, less traditional approach to development. That was in September 1999.

The company's first step was to recruit a manager with experience in both databases and financial investments. Second, a software development team was assembled around this individual, and that new team was given the autonomy and resources it needed for a rapid, focused attack.

The team's first major move was to create a new design concept. Rather than develop a single solution and sell it to traders and portfolio managers, it made more sense to reposition the new offering as a tool that customers could adapt to their unique needs. The team also agreed that the target customers would be IT professionals and quantitative gurus who would, in turn, build applications for traders and portfolio managers. Those customers currently had statistical tools such as SAS, but few tools were as interactive or as ideal for simulation and modeling as MATLAB. Banks, insurance companies, brokerage firms, and investment houses had massive proprietary, internally developed programs that solved immediate problems. The new software had to be able to read data from these applications and integrate results with them.

The team's second big decision involved its approach to prototyping. Instead of developing product prototypes and testing them internally, it would develop them *in concert with users*. To accomplish this, the company set about staging seminars for "quant jocks" and IT professionals in financial services. Hotel and conference rooms were booked in five major financial centers, and seminars were scheduled over the course of the next six months. In preparation for these seminars, the team developed add-on tools for designing financial derivatives and managing portfolios.

The first seminar was held in Boston. Only 25 prospective users attended. Nevertheless, the team showed its prototypes and worked with attendees to make improvements. The team and seminar attendees were both excited by that experience. They all felt like they were breaking new ground in quantitative modeling for the financial arena.

The second event did much better, attracting 85 people. Word spread that something special was happening at these sessions. The next seminar, held in New York City, drew 120 people. Events in San Francisco and London attracted even large crowds.

Just as instructors learn from the process of teaching good students, The MathWorks innovation team took great steps forward with each seminar. The attendees were often brilliant quantitative financial analysts, advanced programmers, or IT managers—people who built proprietary applications for brokers and traders. They taught the innovation team how to enhance and tune its domain-specific tools. The team also learned how its tools would have to be integrated into both the development and production environments of financial organizations. By the fourth seminar, the team was able to demonstrate real-time connections with data streams available from Bloomberg financial news and commodity exchanges. Brokers and traders also wanted to use Microsoft's Excel as their primary graphical user interface. This meant that The MathWorks had to create a link between its mathematical modeling engine, on one hand, and Excel on the other. MATLAB was far more efficient—actually 95 percent faster—as a large matrix math engine than programs written only in Visual Basic or C to run within Excel.

The seminars continued over the next three months. By the beginning of 2000, the team was ready to step back from its prototypes and more fully consider the architecture and toolkit functionality needed for a strong commercial offering. (This can be considered the product line and platform development phase of our management framework for new market applications development.) Fortunately for The MathWorks, this development took place on highly stable and robust platforms: MATLAB and Simulink. Even so, it took another 18 months of intensive work to complete development for the first release. That work included one-on-one development with lead customers in New York, London, and Boston.

When the launch occurred for The MathWorks financial services toolkit, it was great success, and since then, the software has become widely popular within the quantitative financial community. But instead of resting on its laurels, the innovation team immediately began to add new tool sets to the product offering. The extent of those new developments can be seen on the company's Web site. And the next wave of enterprise growth for The MathWorks continued with a similarly designed entry into another new and equally attractive market segment: the life sciences.[8]

## Validating Design Choices with Users

A number of the companies that I studied found "conjoint analysis" useful in validating their product designs for new market applications. Conjoint analysis is a statistical technique used to understand how customers will prioritize or make trade-offs between relevant attributes of an offer: price, performance, various features, and so forth. Using this method, an innovation team can quickly identify the features or attributes that target users prefer most and the extent to which they are willing to pay for them. A statistical technique weights their preferences.[9] The results provide directional guidance, telling us which features users prefer more than others and the price they will pay for those features. Thanks to commercially available software packages, conjoint studies have become much easier to use, to the point where any computer-fluent person can put together a prototype study in a few hours, test it, and then deploy a questionnaire on a Web server so that prospective users can complete the interview process at their leisure.[10]

In many cases, the most difficult and time-consuming aspect of conjoint analysis is finding enough potential users willing to participate in the interview process. One should aim for about 100 respondents in each specific target user group. This sample size lends robustness to the results. Some companies studied employed outside market research firms to recruit respondents. If you choose this route, however, you must still work closely with the research firm to develop a screening mechanism for potential panel members. Anyone involved in a conjoint study should also take the time to learn the software package that the firm is using, request the source data, and run simulations of purchase intent for different product, package, and price variations. Hands-on experience with conjoint analysis provides insights that cannot be obtained by simply looking at a report developed by someone else.

In *The Power of Product Platforms,* Al Lehnerd and I described the application of the conjoint method to a next-generation steam/dry clothing iron.[11] In that example, the manufacturer formed user panels in three different countries—the United States (500 interviewees), Mexico (300), and France (300)—and found strong differences in consumer preferences between regions. The French strongly preferred a heavy iron, even though weight has little to do with ironing effectiveness; it is the steam that relaxes the fibers and allows the iron to do its work. Americans, on the other hand, had a preference for irons with many steam holes in the surface plate, believing that the more holes, the better the steaming effect. They, too, were operating under a misconception; too many holes actually dilute the force with which the steam exits the iron and reduces ironing performance. Mexican interviewees preferred a balance of features but had little interest in higher priced items. All three groups agreed on two features: they wanted a larger water tank and an automatic shutoff.

The conjoint study provided the iron maker with direction for both market communications and technical specifications suited to different geographic markets. Using a common product platform, it could efficiently manufacture different versions of its iron, each designed to meet regional requirements.

## Conjoint Analysis for Services

The conjoint method is also effective in validating service designs. To test a service design, the variations might be based on features, price, and bundling—for example, a checking account with (1) a $10 monthly fee, free printed checks, and interest paid on the average monthly balance versus (2) no monthly fee, $5 per 100 printed checks, and no interest on the average monthly balance. Time of service can be another important design feature, such as the next-day and successive day packages offered by Federal Express, UPS, and others.

To see some actual results from a simple conjoint study, we can turn to a task force at a large university that recently redesigned one of the school's MBA programs. The task force itself was multifunctional, with faculty, marketing personnel, and administrators.

The team realized that its MBA program had two very different sets of customers: students and the businesses that would ultimately employ them. The needs of both had to be considered.

To understand the needs of the former, task force members visited several dozen employers in the New England region and asked them to identify the skills they desired most in freshly minted MBA students who had had several years of work experience. These employers were clear in their responses; they wanted people with strong interpersonal communication capabilities, an ability to work well in teams, and technical know-how in one of three likely career tracks: marketing, finance, and supply chain management. Based on this information, the task force designed a prototype curriculum that, in addition to standard core courses, featured intensive training in teamwork, oral and written communications, and negotiations. A cooperative internship, sponsored by partner companies, was also designed.

But how would primary customers—prospective students—respond? To find out, the task force developed a Web-based conjoint survey and asked respondents to choose between various combinations of the following two variables: (1) A general MBA with many electives versus an MBA with specific career tracks; and (2) A six-month cooperative program versus a three-month summer cooperative program.

To encourage respondent participation, the task force acquired a list of recent undergraduates (a proxy for prospective MBA students) and offered an iTunes gift certificate for completing the survey, which 130 of them did. Figure 5.5 shows the results. Once again, in a conjoint study, the results are directional; there is no statistical significance to the numbers shown for each variable (in fact, they simply add up to "0"). In this case, the study found that twice as many prospective students preferred the career track concept over the general MBA approach. And they perceived company internships as more important than anything they might learn in the classroom (which duly humbled the professors on the task force). In figure 5.5, the preferences within the study variables come under the heading "Utility values." Then, the conjoint software computes market simulations based on alternative packages. These come under the heading "Product shares of preference." The software used here can also run the analysis for different customer groups if such data are gathered somewhere in the interview process. In this case, the "ideal customer" panel consisted of college graduates with between two and five years of work experience.

| *Average Utility Values* | |
| --- | --- |
| General MBA | −42.87 |
| Career Track MBA | 42.87 |
| | |
| No Co-op | −55.19 |
| 3-Month Co-op | 21.36 |
| 6-Month Co-op | 33.83 |
| *Product Shares of Preference by Ideal Customer* | |
| | |
| General MBA | **32.62** |
| Career Track MBA with 3-Month Coop | 34.77 |
| Career Track MBA with 6-Month Coop | 32.60 |
| Career Track Overall | **67.38** |

FIGURE 5.5 The MBA Conjoint Study (Marc H. Meyer)

Using this understanding of employers' needs and student preferences, the task force created a new MBA program that emphasized communication and team skills, specialized career-track courses, and an intensive six-month coop. The program branded its product "Partnership with Industry."[12]

## Putting Product or Service Variations into the Hands of the User

Conjoint tests of concepts can be taken to an even more pragmatic level by asking users to make trade-offs between actual prototypes with different attributes. For example, users might be asked to choose between different colors on actual mockups of a new product, or try driving test vehicles with different transmissions.

Mars provides yet another good example of putting prototype variations into user hands. Its prototype was the dog food bone described earlier. Using a conjoint study, the company's innovation team created different versions of the new product to validate its design. Three hundred dog owners from around the United States, segmented into equal panels of small, medium, and large dog owners, were recruited.

Over the course of five weeks (see figure 5.6), each participant was sent product prototypes. During the first week, they were asked to feed their dogs a standard version of the product—to establish a baseline for future comparisons. During the subsequent weeks, variations on bone size and texture were

The online surveys consisted of 1–5 scale questions rating the attributes that the products were tailored to that week. For example, Week 2 surveys consisted of questions related to the product's size. Each survey also consisted of preference questions, asking respondents to choose between the product samples for that week based on the varying attributes. In Week 5, respondents were also asked overall questions on usage and habits of feeding.

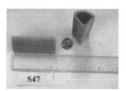 

Two sample variations for Week 5

FIGURE 5.6 In-Home Use Test Study Design (Mars, Inc. Reproduced with permission)

sent to the three different panels. Again, owners fed their dogs these new variations. They were then asked to indicate their preferences (Bone X versus Bone Y versus Bone Z) on a special Web site. Each reported preference, of course, was the owner's assessment of his or her dog's response to size and texture variations in the product. By the end of study, the team felt that it knew exactly what to make for three very different sets of target users.

## Prelaunch Market Testing

A conjoint study is an excellent method for determining customer preferences and validating prototypes. The ultimate form of validation for a new product or service, however, is a market test. Here, variations are not usually attempted. Instead, the first release product or service is marketed to a subsection of the total market—to a specific region or through a specific channel. Market tests are a practical way to (1) assess the attractiveness of a product or service to real people spending real money, (2) forecast future sales, and (3) see how customers respond to different pricing, advertising and merchandising programs, store placements, and so forth. They can even be used to test new distribution channels and the robustness of a new business model.

A market test is an essential part of the launch and learn approach to new product line and service development in the management framework (figure 2.1). There are many creative ways to conduct market tests without tipping one's hand to competitors, taking too much time, or spending too much money. One of the most common is to focus on a select group of customers or a distribution partner in a specific region. Small independent retailers might be most appropriate for some industries; the Web or some other type of direct-to-consumer channel might be best for others. The test may affect the business plan and help refine the product, its positioning, and the messages surrounding the product. However conducted, positive test results should be a precondition for full-scale launch and market expansion.

Among the companies studied, consumer product makers used limited regional launches to market-test new product lines. Equipment manufacturers used certain key accounts, more for field-testing than for anything else. Other companies established direct-to-consumer channels, through the Web, for example, to test responses to new products prior to launching through standard channels. Software companies in the research set all used beta site programs for new products. Whatever the mechanism, programs such as these can be a highly effective way to test products and business plans before committing the tens of millions of dollars needed to ramp up manufacturing and distribution.

## The IBM Method

Of course, there are many other ways to validate product designs that can be used to complement conjoint analysis and market testing. IBM has developed a rigorous, elegant method that it applies to both hardware and software products. Developed as part of the overall business renewal during the 1990s, CUSTOMER $APPEALS focuses on the attributes that products must have to be successful. The $APPEALS model, adapted from Peter Marks of Design Insight, is built on eight facets of customer buying decisions:

— **$**Price
— **A**ssurances and/or fears inherent in the product
— **P**erformance/functionality
— **P**ackaging and the customer's visual appraisal of the product
— **E**ase of use
— **A**vailability through channels
— **L**ife cycle cost—the true cost of ownership
— **S**ocial influences

If the reader strings together the first character of each of these attributes, the word $APPEALS emerges. Products are scored against these dimensions on a scale where 1 is totally inadequate, 5 is acceptable, and 10 is the absolute best possible.

IBM segments its overall markets and applies this method to the specific customer groups to which a new product or solution is targeted. The method is then applied to that target user to help organize and appreciate user needs and to assess how well a design concept satisfies or exceeds those needs at different stages of development. Products are run through the method once again just prior to launch as a final check. Staff also try to apply $APPEALS to users who are not current IBM customers in the continuing effort to grow share and increase revenue.

For IBM, $APPEALS is a powerful template that innovation teams throughout its businesses have applied to new product line development. IBM's services teams have adapted this train of thought to their own work as well. My advice to the reader to construct a prelaunch validation method appropriate for his or her line of business.

Some companies apply a similar method—called perceptual mapping—to the front end of their concept developments in order to develop distinct product positioning within seemingly mature product categories. My colleague Fred Crane describes how perceptual mapping can lead to a visual awakening for product developers by allowing them to visually observe holes or gaps in existing markets. The example he uses is a beverage manufacturer that, in an effort to increase milk sales, mapped existing milk beverages on a grid contrasting nutrition and the age of consumer (children versus adults). This grid showed a gap at that time for nutritious drinks targeting adults. The company then developed a tasty chocolate milk beverage that was fortified with calcium and vitamins and packaged appropriately for adults.[13] In our next chapter, we will see how perceptual mapping was also part of Honda's development of a new sports utility vehicle.

We have now completed our tour through the "market innovation" dimension of enterprise growth. Table 5.1 summarizes that journey with a simple roadmap of topics and templates.

## Reader Exercises

You should now apply the methods presented in this chapter to a new market application of your choosing. You should already be armed with preliminary market segmentation from the chapter 3 reader exercises and a use case scenario and persona description from chapter 4. Now it is time to try your hand at applying the template shown in figure 5.1 to your own new market application.

**Exercise 1** Begin with the user needs developed from work in the prior chapter. Try to crystallize those needs into a focused set of important perceived and latent needs. Some innovation teams find it useful to place Post-It notes on whiteboards and then consolidate them into logical groups. If you are having difficulty consolidating needs into a powerful, consolidated set of needs, you might try grouping needs into IBM's $APPEALS method or something like the Honda hierarchy of needs shown earlier in this chapter, as a starting point. Avoid making that hierarchy too complicated or spending time on trivial needs. If it can't fit on a page—or on your whiteboard—it is probably too complex to be readily managed for subsequent development. If, however, the needs on your short list seem no different than what other competitors are doing for target users, take another "deep dive" with users until you find those compelling but unserved needs.

**Exercise 2** Armed with a consolidated set of needs, develop design concepts to serve each need. A design concept may be product styling. It can also be a

TABLE 5.1 Tasks and Associated Templates

| Topic | Template |
|---|---|
| Segment markets to identify new users or uses | Market segmentation template Figure 3.2 |
| Define new product lines and/or services (and staff your innovation teams) | Product market strategy template Figure 3.3 |
| Understand target user needs, perceived and latent, from a "systems perspective" that pinpoints users' pains and pleasures across the total user experience | Use case scenario template Figure 4.3 |
| Create design concepts that focus subsystem innovation and, when combined, bring satisfaction and pleasure to users | Map user needs to design concepts, to subsystem innovations template. Figure 5.1 |
| Validate the implementations of those designs with actual target users | Methods/Templates<br>– Conjoint method<br>– In-home/field use tests<br>– Prelaunch filters (like IBM's $APPEALS) |

level of product performance or functionality. The design concept might also be an architectural approach—such as plug-in interfaces for a piece of software. Engage teammates in design concept creation; many heads are usually better than one. Examples of existing products arrayed before them on a conference table may spark greater creativity. *The best teams reach outside their industries.* For example, in styling, an SUV or cross-vehicle manufacturer might look at the design of sports accessories. Or a snack foods manufacturer might consider innovative packaging alternatives used for household products.

**Exercise 3** Think about the architecture of the product, system, or service. What are its major subsystems? Don't overlook external interfaces with the user—for example, packaging. Make a list of these subsystems on a whiteboard. Now, which subsystems are best suited as carriers of the design concepts you created? Be specific. If a design concept appears to not have a "home" in your architecture, then a level of architecture or a subsystem is missing.

**Exercise 4** Next, look inside your company's repository of working technologies, as well as its internal R&D. Talk to your industrial designers. Consider how to best implement the design concepts into specific subsystems or interfaces. If your company does not have an innovative subsystem solution to serve as a carrier for your design concepts, consider your current suppliers, and if not them, look at new suppliers. The answer to the user's need is mostly likely sitting somewhere inside your company's R&D facility or in that of another company. You just need to find it and use it for your own purposes.

The mapping method shown in figure 5.1—from user needs to design concepts to subsystem innovations—will help you create the implementation strategy for your new market application. After you have done this work, sit back and ask yourself, "Will the combination of my design concepts and their implementation as subsystem innovations make a strong and lasting impact on the market?" If the answer is no or maybe, go back the drawing board. Do not be discouraged! World-beating products and services are not invented overnight.

## Notes

1. Donald A. Norman, "Emotion and Design: Attractive Things Work Better," *Interactions Magazine*, 2002, 9(4): 36–42. Readers working on tangible, physical products will find Norman's *The Design of Everyday Things* (New York: Basic Books, 2002) worth reading.

2. Ikujiru Nonaka, "A Dynamic Theory of Organizational Knowledge Creation," *Organization Science*, 1994, 5(1): 14–37.

3. A good resource for QFD methods and examples is Glenn Mazur's Web site at www.mazur.net/publishe.htm, where, for example, you can download his white paper "Voice of Customer Analysis: A Modern System of Front-End QFD Tools, with Case Studies."

4. Abbie Griffin and John Hauser, "The Voice of the Customer," *Marketing Science*, 1993, 12(1): 1–27.

5. Roger Schreffler, "Shrinking Time: Can the Japanese Bring a Car to Market in 18 Months?" *Ward's Auto World*, March 1, 1998. See www.findarticles.com/p/articles/mi_m3165/is_n3_v34/ai_20393261/.

6. Marc H. Meyer and Arthur D. DeTore, "Product Development for Services," *Academy of Management Executive*, 1999, 13(3): 64–76.

7. Stefan Thomke, "Enlightened Experimentation: The New Imperative for Innovation," *Harvard Business Review*, February 2001, 67–75.

8. The financial services venture was so successful that senior management wanted to do it again! The team leader was asked to lead a new innovation group to leverage MATLAB and Simulink to life sciences. As a market segment, the life sciences were clearly growing strongly and demanded both modeling and quantitative analysis on massive data sets regarding the interactions between specific chemistries and specific cell biologies. This new internal venture—pursued with a similar approach—has since come to yield results comparable to those enjoyed in the financial sector.

9. Many articles have been published on the application of conjoint analysis to new product or service development. Two articles that I have found interesting and

useful are P. E. Green and V. Srinivasan, "Conjoint Analysis in Marketing: New Developments with Implications for Research and Practice," *Journal of Marketing*, 1993, 54(3): 122–40; and W. Moore, J. Louviere, and R. Verma, "Using Conjoint Analysis to Help Design Product Platforms," *Journal of Product Innovation Management*, 1999, 16, 27–39.

10. I encourage readers to look at Sawtooth Software's offerings. I have used this company's conjoint package (with several techniques, specifically a "choice-based" method and an "adaptive" method, and support staff at Sawtooth will provide excellent advice on which technique is best for your application) on a number of projects and have had dozens of MBA student teams apply the tool to sponsored company projects. It works! Also, that firm's Web site is a good source of educational materials. See www.sawtoothsoftware.com.

11. Marc H. Meyer and Alvin Lehnerd, *The Power of Product Platforms* (New York: Free Press, 1997), 105–16.

12. Glenn Urban and John Hauser, in the *Design and Marketing of New Products* (New York: Prentice-Hall, 1993), provide another MBA design validation example, in this case for a technology-focused MBA program at MIT.

13. Frederick Crane, *Marketing, 6th Canadian Edition* (Burr Ridge, IL: McGraw-Hill, 2006).

# CHAPTER SIX

# How Honda Innovates

*A history of organic growth—Honda's light trucks—*
*Understanding new target users—Positioning the Element—*
*Translating concepts to subsystem designs—Making*
*the business case—Getting executives to live*
*the new product experience.*

Previous chapters have explored both the market innovation and the concept development dimensions of enterprise growth. We've seen how segmentation can be the basis for a growth strategy and how user research can lead to concepts that, when tested through prototypes and user feedback, can result in customer-pleasing new products and services.

This chapter offers an inside look at how one company, Honda Motor Company Ltd., used that methodology to develop a remarkable new vehicle: the Element. First introduced in early 2003, this unusual-looking SUV has made a mark in the U.S. auto market, among both young drivers and older ones who are young at heart. Honda's work on the Element exemplifies best practice in the user-centered design and development methods advocated in this book.

Honda provides a rich example of organic (i.e., internally generated) enterprise growth. With more than 130,000 individuals working throughout North America, Europe, Asia, South America, the Middle East, and Australia, Honda has developed methods that help it systematically identify emerging market needs, understand those needs, and then create products to serve them. Honda's deep-rooted company culture of invention and application has resulted in total worldwide sales in excess of $84 billion for its 2005 fiscal year (ending in March 2006), a 14.5 percent increase over the prior year. Globally, 55 percent of that revenue was derived from automobile production, with motorcycles, power products, and financial services operations making up the rest.

This was also a banner year for Honda in terms of its 2006 automotive products. It captured five of the ten #1 spots in the *Consumer Reports* rankings. For passenger sedans, Honda basically ran the table: The Civic won the under $20,000 sedan category, the Accord won the $20,000–$30,000 sedan category, and the Acura TL won for the best $30,000–$40,000 sedan. Honda's Odyssey won the highly coveted best in the minivan class. A brand new Honda product, the Ridgeline, was named the best pickup truck.

The company produced nearly 3.5 million vehicles during fiscal year 2005, 55 percent of which were made in North America. For these North American units, the vast majority of components were also sourced from North American suppliers. The thinking behind product development for all these successes is also revealed in the story of the Element.

Although this chapter focuses on motor vehicles, the full extent of Honda's innovative culture can be appreciated only by looking at the full scope of its far-reaching enterprises. In 1965, for example, Honda introduced its first portable, fuel-efficient generator, the e300. Today, it has an entire line of generators for homeowners and tradespeople. Like its car engines—for which the company is famous—Honda generators feature fuel economy, reliability, and quietness at competitive prices. The company has also leveraged its engine technology into other fields: lawnmowers, tillers, trimmers, brush cutters, snowblowers, all-terrain vehicles, personal watercraft (Aqua Trax), and four-stroke outboard marine engines. In 2003, the company boldly entered the aviation business as a jet engine OEM supplier and with a twin-engine small business jet aircraft, which made its formal debut at the Oshkosh air show in July 2005.

A backward glance at Honda's history indicates that it has embarked on a major new market application every 15 to 20 years—each time leveraging its engine technology. In the 1950s, it was motorcycles; in the 1970s, passenger cars; and in the 1990s, sport utility vehicles and minivans. The cycle now appears to be accelerating to every decade, with jet engine and other applications taking flight. Leveraging core technology to new market applications is something that Honda does well and does often.

Honda's foray into passenger vehicles follows a path of continuous innovation and market growth, free of internal upheavals or acquisitions. Soichiro Honda established the Honda Technical Research Institute in 1946. A year later, he developed the institute's first product, a small engine for powering bicycles. By 1949, Honda's team had produced a 98-cc two-cycle engine for motorcycles. Its first motorcycle, the Super Cub, followed in 1958. Recognizing the size and strength of the postwar U.S. market, Honda opened its U.S. division in Los Angeles in 1958. This event was a major milestone in the company's history; it marks the beginning of Honda's consistent strategy of leveraging its growing engine capabilities with the needs and tastes of American consumers.

The transition from motorcycles to automobiles began in 1963 with the launch of a sports car for the Japanese market. Formula One auto racing followed as a means of understanding the most demanding engine applications. In 1966, Honda introduced the N360, a mini-compact car with a highly efficient air-cooled engine. The now ubiquitous, fuel-stingy Civic came next, in 1973. It hit North American shores just as the United States was coming to grips with its first energy crisis. The timing could not have been better.

While the Civic was winning awards for fuel economy, Honda was beginning development work on a larger sedan, one that would meet the needs of American families. That vehicle, the Accord, hit the market in 1976 and quickly began winning awards from auto magazines such as *Car & Driver* and *Road & Track*. Within five years, it was the best-selling car model in the United States. In search of new uses and new users, Honda then moved into both upscale passenger cars and light trucks.

## The Light Truck Category

The light truck product category includes SUVs, minivans, and pickup trucks. The SUV profiled in this chapter, the Element, is merely the most recent in the Honda light truck series. The company's first entry in this category was the Odyssey minivan.

The minivan subcategory was already well established and contained many fierce competitors, led by Chrysler. In many ways, the Odyssey minivan concept was a natural extension of Honda's understanding of the family as a user. Consequently, the vehicle was styled to please the mature eye, with more interior space than current competitors, great driving comfort, and high reliability. The first-generation Odyssey was launched in 1995; the second and third generations followed in 1999 and late 2004, respectively. Within two years of the initial launch, Odyssey unit sales exceeded 100,000 units per year; by the end of 2004, U.S. sales exceeded 150,000 units.

Honda next attacked the sub-$20,000 SUV category with its five-passenger CR-V. The CR-V leveraged many of the basic subsystems in Honda's passenger cars, especially the Civic. The reliability, simplicity, drivability, and price of the CR-V resulted in a warm reception in the United States upon its introduction at the end of 1996. The results were impressive. The CR-V achieved more than 73,000 units by the end of 1997. By 2004, Honda was producing more than 120,000 units for the North American market. Like the Odyssey, Honda refreshed the CR-V with major model changes every four to five years.

By the mid-1990s, American consumers desired a larger family-focused SUV as an alternative to the minivan. The U.S. Big Three responded with the Chrysler Jeep Cherokee, the Ford Explorer, and the Chevy Blazer. Honda decided to first target the high-end segment of that market, whose lower unit volumes were in balance with its North American manufacturing capacity at the time. The newness of the target market made MDX development challenging and fun. First-year sales of the MDX were 52,000 units. Next came an even larger SUV, the Pilot, which it launched in late 2001. First-year sales of the Pilot were 50,000 units in North America, which more than doubled over the next several years to about 120,000 units by 2004. Honda's strategy to grow its light truck product line led to the development of the company's first pickup truck, the Ridgeline, which entered the market in 2005.

The collective impact of these various passenger car and light truck product developments (see figure 6.1) was that Honda became a major force in the U.S. market, where its market share had grown by almost 250 percent since 1985. Not only was Honda making vehicles that people wanted to buy but also it was making money, thanks in part to its product line architectures and shared platforms, such as engines and chassis across those architectures.

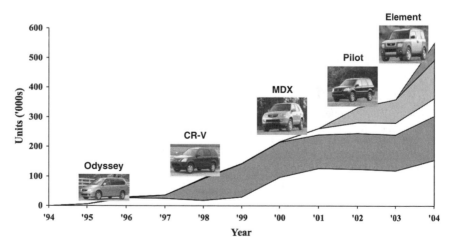

FIGURE 6.1  Innovation in the Light Truck Category (Honda Motor Company. Reproduced with permission)

## Leveraging Technology to a New Target User

Invention and new product development is such a core part of Honda's mission and culture that it should be no surprise that another new SUV was under development even as Honda was bringing the Pilot to market in 2002. That vehicle, the Element (figure 6.2), was the result of five years of intensive concept, product, and manufacturing process development. It targeted a different user and use.

### New Users

If you have seen an Element on the road, you know that it looks quite different from any other SUV made by Honda—or by any other manufacturer. Some people find the look intriguing; others are puzzled by its boxy look. Honda designed the Element for the Generation Y first-time car-buying male, which Honda defined as men between 19 and 29 years old. This was a new target user for Honda America. Said one senior sales executive, "We had products for young women and families, but nothing focused on young men." Senior management knew

FIGURE 6.2 The Honda Element (Honda Motor Company. Reproduced with permission)

that Honda was losing the opportunity to bring these first-time car buyers into the brand and keep them there as they grew older and more affluent with successive targeted offerings, such as the Pilot or the Acura MDX.

## A Four-Stage Development Approach

New vehicle developments at Honda go through four major stages, and the Element was no exception.

1. *Business planning.* A concise yet comprehensive statement of target market, user needs, design focus, addressable market, projected sales, costs, and operating profit. Team and development time lines are assigned based on approval by executives of a new vehicle concept.
2. *Subsystem planning.* A series of design reviews for exterior and interior subsystems, as well as a time line for manufacturing and sales.
3. *Prototyping.* Integration, confirmation, and review of all vehicle requirements.
4. *Preproduction review.* Confirmation of the manufacturability of all specifications. This results in approval for mass production go-ahead.

An executive chairs the business planning process for all new vehicle developments. Together with other company executives, this individual reviews a range of new product proposals on a regular basis. The proposals deemed worthiest are assigned to concept development teams staffed largely with automotive engineers and stylists. Given the intensity of the work involved, management is highly selective in its choice of which ideas win approval to move forward.

Each concept development team aims to refine the product concept, create specific test vehicles (often by modifying parts of existing vehicles), and prepare a comprehensive yet concise business plan. Once Honda's executives approve that plan, the concept proceeds through subsequent stages of intense product and manufacturing process development, leading to launch. Engineers from the concept development team often move onto the formal product development team, ensuring the continuity of market insights and technical designs created earlier. Once a new vehicle is launched, team leaders continue to meet for a number of months for postlaunch reviews, searching for lessons learned that can be applied to future developments.

Honda's R&D division has its own front-end marketing professionals, called product planners. These individuals are highly skilled in segmenting markets, identifying user needs, and translating those needs into brandable concepts. The product planning staff works with different concept development teams in parallel.

## Understanding Target Users

Honda formed the Element concept development team in early 1998 at its Torrance, California, styling studio. At that time, the project was called the Model X. The team's goal was to create a compelling design, with features and a price that would harmonize with the core values and beliefs of target users. Understanding core values and beliefs is no trivial matter, particularly for a new and unfamiliar user group. Those values and beliefs cannot be obtained from a book or purchased from a consulting firm. Rather, an analyst "must go to ground" and perform careful user research. Learning about the competitive environment is important, and the insights into users and uses become the foundation for a compelling design, as described in the previous chapters. (The reader might wish to refer back to the aspirational side of figure 4.2.) Honda's product designers had done this many times before. For example, in creating the Odyssey minivan, the Honda concept development team observed the pleasures, frustrations, and needs of families in terms of their personal transportation. Those observations led to innovative designs for interior space and versatility.

For the Element team, achieving the design concept first meant observing Gen Y males in their environments. And there seemed to be no better place to get started than at the notorious X-Games, which feature daredevil competitions in "hot dog" skiing and snowboarding, dirt course motorcycle racing, skateboarding, and other hair-raising "extreme" sports. Eager for insights into this segment of male society, a group of young engineers and marketers was dispatched to the 1998 X-Games competitions. Armed with cameras and camcorders, field researchers closely observed what X-Gamers were doing before, during, and after the various competitions. Many of the team members themselves were on the youthful side of 30.

Ethnography at the X-Games was quickly followed by other "scene-hunting" studies—where young men lived and played—to develop specific use case scenarios. Some of the specific behaviors observed included apartment move-in, move-out and sports-active and social weekend living. Each was later translated in specific design concepts for vehicle subsystems, such as flexible seating. Figure 6.3 shows some prime examples of scene hunting. Note, for example, the unintended storage area under the sleeping mat in the top left photograph. Designing special storage areas in interiors has become a strength of Honda automotive engineering.

Through these efforts, the concept team arrived at a coherent profile of its target user. Gen Y males exhibited strong cohort identification. They were highly social and enjoyed doing things in groups. In addition, they were inclined to be community-sensitive and supportive of broader social and environmental causes. Target Gen Ys were also well educated, many being college

Active Lifestyles

Dorm Move-In

Weekend Fun

FIGURE 6.3 Scene Hunting to Develop Use Case Scenarios (Honda Motor Company. Reproduced with permission)

graduates. Nevertheless, they were not as career-driven as their Gen X predecessors (30-somethings at the time of the study). The team observed that Gen Y men "worked to live," as opposed to their Boomer parents, who "lived to work." Even those Gen Ys who followed traditional career paths refused to allow work to take over their lives. The team developed its persona for the target user, as shown in figure 6.4. And as observed by Marc Gobe in *Emotional Branding*, Gen Y men responded to a different set of marketing cues than other users such as young women or families.[1] Word-of-mouth, buzz marketing might prove far more effective than traditional advertising strategies.

Translating observations about Gen Y males into an appealing new vehicle would require designs and features that spoke to the target user's personal identity. In other words, the vehicle had to exude a certain attitude and expression in its styling, shouting out to the world, "I'm a Gen Y guy." That expression had to authentic, credible, and pervasive.

Product planners began talking about an Endless Summer vision, wherein the young man's vehicle would carry friends and gear. Together, they would

- 19–28 Year Old Males

- Single

- Active (hobby enthusiast)

- Social (many friends)

- College Graduate

- Well-Traveled

- "Work to live"

- 45% of First-Time Car Buyers

FIGURE 6.4 The Persona of the Gen Y Male (Honda Motor Company. Reproduced with permission)

hit the road and have fun: biking, hiking, windsurfing, skiing, and partying at the beach. The vehicle would have to be capable of carrying sports equipment, furniture, and friends and providing sleeping space on weekend excursions. Ironically, this very flexibility in interior design turned out to be equally appealing to older males seeking a youthful vehicle.[2]

The multifaceted consumer understandings garnered by Honda's product planners supplied the "edge" that designers gave to the emerging Element—an edge that had to go well beyond superficial cosmetics that competitors could easily replicate.

## Product Positioning

User research helped produce a clear and distinctive product position for the Element relative to minivans and other SUVs in the lineup. Drawing on its knowledge of target users, it positioned the Element in terms of *lifestyle* and *life stage*. As shown in figure 6.5, the CR-V was primarily targeted at single and fairly active individuals in stable lifestyles; the Pilot targeted families with

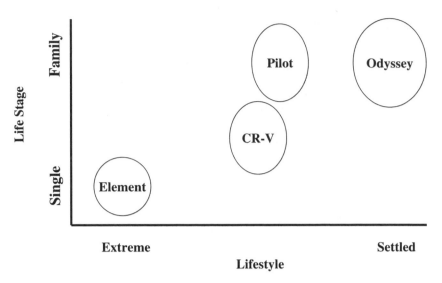

FIGURE 6.5 Positioning the Element (Honda Motor Company. Reproduced with permission)

similar dispositions. The Odyssey, on the other hand, was positioned to appeal to families with settled lifestyles. The Element filled a gap in the positioning framework: the single individual with an extreme or unconventional lifestyle. This became the "sweet spot" and a focus for the project.

This positioning matrix appears simple, but product breakthroughs often emerge from such elegantly simple understandings. The Element's positioning made the vision clear to the hundreds of individuals who would be involved with the project in the years ahead: executives, managers, designers and engineers, marketers, and suppliers.

## From Consumer Characteristics to Product Concepts

Armed with knowledge of Gen Y core beliefs and values and the positioning of the Element relative to Honda's other light trucks, the concept development team raced forward. Endless Summer began to take a more tangible form, as a period in life when a young man had few family responsibilities, abundant personal freedom, and a need for a vehicle capable of supporting that lifestyle. The person who fit that mold would want to put many things into his vehicle:

friends, bikes and surfboards, furniture bound to or from an apartment, stereo equipment, and so forth.

Appearance and driving feel were also important. This vehicle had to look solid and "edgy." Plus, it had to have enjoyable driving dynamics—rapid acceleration, quick turning, and a sporty suspension.

Analogies are critically important for helping teams develop fresh, original designs. After a few months of user-centered design activity, the concept development team was drawn to several concepts as sources of further design inspiration. One of these was the lifeguard station on the beach: strong, able to withstand the elements, an expansive view of the surroundings, and unfettered internal space in which to store gear and equipment.

The Element team then distilled all it had learned from observational research into four major design themes for its new vehicle:

1. Adaptability and modularity
2. Credibility and authenticity
3. Pragmatic/function-oriented
4. Attitude and expression

To these it added the overarching themes common to all Honda automotive products: driving performance, safety, and value for money. Each of these seven design themes became the focus of specific solution developments for the team's stylists and engineers. Some already existed within Honda's arsenal of technologies. For example, the power train solution was already under development in Honda's central engine R&D facility. Other technical solutions had to be adapted from other products or developed from scratch. For example, exterior styling for the Element had to be very new.

Let's consider how the product planning team tackled the "attitude and expression" design theme. At first, this took a radical form: the "brain cage on wheels" shown in figure 6.6. This early drawing made the vehicle appear more like a truck than a passenger car. It featured a large interior space, open detachable hardtops, and a short, stubby front. And yes, there were those large wheels.

Many versions of the brain cage were created, first as a series of sketches and then as physical prototypes with bold, innovative exterior styling concepts and colors. The phrase Endless Summer was joined by Animal House on Wheels and Free to be Extreme. This was unusual in the auto industry. Given the huge cost of developing a new vehicle line, automakers are tempted to play it safe and water down designs that are bold, edgy, or very different than their current vehicle lines. With more conventional manufacturers, management reviews tend to force a bold new design to regress toward the mean, so that before

FIGURE 6.6 The Brain Cage on Wheels: An Early Design Concept (Honda Motor Company. Reproduced with permission)

long, new vehicles have that "me too" look. Honda executives avoid this behavior. As noted earlier, staying true to the vision is deemed essential. That might mean more conservative styling for a family sedan, aggressive styling for a sports coupe, or in this case, a very edgy appearance for a sporty active user. Executives took steps to ensure the Element's distinctiveness within the company's more traditionally styled lineup.

Engineers on the concept team tackled other key design themes in parallel. Figure 6.7 maps the process the team used to translate core user beliefs into design themes in its new SUV. The figure illustrates the approach applied to the "adaptability and modularity" design theme. The vehicle had to be good for moving furniture, carrying sports equipment, and partying on the beach with friends. Within each use, the SUV had to pragmatic and function oriented. In the figure, we show how this can be served by special designs for two major subsystems: the interior and the exterior.

## General Process

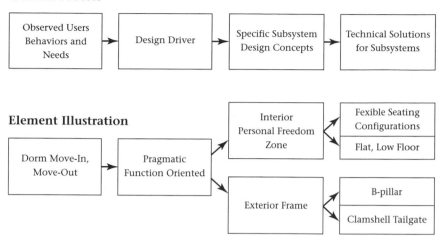

## Element Illustration

FIGURE 6.7 From User Needs to Technical Design Solutions

Specific design concepts for the interior subsystem featured flexible fold-away seats. This facilitated substantial cargo capacity, partying space, and, if need be, sleeping space in a relatively small SUV package. For the exterior sub-system, the team also designed a b-pillarless frame[3] that allowed clamshell-style doors for maximum move-in, move-out entry and exit. The tailgate was also designed with a clamshell function, providing far greater entry/exit utility than traditional tailgates. The same held true for the removable sunroof. In short, the Element design incorporated many innovative, function-providing subsystems. Each subsystem design was reviewed, in sketch form, within the team and again with panels of target Gen Y men users.

Those sketches moved on to R&D's prototyping shop, where major subsystems such as the frame, the tailgates, and interior seating were milled out of foam or formed from clay in a quarter of the actual size. After numerous re-views and adjustments, these prototypes were recast at the actual size. A life-size Element prototype began to take form.

The concept development team was pleased with the design that was taking shape. But would target customers be equally pleased? To answer this impor-tant question, members of the team vetted their design sketches with college students in different parts of the United States. Over the next several months, team members visited the University of Washington, the University of South-ern California, Syracuse University, the University of Texas, and the University of Colorado, often using fraternity houses as meeting places. Honda engineers and marketers showed the students their sketches, sought feedback, and did quick-turn improvements.

## Making the Business Case

While target users were commenting on initial design sketches, the business case for the vehicle was being formulated. That case rested on simple yet powerful data.

— Gen Y represented a major population expansion in North America, almost matching the Baby Boom generation. Children of Boomers, the number of individuals in the 15- to 25-year-old age bracket, had grown by 719 percent from 1995 to 2002. By 2010, more than 70 million Gen Y individuals would be driving vehicles in North America. Gen Y had arrived as a major consumer force.

— Gen Y people were *more than half* of all first-time car buyers (52 percent).

— No other SUV-type vehicle directly appealed to Gen Y male tastes and price inclinations in the $20,000 range.

These data made a powerful argument for pursuing the Gen Y man with a new vehicle concept. Some of the data used to make that argument are shown in figure 6.8.

Management was confident that once this new customer adopted the Honda brand, he would remain loyal and trade up to different Honda vehicles as his lifestyle and bank account changed over time—just as women had moved from Civics, to Accords, and then to Odyssey minivans. Today's Gen Y Element owner would very likely have a Pilot or Odyssey as he matured, married, and had a family—or to a hot S2000 convertible if he remained single.

## Financial Forecasts

At this point, the team had to create a financial plan with projected revenues, manufacturing costs, and capital requirements. The first challenge was to forecast sales revenues, based on two factors: projected unit sales and the vehicle's wholesale price. Here, Honda's experience with light truck and SUV sales provided some guidance; at bottom, the Element shared characteristics with both subcategories. The most suitable benchmark was the CR-V, which Honda was then producing at a rate of about 100,000 units each year. Because the CR-V

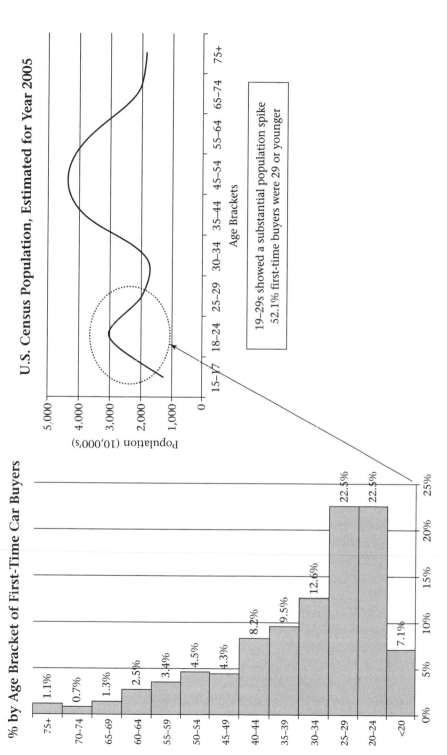

FIGURE 6.8 Demographics of First-Time New Car Buyers (Honda Motor Company. Reproduced with permission)

targeted a broader population—single people and young families—it made sense that Element unit sales would be fewer, particularly as a new concept going after an emerging market. Consequently, projections were set at 50,000 units for the first year, and capital plans were set accordingly. Management knew that they could scale up production if that estimate proved to be too conservative; overshooting a realistic sales goal, on the other hand, would tie up tens of millions of dollars in unused plant and equipment.

The other part of the financial forecast concerned variable costs based on 50,000 projected units. Honda R&D maintained a computerized database of costs for different components and manufacturing processes pegged at different levels of procurement for current vehicles. The concept development team used this database in creating its cost-of-goods estimate. Because many of the power train elements, as well as certain aspects of the underlying chassis and the driver controls, would be common to other Honda products, the database approximated the numbers eventually realized in mass production of the Element.

Engineering development budgets were prepared in a similar fashion, using prior projects as benchmarks and making sure that the budgets had enough slack to accommodate unanticipated problems. The team also estimated the capital required for retooling in this way. Given the intent to sell the vehicle in North America only, management wanted to manufacture it domestically, but building it would require major retooling of one of the company's assembly lines.

## The Green Light from Management

The concept team knew that the success of its business plan depended on strong support at the top, which would require executives to buy into the vision. Because ethnography had worked so well for the product planning team itself, team members came up with the notion of having the executive team "live the life." Being an "experience" as well as a product, the Element was a natural for immersing executives into the target user's environment. This is a lesson well-learned for corporate innovators seeking executive endorsement for new market applications.

The team invited Honda executives to participate in a weekend camping trip on California's San Onofre Surf Beach. Some 30 Japanese and American participants, representing all major corporate functions—including U.S. sales and R&D executives—joined the Element team at the beach. Honda's top executives are, in the words of a Honda R&D director, "absolute car nuts." They are passionate about their products and are active test drivers throughout development.

The group assembled on the San Onofre beach talked about their shared passion for driving performance, about the unique Gen Y lifestyle, and what these two factors meant for the Element and for Honda as a business. The major review meeting soon thereafter drew on the consensus achieved during that weekend on the beach. Key human resource decisions were made, including the selection of the development team leader and key staff.

Another crucial executive decision was where to assemble the new SUV. Honda had four major auto manufacturing facilities in North America: Line 1, at the Alliston, Canada, plant made Civics but was running at near full capacity. Line 2, also in Alliston, produced the Acura MDX and the Odyssey (and by 2004, the Pilot). It was also near full capacity. The third Honda plant was located in Alabama. It made the Odyssey and the Pilot, but given the surging demand for these vehicles, it, too, was running at full tilt. That left the company's fourth North American plant at East Liberty, Ohio (ELP). At the time, ELP was churning out Civics and operating near full capacity. However, demand for Civics was anticipated to plateau.

Getting ELP ready to build the Element would not be easy. The Element would weigh much more than the sprightly Civic, so substantial upgrades to the conveyor systems and other manufacturing processes would be required. However, the manufacturing team at East Liberty had an outstanding reputation and appeared up to the challenge. The proximity of East Liberty to Honda's engineering center in Raymond, Ohio, was another plus—one that tipped the decision in its favor.

The Element team was now prepared to embark on the product and platform development phase of our new market applications framework. Driving everything was an aggressive launch target set by executives for December 2003.

The concept development for the Honda Element richly illustrates user-centered design. We will pick up on how Honda transformed these design concepts into real steel on wheels later. But first, we must examine some underlying principles of product line and platform development.

### Notes

1. Marc Gobe, *Emotional Branding* (New York: Allworth Press, 2001).
2. Flexibility in the Element's interior design later proved to be attractive to a much broader age range of men.
3. A b-pillarless frame eliminates the vertical steel support structure running from roof to floor between the front and passenger doors.

CHAPTER SEVEN

# Product Line and Platform Development

*Product line architecture, subsystems, and interfaces for new market applications—Platforms as shared subsystems—The power of subsystem and user interfaces—The bloody reality in most companies—Developing a platform strategy for new market applications—Templates—Bottom-up resource planning—Using architecture to embrace complementary innovators—Reader exercises*

As we saw in previous chapters, an overall product or service concept is the composite of more specific design concepts that serve specific needs and that are targeted for implementation within the major subsystems of the product or service. Now we turn to implementing these technical solutions.

The ability of companies to leverage their core technologies to new market applications rests on the increasing modularity in the design and implementation of technology. As noted by Carliss Baldwin and Kim Clark, this modularity allows firms to more easily mix and match specific technical components into final products or services.[1] When a technology is not modular—not like LEGO—but monolithic with inseparable parts, it is very difficult to apply that technology to any purpose other than the one for which it was originally designed.

Experience shows that the best way to leverage technologies for new market applications begins with the development of a robust, modular architecture composed of subsystems, each of which has a specific purpose. Let's consider how this works for physical products first, and then extend our thinking to software systems and services.

The product line architecture shows the major subsystems common to a closely related set of products, i.e., a product family. A subsystem is the aggregation of specific components, modules, or processes that constitute an important subset of the overall functionality of those products. The product line architecture also shows how and where these subsystems connect to one another. These connections are called the *internal interfaces* within the architecture. The product line architecture also indicates the *external interfaces* needed by the products, be it for pumping gasoline into a car or receiving electricity into a computer. One type of external interface is the *user interface,* which enables a user to interact with a product. Another type of external interface facilitates interactions with other products.

The product line architecture also indicates how and where specific customizations can be performed to tailor products for specific users and uses. The architecture shows the boundary points after which standard products can be made specific solutions, either through more engineering or services. Cost effective mass customization requires strong underlying product line architecture.

Then, there is the "platform"—a popular but often misused concept. A product platform is a subsystem that can be used across many products, both within a product line, and sometimes, across multiple product lines. IBM's 64 bit RISC processor is a platform that is used across many different models; so is Honda's 2.4 liter engine, which is found in many of that company's cars and light trucks. Unfortunately, many companies make the mistake of viewing architecture as the platform, then try to force fit it into widely different applications. Companies make this mistake when they try to extend their reach into an emerging market application using existing product lines rather than developing a new product line architecture directly suited for the opportunity at hand.

Product line architectures and product platforms are different and should have a different focus. A robust product line architecture produces new revenue by serving as the foundation for new products for new users and new uses. Robust product platforms, on the other hand, can reduce the cost of goods, engineering expense, and time to market. Both are needed for enterprise growth.

Subsystems with modular architectures can be independently upgraded over the life of the product line. For example, a computer has a modular architecture; it memory and peripherals can be upgraded readily. Further, these same subsystems can be more readily adapted to new market applications. A "blade server" architecture, for example, can be leveraged across a wide range of applications.

As these cases show, time dedicated to product line architecture and subsystem design is time well spent. In the long term, it results in greater product functionality, reliability, and faster time to market.

In theory, the more modular a product line architecture, the longer it should last because it is designed to be extended. That extension is essential for sustaining enterprise growth. Once extensions become painful in terms of engineering effort, cost, and time to market, a clean-sheet approach to the product line architecture is warranted. Sooner or later, the vast majority of product line architectures fail to incorporate new technological breakthroughs.[2] Had IBM followed this clean-sheet approach earlier, during the late 1980s instead of 1993, its near-death experience described in chapter 1 might have been avoided.

Unfortunately, selling R&D investments for the development of next generation product line architecture and subsystems is an uphill battle in most corporations. Management often wants to maximize profit today at the expense of future product line growth. By the time a company recognizes that forcing new functionality on top of an aging product line architecture is a losing game, market share is irretrievably lost. As one team leader remarked, "Few people understand architecture and how it enables progress. It is the hardest darn thing to sell to management. Every time I bring up the subject, they say that customers don't buy architecture, just products. Either they don't understand that architecture is the foundation of all good products, or they want to leave the expense of designing and implementing new architecture to their successors."

That frustrated manager was not talking to managers at Gillette, who clearly understand the importance of architecture innovation. Gillette introduced a new product line architecture for its shaving systems in 2004: it had three major subsystems: the handle, the blade cartridge, and an internal, battery-powered, micro-pulsing subsystem that promised to provide an even closer shave. Gillette used this architecture to create a new dimension in high-performance shaving, and also to counter its competitor's four-blade system. The results were telling. Strong consumer demand for the new product, M3Power, drove six consecutive months of U.S. market share gain for Gillette and increased the company's UK share substantially.[3] Gillette entered 2006 with more than 70 percent global share for razors and blades, five times greater than its nearest competitor.

## Defining Product Line Architecture

Architecture is the foundation for developing a fully featured product line where each member uses common technologies and capabilities. It defines how subsystems within a product, system, or service interact. Architecture is also the best way to ensure that those products and services connect well with

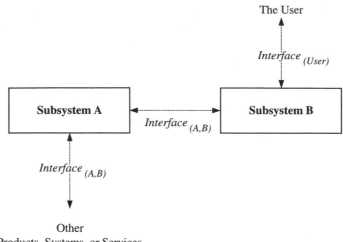

FIGURE 7.1  A Simple Architecture with Two Subsystems
and Three Interfaces

other products or services in the user's environment. Is architecture important? You bet it is, and developing a good architecture requires a dedicated, focused commitment—before getting down to the details of implementing particular designs and features.

As noted above, product line architecture *defines the subsystems and the interfaces* that connect those subsystems, as shown in figure 7.1. Here the product line architecture is defined by just two subsystems, A and B. Each is connected to its neighbor by an interface, labeled Interface$_{(A,B)}$. The user interface is labeled Interface$_{(User)}$.

The product line itself has a structure—an architecture—that defines the key subsystems and the interfaces between subsystems and users. Then, each subsystem and interface has a design. Therefore, architecture exists at two levels: the product line as a whole, and the key subsystems within it. Both are equally important. If done well, the product line can be easily evolved and key subsystems can be leveraged to other product lines. As applied to the Element, Honda will upgrade the vehicle based on new market learning; it also deploys the engine used in the Element to other cars and light trucks.

The same thinking applies to systems and services. The architecture for a system, such as a management information system, not only shows the major parts of the system—such as the user interface, the analysis routines, and the reporting modules—but also how external systems are accessed by the system itself.

Services also have architecture, as seen in the workers compensation services innovation example described earlier in chapter 5. In that example, distinct subsystems included injury prevention, accident reporting, treatment, and claims management. However, relative to physical products, the subsystems in a service tend to be specific processes within a larger workflow. The workflow itself defines all the processes required, the connections between those processes, and typically, the information systems needed to support each process and measure performance. The workflow is often the product line architecture for a service.

Few product lines are as simply architected as the one shown in figure 7.1, with just two major subsystems and a single interface joining them. But there are some. Consider once again the shaving system that many of us use daily. The architecture of the Gillette's product consists of the handle and the blade cartridge, and for newer versions, a battery power supply. This same architecture is used for men's and women's shavers. The handles are designed differently to suit the needs and tastes of the two genders, but within each generation of these product lines, the blades themselves are common. The interface architecture (between the handle and blade cartridge) developed by Gillette's engineers makes this reuse possible, and the company enjoys cost of goods and capital efficiency advantages of sharing a major subsystem between two different product lines.

In other cases, packaging is an important subsystem. For many consumer product companies, product packaging can be just as important as the product itself. In such cases, an innovation team must consider the packaging as an important element of the architecture. Otherwise, it will be left as an afterthought.

Although architecture can focus on a single product (such as a custom-designed residential dwelling), our purpose here is to help corporations develop multimember product lines or services. That is why instead of talking about product architecture, we refer to this as *product line architecture* for products, systems, or services. Product line architecture serves as the basis for a stream of products, systems, or services. All members of the line have the same number of subsystems and the connections between those subsystems as specified in the product line architecture.

Architecture structures a set of separate and distinct technical building blocks into a unified whole that serves users and uses. Architecture is most often hierarchical. An automotive power-train architecture, for example, encompasses lower level subsystems: the engine, transmission, and exhaust systems. These are subsystems within a subsystem.

The most robust architectures are modular. Their subsystems can be readily replaced with improved or upgraded versions without violating the functions of other subsystems by adhering to the interface definitions. The reader's antivirus software is a perfect example. Leading packages automatically access Web servers to download and install specific new virus detection software and to clean up plug-ins. This would not be possible without the modular design of the software itself. For an automobile manufacturer such as Honda, modular architecture rules supreme. Automakers cannot afford to redesign a vehicle every model year. Instead, they replace particular subsystems with improved versions, for example, for engine controls, on-board navigation systems, or interior finishing. Each of those subsystems is sufficiently modular that it can be replaced without redesigning the entire vehicle. In both cases—the antivirus software and the automobile—the modular architecture provides opportunities to improve the total product, system, or service piece by piece over time without having to start from scratch.

A company that sets out to develop a new market application must typically construct a new product line or service architecture. The exception is when the company already has a robust, modular product line architecture that can be readily adapted to the new user or use. For example, the product line architecture of Honda's Element is not all that different than that for the CR-V, although the implementation of many major subsystems is indeed very different. In contrast, IBM had to discard its then current bipolar architecture before it could create a winning CMOS-based product line architecture that could run Linux for open systems, e-business applications.

## Subsystem Interfaces

If subsystems are the key to product line architecture, be it for physical products, systems, or services, the interchangeability of those subsystems is the key to subsequent generations of product improvements. Interchangeability is a function of the connections, or *interfaces*, between subsystems.

As noted above, interfaces take one of three forms: internal interfaces that connect one subsystem to another; external interfaces that connect the product, system, or service to others; and user interfaces through which people (and of course, their pets) interact with the product, system, or service.

Simplicity and elegance in user interface design is the goal to which industry leaders across nearly all categories should aspire, be it the controls in a car, the snap-in replacement of cartridges in an inkjet printer, or the reporting of claims to an insurer. Kludgy, clumsy products fail to win over customers. They are far less tolerant of poorly designed, hard-to-use products today than even just five years ago.

The key to good user interface design is to think of it as bidirectional and interactive: "The system tells me this; I tell it to do that. The system responds, and we both continue forward." Unfortunately, much if not most software is still a unidirectional error message, leaving the user lost and hungry for a more helpful interaction.[4]

Many products and services must also connect with other products and services in the user's environment. Careful design of these external interfaces has been an enabling technology for a host of technology-intensive products. For example, IBM's software development tools must connect with other tools, and its computers must access data through various protocols used in both storage and communications networks. Developing good interface technology takes just as much work as developing good subsystem technology; in fact, an interface is just a special case of a subsystem within a product or service architecture.

In an industrial landscape with ever improving subsystem technologies, the interfaces between subsystems are often the most important platforms. They allow a product line to evolve in a stepwise fashion. This provides a much more comfortable situation for users who have invested time and money in learning and integrating the current product line architecture—be it for a product, system, or service—into their work and lives.

## Platforms

Modular architecture enables the development of powerful product and process platforms. *A platform is a subsystem or interface that is used in more than one product, system, or service.* The Gillette blade cartridge noted earlier is a simple but powerful example of a product platform. First a single blade, then a double blade, then three, and now five, these cartridge configurations define successive generations of the company's shaving systems and have been shared between male and female shaving systems.

A product platform might also be a motor used across different power tools or a library of graphic interface objects used across word processor, spreadsheet, and charting applications. Swatch Watch designed a series of common subsystems (the battery power supply and the mechanical innards) that are common to a wide variety of timepiece styles: sports watches, dress-up watches, kids' watches, and so forth. High levels of customization can be achieved through well-designed interfaces between the underlying platform subsystems and other subsystems that are tailored for specific applications. In a watch, those tailored subsystems might be the watch face or hands.

A platform might also be a common process within a line of services. Many insurers deploy common underwriting processes used across multiple lines of property and casualty insurance, or different lines of life and health insurance, using different data and decision rules to derive particular risk ratings for new cases across these various lines of business. [5]

The most powerful platforms can be leveraged across several product line architectures. In our book *The Power of Product Platforms*, Al Lehnerd and I provided examples of platforms that enabled next-generation product line development and new market applications. Those examples included the common, scalable motor design for Black & Decker's consumer power tools, the ink-jet cartridge in Hewlett Packard's printers, the common disk and electronics in EMC's storage systems, and the common frame, wing, seating, and overhead storage bins used across different short- and long-range models of Boeing's 777 airplanes. Each of these examples represented a new market application development for the respective firms. Common production processes can also serve as powerful engines for profitability and revenue growth (see sidebar.)

Though many books and scholarly papers about modular architecture have appeared in recent years, the idea is not new. Henry Ford's *Today and Tomorrow*, an exacting treatment of the modular design applied to automobile manufacturing, was first published in 1926![7] Ford described the seating subsystem, its components and the different materials (such as fabric) and processes used for each component, and the processes used for final subassembly.

Ford's thoughts have been picked up by current students of product line architecture and platforms. Thomas Johnson and Anders Broms, for example, describe in *Profit beyond Measure* how the Scania truck division created customized designs for fleet owners by combining different variations of what may be generally considered as "good, better, best" versions of each of four basic subsystems: the engine, the chassis, the driver compartment, and the electronics used for GPS and communications.[8] Each year, Scania's engineering groups would improve features within these subsystems. None of these improvements would have been so rapidly introduced and commercialized were there not absolutely clear, inviolable interfaces or methods of connecting the subsystems, such as the engine to the chassis or the electronics within the cab.

### Reusing Subsystems

Subsystems can and should be shared across product lines. To appreciate why, consider one of the companies I studied: a leader in health care systems and technology. Over the years, it grew through a combination of internal developments and the acquisition of various product lines that addressed both the

---

**Process as Platform**

A platform can also be a process. For many corporations, manufacturing or service processes are their most important platforms. For these companies, the manufacturing line has an architecture that provides for the integration of certain key processes. For example, at Mars Incorporated, the snack and pet foods manufacturer, a candy bar line has a bar-fill process followed by a flow-wrap process; each uses expensive machinery that can operate at incredibly high volumes and can be deployed for different brands if the company so chooses. A baker, on the other hand, will have automated processes for ingredient preparation and forming, baking, and packaging. In the technology sector, one of the sample companies studied for this book was a leading semiconductor manufacturer. An internal team showed how a platform-centric approach to semiconductor design and manufacturing led to substantially improved engineering cycle times and revenue generation when compared with product lines where little in the way of design, process, or people carried through from product to product.[6] Processes such as these can power the corporation, just as a jet engine powers an airplane.

There are two major benefits of a process platform. First, it allows the firm to enjoy improved asset utilization. Production processes are typically capital intensive, whether it's a Honda assembly line or the computers, storage systems, and networking devices used by a bank to manage its retail accounts. Any time a single process can be shared across multiple products or services, the cost of that capital is amortized over more business or revenue volume.

Second, like one of Honda's engines, a common process can be the focus of intensive quality control and improvement. All products or services produced by that process enjoy the benefits that effort.

---

administrative and clinical activities of hospitals. Unfortunately, the user interfaces across many of these systems were different, as were internal databases and error-handling methods. Services were sold to "patch" these systems together. Customers, however, expressed dissatisfaction with this approach. So the company embarked on a major effort to create common layers of technology capable of spanning all of its offerings: a single database interface, one protocol of providing user access to all applications, a common programming library for constructing graphical user interfaces, and so forth.

|  | Monitors | | | | Imaging | | CathLab | |
|---|---|---|---|---|---|---|---|---|
|  | System 1 | System 2 | System 3 | System 4 | System 5 | System 6 | System 7 | System 8 |
| **Real-time Acq.** | Unique | Unique | Unique | Unique | Unique | Unique | Unique | Unique |
| **Data Review** | Unique | Unique | Unique | Unique | Unique | Unique | Unique | Unique |
| **Documentation** | Unique | Unique | Unique | N/A | Unique | Unique | Unique | Unique |
| **Decision Support** | Unique | Unique | N/A | Unique | Unique | Unique | Unique | Unique |
| **Workflow Mgt.** | Unique | Unique | N/A | N/A | Unique | Unique | Unique | Unique |
| **Database** | Sybase | Sybase | Sybase | N/A | SQLServer | SQLServer | Oracle | Informix |
| **Networks** | TCP/IP | Lan Mgr | TCP/IP | TCP/IP | TCP/IP | TCP/IP | TCP/IP | TCP/IP |
| **OS** | NT,Unix | NT | NT | Windows | NT | OS/2 | NT | Unix |

FIGURE 7.2  Little Reuse across Three Medical System Product Lines

This company was not an exception. Figure 7.2 is based on data gathered during the late 1990s for the family of information systems used by hospitals for patient monitoring and imaging applications. Each column in the figure had been, at one time or another, a new market application, typically targeting a specialized new use for hospital medical technology. Notice how few systems are shared across or within the three product lines. As a division of a much larger corporation, R&D had always been decentralized with no formal mechanism for sharing subsystem technology. Reuse of major subsystem technology, if it existed, was done as an act of good citizenship by product line managers.

Studying figure 7.2 is a good exercise for anyone who works for a company that fails to exploit platform opportunities. The different columns in that figure represent the company's various medical devices. The rows are the subsystems that were common to these devices. In reality, when we examined the implementation of these subsystems, each product development team had implemented its very own solution. The three product lines—bedside patient monitoring, heart imaging, and cardiology laboratory procedures—had common needs: gathering data in real time from medical devices, reviewing these data to detect patient health signals, and supporting and documenting physician or nurse actions during a patient's stay in the ward. Despite these common needs, each product line had its own software modules; there was virtually no code reuse across product lines. At the infrastructure level, where one would expect substantial commonality, commonality was found only at the networking layer in TCP/IP. All the rest, even the operating systems, were different.

The result was that the company's development cycles were long and often over budget. Customers who had purchased all three systems wanted information centralized into a common patient information repository for physician access and tracking. With hardly any commonality in the lower layers of technology across these product lines, achieving that integration was costly and time consuming. No one in management viewed this situation as desirable, but no one had taken steps to develop common tools and subsystem platforms.

Many successful companies diversify within closely related product and service categories, and not into unrelated pursuits.[9] Yet, they do not always take advantage of that relatedness as they make and execute product line decisions. Instead, each product line is treated as a separate business. They compound this problem by housing development teams in separate locations, where they have few opportunities to interact. Inter-product line engineering meetings fail to focus on product line architectures and common subsystems within those architectures. The result is that opportunities to create commonalities between product lines are overlooked.

### Reusing Interfaces

Effective product-user interfaces are also often lacking; the problem is even worse for internal interfaces—the interfaces between subsystems. This problem is not difficult to understand. As engineers add new functionality to key subsystems, they tend to build new, custom interfaces to get into or connect with them. Over time, this multiplicity of interfaces becomes a tremendous impediment to both subsystem innovation and value-added product development. Development time and costs skyrocket as even the simplest product enhancements become difficult to execute.

For example, one of my MBA students, a mid-level engineering manager, was trying to support a new platform by using an existing code base. His challenge was how to make code changes in the hardware infrastructure code without affecting the rest of the overlaying code. Take a look at figure 7.3. This is an engineer's worst nightmare. That figure is a snapshot of the product line architecture, showing the major subsystems (the boxes in the figure) and the interfaces between them (the lines). Change any single subsystem (or box), and one must check and often revise all the interfaces (lines) leading to and from it. This becomes even messier when changes in one subsystem affect a second subsystem, which then affects the first subsystem—all through uniquely designed interfaces! Recursive procedure calls create havoc in complex systems because it is

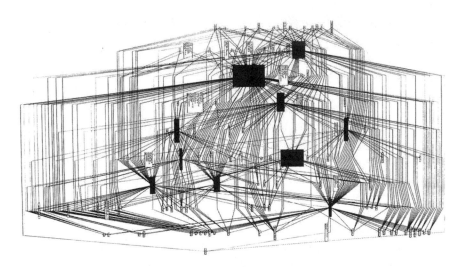

FIGURE 7.3 An Engineer's Nightmare: No Interface Discipline

hard to track down the root causes of problems or fully know their ripple effects.

This student quickly understood the larger issue. He applied a feature in software compilers that shows procedure calls from one module to the next and then plotted the result as shown in the figure. He used that visually abhorrent figure to secure the funding needed to clean up the mess, subsystem by subsystem. As noted earlier, pushing a change like that is not easy because you invariably hear the argument that "customers never pay for architecture, so why bother?" However, my student convinced senior management and used a step-by-step methodology to eliminate the "spaghetti code." His team cleaned up major interfaces and created a layered access to the hardware infrastructure code. Several years after the completion of this effort, the company has found the results to be remarkable in terms of R&D productivity. Time to market for new systems has been cut by about 20 percent! And, he deservingly became the chief architect of the company's major product line.

All the large technology corporations studied experienced varying degrees of interface problems as they developed software. Like the case above, the problem was so bad for another software company that management created a dedicated team of more than a dozen programmers to clean up its tangle of internal interfaces, to eliminate redundancy and improve flexibility among the internal interfaces. After several years of work, it had reduced the amount of code dedicated to software interfaces by a substantial percentage, in the words of one engineer, from "a mountain of code" to something far more structured and manageable. This made new features far easier and less expensive to add. The complexity of the old internal interfaces also made some of the external user interfaces cumbersome. After the revision, the new software was far easier to use.

## Three Steps to Modular Architectures and Platforms

To develop architecture, platforms, and interfaces for new market applications, consider following the three following steps:

1. Design a modular architecture for the new product line or service. That architecture should show specific *layers* of technology or functionality that, together, are the total solution. The goal is that over time, new technology and/or functionality can be added to a specific layer without violating the other layers, leading to continuous evolutionary improvement with minimum disruption to the user.
2. Define the common *and* unique subsystems and interfaces that must exist within the architecture to yield winning products, systems, and services. For the common subsystems, developers must try to design and implement *scalability* in the performance or functionality of those subsystems so that they may be used across multiple applications.
3. Plan the evolution of products, systems, or services over time. That planning includes the forward migration of end user solutions—the product and services—as well as the underlying platform subsystems and interfaces that are the foundation for those solutions. These two types of improvements, to the solution and the underlying platforms, should be synchronized in a stepwise fashion. Making this planning work requires good communications between specific product development teams and the more centralized subsystem platform development teams.

Now, let us examine each of these complementary steps.

## Step 1: Design a Modular Architecture for the New Product Line or Service

A modular architecture can be expressed as a *block diagram* showing major subsystems within the architecture and the interfaces between those major subsystems. For definition purposes, a team should specify three types of interfaces in its block diagrams:

— Internal interfaces: How specific subsystems in the product line architecture connect with one another, as well as the functionality within that connection.

— External interfaces with users: For a software product, this is often called the graphical user interface. Anything that touches the end user has some form of user interface, be it a control switch on a power tool or the shelf layout in a supermarket.

— External interfaces that connect to other products, systems, or services in the user's environment: These connections can have an important if not even decisive impact on the user's impression of the product. When my cell phone works just as well in Amsterdam as in Boston, I am delighted. When my ATM card works just as well on the island of Bali as it does in Boston, I am doubly pleased. Both are made possible through external interfaces that users appreciate but never see.

Figure 7.4 is a block diagram for one product line architecture. Consider this figure a planning template for new market applications development. That architecture is modular by virtue of specific subsystems connected through specific interfaces. It also shows the use of *layering* within the architecture. Layering is an important organizing principle for many types of products and systems. Each layer in the architecture is a logical group of subsystems that together provide a specific set of functionality. For example, one layer in software architecture might include all subsystems dealing with the user interface, and another, all subsystems for accessing data. Layering helps development teams specify and isolate functionality to specific subsystems and the connections between them. In this example, a software user gives a command to start a database query without having to know anything about the structure of the underlying database itself or the composition of the storage network where the data physically reside.[10]

Layering also gives a clear focus to roadmapping future subsystem improvements. Let's consider M&M's Candies, the forever youthful brand of Mars Incorporated. M&M's has three major subsystems: the center, the shell, and the packaging. The power of layering comes in how the company has innovated within recipes, materials, and other technology at each respective layer:

— The center: There are different centers such as peanut and almond. A variety of process technology for cocoa and peanuts has resulted in manufacturing platforms that create rich flavoring across the company's many candies. Focused efforts have continued to improve the quality and variety of an M&M's center.

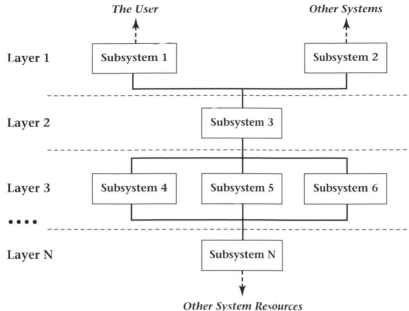

For each subsystem specify:
   Purpose, focus, organizational owner
   Links to specific design documents
   Potential and/or status of IP (intellectual property)

FIGURE 7.4 The Product Line Architecture Template

— The shell. Color is the shell subsystem driver and a big deal for dedicated M&M's fans. The company hosts a periodic "color vote" through which consumers help it decide which new colors to add to its current palette. Millions cast their votes on the company's Web site. In a later chapter, we will see how the company has created an entirely new business based on innovation to this subsystem—printing personalized messages on the shell!

— Packaging. M&M's Mini's have been especially popular with children. Instead of using the company's traditional flow-wrap packaging, Mini's are packed in tubes with unique graphics.

In sum, we can see how Mars has applied innovation to specific subsystems to meet new and emerging needs for taste, color, or tactile pleasure. By breaking a monolithic architecture into its logical parts, or layers, the company has been able to focus R&D on the different features that matter to users.

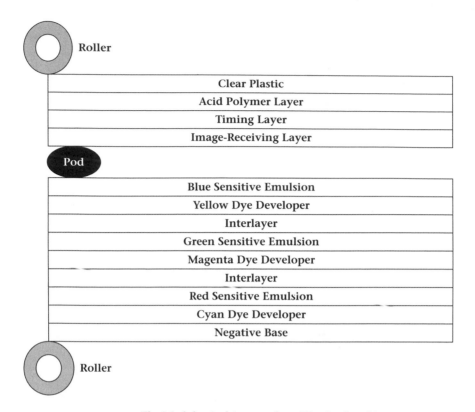

FIGURE 7.5 The Modular Architecture for a Film Product Line.
(This originally appeared in Marc H. Meyer and Dalal Dhaval, "Managing Platform
Architectures and Manufacturing Processes for Nonassembled Products," *Journal of
Product Innovation Management,* 2002, 10:277–93)

Film and materials manufacturers also use a layer approach to product architecture. The ones I studied, for example, found it best to express their product line architectures as a number of laminates—more than a dozen in some cases. These layers are bound together through a combination of chemicals, temperature, and precise timing. Figure 7.5 shows the block diagram for the core product line of a film manufacturer, with the various chemistries disguised.[11]

As your team creates its layered block diagram of the product line architecture (be it for a product, system, or service), pay particular attention to the proprietary subsystems that may give your company a competitive advantage, such as potentially patentable subsystems and interfaces. Highlight every subsystem with intellectual property advantages with colors, italics, or special fonts. It is important to innovate in areas where your company has distinctive competence and where achievements cannot be easily copied. Make sure that you have colleagues present who truly understand the functionality of each subsystem, the underlying technologies involved, the suppliers or sources of those technologies, and the strategies of competitors.

Remember, too, that the architecture block diagram can be used to communicate with senior management. Company executives must understand the product line or service architecture and the benefits of developing modularity and reusable platforms. Describe everything clearly on a single page in a font size large enough to make all items seem important. Follow-up pages for each major subsystem or set of interfaces can be created for more detailed discussion among technical members of the team.

### Step 2: Define Common and Unique Subsystems and Interfaces

Figure 7.6 shows a template for identifying common subsystems and interfaces ranging across multiple product lines and those that are unique to each product line. Common subsystems and interfaces help leverage company technologies and reduce time to market.

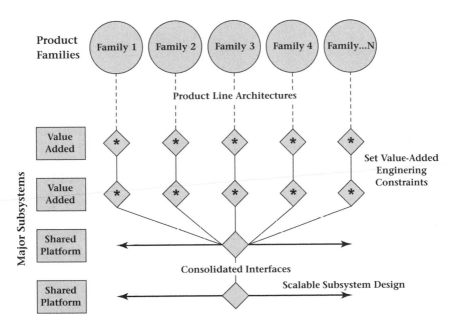

FIGURE 7.6 Achieving the Right Balance between Shared Platforms and Uniquely Designed Subsystems

Although commonality is generally beneficial, force-fitting all subsystems or interfaces to a new application usually disappoints users. Creating value-added on top of common subsystems creates that special product, system, or service for the new target user. A balance must be struck between common and unique. In the Element, for example, Honda tuned its exterior and interior subsystems for Gen Y users and at the same time leveraged its power train technologies across multiple SUVs. We shall learn the particulars of this in the next chapter.

The template in figure 7.6 represents how I think about that balance, and it is an important element in Phase 2 of the management framework for new market applications development presented in chapter 2 (figure 2.2). As a team transforms its prototypes into concrete product lines, it must seek to engineer robust product and process platforms.

In that figure, each product line is shown to have a distinct architecture. Over time, that product line architecture evolves to meet new user requirements and embrace new core technology. Each version of the architecture may be referred to as a generation of the product line. In well-managed firms, architecture changes with a frequency that, at a minimum, keeps the product line abreast of competitors' generational changes. The value-added engineering performed for individual products should be only a portion of the total engineering effort; in some cases, the majority of that effort should focus on shared platforms; in other cases, it might be about half. The balance between using shared platforms and value-added engineering for the specific application is one that executives and innovation teams should try to consciously determine. Figure 7.6 represents that balance for discussion purposes as "50-50." This decision on balancing platform R&D with specific product line R&D is labeled "Set value-added engineering constraints" in the figure.

It is important that value-added engineering be focused on specific subsystems or layers of technology containing a group of subsystems. Thus, for a new automobile targeting a youthful population, exterior styling might be one customized layer. Electronics, the power train, steering systems, and other subsystems might be reasonably leveraged as common platforms. Just be careful: Too much commonality or reuse does a disservice to the user-centered design methods described in prior chapters. It might reduce costs, but at the expense of user satisfaction.

## Creating World-Class Subsystems with Intellectual Property Protection

The logic of using common subsystems is fairly obvious; common subsystems make it possible to create a new market application without starting from scratch with every component, which reduces development expense and the

---

**Make IP Your Ally**

A common approach to IP emerged from the seasoned innovation managers in the companies I studied:

— Identify existing patent coverage as these patents might apply to the utility of a core technology, subsystem, or product within the new market application.
— Check with corporate counsel to see which patent applications have been filed or are in the process of filing.
— Determine which potential IP is best reserved as a "trade secret," and make sure that employees working on the project have appropriate contracts to protect that know-how.
— Apply for specific design patents on products and for other forms of protection on styling and appearance, such as copyrights and trademarks.
— Compile IP strategies and compare them with those known for competitors who are already serving the new market application spaces.

These steps should be of no surprise to practitioners. However, putting them into action in a systematic manner remains a challenge for most companies. IP will not *manage itself*! A new market applications development team must make discussions on IP an early and regular part of its work, both during the prototyping phase as well as in later product line and platform development.

---

cost of goods. But common subsystems must be world-class; otherwise, all the product lines that use them, old and new, will suffer in terms of performance. For example, the soul of IBM's new high-end servers described in the first chapter was a multiplexing "intelligent resource director" implemented as special-purpose firmware on 64-bit RISC microprocessors. That subsystem allowed tasks to be portioned out to different on-board processors for calculations and input/output in an incredibly flexible and scalable manner. IBM managers considered this project amongst the largest microcode development efforts ever undertaken in its industry. Had this core subsystem been inferior in any way, all new IBM machines would have failed the test of customer satisfaction. They would have lacked the speed and scalability needed for today's demanding computing applications.

World-class systems and technology should be protected whenever possible. All of the successful companies in my study were proactive about identifying

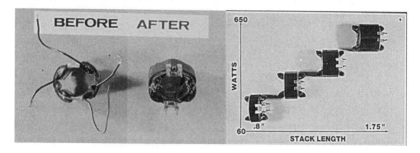

FIGURE 7.7 A Black & Decker Product Platform (this originally appeared in *The Power of Product Platforms*, Free Press, 1997)

potential intellectual property (IP), whether for core technologies or for product or process subsystems. Even service companies were highly attentive to IP.

### Scalable Subsystems with Plug-in Interfaces

It takes a lot of effort to create truly scalable subsystems that provide functionality across multiple market applications, both new and old. But the payoff can be substantial. Consider how Black & Decker revolutionized the manufacturing of power tools by treating motors, armatures, power cords, and switches as its platforms. Figure 7.7 shows a single "universal" motor designed to serve the needs of *all* Black & Decker consumer power tools up to 650 watts. This motor had a plug-in interface to the rest of the motor assembly, and the entire assembly was designed for automated balancing. Prior to these innovations, the firm had more than 120 different motors for its various consumer power tools; these were attached manually to the motor assembly and balanced through operator-assisted machinery.

Black & Decker's scalable subsystem facilitated the manufacture of a wide range of motors through a *single* production process, using the same materials and the same quality control process. That motor was a classic product platform, combining a scalable engineering design with automated manufacturing processes to drive down cost of goods and improve quality. The same approach was applied to all the other major subsystems of drills, sanders, circular saws, and jigsaws. Management used its resulting cost advantage to drive most competitors from store shelves. Black & Decker continues this discipline today, sharing many subsystems between its consumer power tool line and its high-powered DeWalt line, which focuses on professional carpenters and other tradespersons.

### Robust Channel Interfaces

Robust interfaces to and from subsystems are as important as scalable plat-forms within modular product line architectures. Robust means that there is one path into and from any given subsystem. The interface technology must have sufficient flexibility to adapt to different external elements. Looking back to our power tool example, imagine how inconvenient it would be if there was not a single, scalable interface between drill bits and the drill itself. In this case an adjustable chuck makes it possible for a single drill to accommodate bits of different sizes. This type of interface can also be an important competitive as-set if the scalable subsystem is patented. Black & Decker did just that, patent-ing its first and subsequent keyless chuck designs.

Designing the interface by no means assures that the pathways in and from the subsystem will automatically be used by other engineering teams. Interface discipline must be enforced by senior R&D management. For example, large computer companies often have several or more competing interface program-ming libraries because there is insufficient organizational force and invest-ment to make any single one "the standard."

One of my favorite examples of elegant, powerful interface design is in an area that I relish as a user: fly-fishing. I have fished in calm streams; in slip-pery, fast-moving rivers; in the ocean; and after hiking overland for extended distances to reach remote areas. For safety and comfort, each one of my per-sonal use case fishing scenarios requires a different type of wading shoe: felt-soled for the calm water, metal-studded for the treacherous water, rubber-soled for saltwater beaches, and hiking boots for the treks to remote fishing spots. The soles of all except rubber-bottomed waders wear out after two or three seasons, requiring the purchase of an entirely new boot. One company, Ko-rkers Footwear, solved the problem by designing a boot with interchangeable soles.

The key to the Korkers solution is the interface between the front of the sole and the front of the boot, as well as the attachment strap on the back of the sole or, in newer versions, a rubber heel strap and nylon hook as the release mechanism (see www.korkers.com). This interface architecture, branded as OmniTrax Sole Technology, makes it easy for the user to switch between dif-ferent soles that include felt, studded felt, rubber, deep rubber tread, and stud-ded rubber. The boots themselves, built on hiking shoe lasts, are comfortable on long, overland treks. A fisherman can walk on roads or trails wearing the rubber soles, upon reaching the river determine if plain felt or studded felt is required, and then replace the rubber sole with whichever one is best suited to the condition. Because the soles weigh very little, they can be carried in a fish-ing vest. They can also be replaced at low cost. Taking this a step further, the

FIGURE 7.8 The Konvertible Wading Boot: Multiple Uses through Simple Means
(Korkers Footwear. Reproduced with permission)

company is licensing its OmniTrax interface technology to other firms for applications beyond fishing.

Interface definition for many categories of products, systems, and services goes far beyond what a company designs itself. Industry standards often fill in nicely for the external interfaces required in a new market application. These standards facilitate plug-in modules and systems integration and save both developers and users considerable time and money. For example, the world of computers survives on industry standards such as USB, wireless 802.11, and Bluetooth (infrared) interface technologies. When these standards exist, use them! Or, in some cases, you will have little choice. Health care providers, for example, must conform to the treatment protocols defined by health care insurers in order to get paid!

## Step 3: Synchronizing Changes in User Needs, Products, and Platforms

Never expect user needs and core technologies to stand still. A company must plan for their evolution through new and improved platforms, as well as new and improved products and services based on those platforms. In effect, you need a roadmap for the future and a plan to integrate improved subsystems within the overall architecture.

Many different types of technology roadmaps have been espoused in the literature.[12] Some create a detailed matrix of technologies and performance requirements as each is expected to evolve over time. Richard Albright and Thomas Kappel present good methods and examples of this sort.[13] A roadmap for a new market application has three essential characteristics:

1. Staged improvements to products, systems, or services, over time. Improvements might also include new SKUs, product line additions, or revisions of current offerings. The inputs for staging these improvements and additions typically come from product and business managers, working in conjunction with engineers and market researchers. All should be members of the innovation team. This roadmapping is shown in the top half of the template.
2. Staged improvements to underlying platforms and their component technologies. Some of these platforms will be common across all products and, hopefully, product lines within the division. Others will be unique to the product line or service. The inputs for staging these improvements come from many sources, including central R&D, platform teams, and suppliers. Participants are not necessarily part of the innovation team but are nonetheless key development partners. The roadmapping of these platform improvements is shown in the bottom half of the figure.
3. Major market drivers (changing customer needs, demographics, or new technologies or materials) that will affect the team's market "space." These should have a pronounced effect on products and platforms. They are shown at the very top of the figure. For example, if a food company knows that health and nutrition will be important drivers in the future, its roadmaps must show recipe platforms that address this market trend.

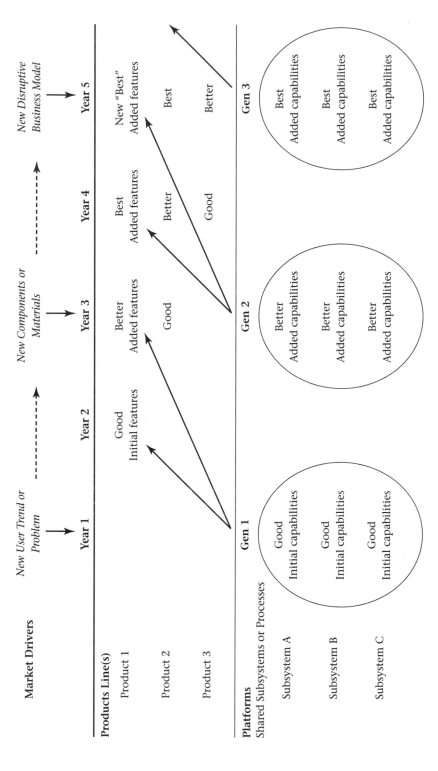

FIGURE 7.9 Synchronizing Market Drivers, Product Line Improvements, and Platform Enhancements

Integration across these three characteristics is obviously important. Ideally, a team will anticipate major market drivers. Core technology and platform implementations of that technology should logically come next. Product improvements that exploit these platforms and meet emerging market needs come third; these should be developed on tested and operational product and process platforms.

In reality, time-to-market pressures make synchronization difficult. The parallel development of new subsystems and specific product or service applications is often an unavoidable fact of life. Yet, using a new platform for a new product release clearly raises the risk. It is far better to have new subsystem innovations ready and tested *before* products using them are made ready for the market. That is the purpose of the arrows and sequencing shown in figure 7.9.

In the figure, I have also used the words "good," "better," and "best" to indicate a sequencing of objectives with respect to achieving excellence in subsystem capability. This concept was first discussed in chapter 3 (figure 3.3) in the context of defining new product strategy. It would be a shame to hold up the release of a solid and appealing product line because perfection cannot be achieved in that development cycle of subsystem technology. Yet, in my study, companies allowed perfection to stand in the way of good with some frequency. Core subsystem developers are often tempted to shoot for the moon, even though users do not require stratospheric levels of functionality, *at least not yet*. Months pass, and the top management team grows distressed with the pace of progress. A year of "Yes, we are working on it," "It's almost there," and "It's more difficult than we expected" delays the point at which early product offerings can be launched for the market learning that will determine with certainty which features are needed, and which are not.

## Reader Exercises

The reader exercises for this chapter ask you to apply the three key templates—the product line architecture diagram, defining common and unique subsystems and interfaces, and roadmapping product and platform changes—to a new market application that you have identified and are preparing to bring to senior management. To apply these templates most effectively, you should already have developed at least preliminary versions of:

1. A market segmentation that shows areas for growth and new product line or service targets.
2. An initial picture of the target user, enhanced with knowledge of the

user's experiences, beliefs, norms, and needs—both perceived and latent.

3. A use case scenario reflecting the primary activity set for the target market application and a list of perceived and latent needs emerging from that scenario.

4. An initial mapping of user needs to design concepts to subsystem innovations.

5. Some design sketches for possible product and service solutions.

Each of these is a powerful planning template. Each can jump-start development activity. Planning templates provide cross-functional innovation teams with a common mechanism for discussing ideas, exploring new horizons, and getting started. If you have the four templates roughed out for your new market application, then you'll be ready to begin working on the next set of technology-focused templates.

**Exercise 1**   Define product line architecture using each of the following guidelines.

— *Create a modular product line architecture* by using the block diagram in figure 7.4 as a template. Try to define the layers in the architecture. Also, identify the user interface, as well as interfaces to other products, systems, or services that users will require. This block diagram need not have dozens of subsystems running across three or four pages. Keep it simple at this point by identifying the highest level subsystems and interfaces in the architecture.

— *Focus on the internal and external interfaces.* Most of us will identify the interfaces but not pay much attention to their design. That's all right, as long as you take a second pass through the entire architecture and focus on the requirements for robust interface design to and from each major subsystem. You might even want to create a separate page for this.

— *Have a strategy for intellectual property protection.* IP is critically important during the planning phase for new market applications. Create a separate page listing IP targets for both major subsystems and interfaces—or IP that your company must license to create a winning solution. Remember, you will most often be entering a market space already served by traditional solutions. If your new product or service is indeed better, competitors will try to imitate it. So have an IP strategy (patents, copyrights, trademarks, or trade secrets) worked out *before* initial launch, the earlier the better. For product designs, paperwork should be filed in parallel with prototype development and testing; for process implementation, proprietary breakthroughs usually become apparent in the "product line and platform development" phase of the management framework for new market applications development (figure 2.2).

**Exercise 2** Create a roadmap that synchronizes market trends, product line improvements, and platform enhancements, using figure 7.9 as a template. Indicate where a product or service line and its underlying technologies are heading before starting your journey. That map will help senior management understand why you might be developing a "good" version as your first step (to get to market quickly), with "better" and "best" scheduled to follow. Your roadmap will also lay the groundwork for investments in underlying product and process platform technologies. So indicate what R&D will be required to build a flourishing product line, system, or service.

Now that you understand architecture, subsystems, and interfaces—and their value in product line development—let's return to the Honda case and see how that company's team readied its unique vehicle, the Element, for the road.

## Notes

1. Carliss Baldwin and Kim B. Clark, *Design Rule: The Power of Modularity* (Cambridge, MA: MIT Press, 2000).

2. These data were gathered from Proctor and Gamble's Gillette Web site.

3. In one of the companies studied (a manufacturer of industrial equipment), we developed a series of interesting metrics that show when a product line architecture is "running out of gas" and failing to allow engineers to quickly serve new user requirements. See Marc H. Meyer, P. Tertzakian, and James M. Utterback, "Metrics for Managing Product Development within a Product Family Context," *Management Science*, 1997, 43(1): 88–111.

4. Alan Cooper, *The Inmates Are Running the Asylum* (Indianapolis: Sams, 2004), 23.

5. Marc H. Meyer and Dalal Dhaval, "Managing Platform Architectures and Manufacturing Processes for Non-Assembled Products," *Journal of Product Innovation Management*, 2002, 10: 277–93.

6. Marc H. Meyer and Arthur DeTore, "Creating Platform-Based Approaches to New Services Development," *Journal of Product Innovation Management*, 2001, 18: 188–204.

7. Henry Ford, *Today and Tomorrow* (Garden City, NY: Doubleday, Tage, and Company, 1926; reprinted by Productivity Press, Cambridge, MA, 1988).

8. H. Thomas Johnson and Anders Broms, *Profit beyond Measure: Extraordinary Results through Attention to Work and People* (New York: Free Press, 2000).

9. Richard Rumelt, *Strategy Structure and Economic Performance* (Boston: Harvard Business School Press, 1974); Marc H. Meyer and Edward B. Roberts, "Focusing New Product Strategy for Corporate Growth," *Sloan Management Review*, 1988, 29(4): 7–16.

10. Marc H. Meyer and Peter Webb, "Modular, Layered Architecture: The Necessary Foundation for Effective Mass Customization in Software," *International Journal of Mass Customization*, 2005, 1(1): 14–36.

11. Meyer and Dhaval, "Managing Platform Architectures."

12. See Steven C. Wheelwright and Kim B. Clark, *Revolutionizing New Product Development* (New York: Free Press, 1992), to learn about aggregate project plans.

13. Richard Albright and Thomas Kappel, "Roadmapping in the Corporation," *Research Technology Management*, 2002, 42(2): 31–40.

CHAPTER EIGHT

# Honda's Element Comes to Life

*Implementing the product line architecture and key*
*subsystems for the Element—The user group helping with*
*user-centered design—The exterior styling—Interior*
*subsystems—The suspension—The power train—The engine*
*roadmap—Manufacturing retooling—The virtues of*
*co-location—Launch—In-market surprises.*

Now that we've discussed the importance of architecture and subsystems in new market applications, let us return to the Honda case and see how that company leveraged some proven subsystems from other vehicles, developed new ones as needed, and brought them all together in a package that appealed to the Gen Y guy's dreams. It is a rich example of how to translate a team's understanding of user needs into innovative design concepts, and those concepts into specific subsystem implementations—the template described earlier in chapter 5 (figure 5.1).

Like the company's other automotive products, the vehicle concept and business plan development for the Element had proceeded under the interdisciplinary Honda R&D's product planning group. With the project approved and a launch date set, Honda formed a larger SED team, where SED stands for sales, engineering (manufacturing), and development (R&D). This SED team reported directly to the executive team.[1]

## Implementing the Product Line Architecture and Its Subsystems

Every type of modern vehicle—sedan, minivan, SUV, pickup truck, and so forth—has its own architecture. That architecture defines the subsystems needed in the manufactured product and how those subsystems connect and operate together. One key to Honda's success as an automaker is its ability to leverage common subsystems across different product lines and yet create very different styles with specific features for different tastes as influenced by the user's culture, age, lifestyle, and gender.

Although subsystems are important, balance in their employment is equally important. If no subsystems were common across its product lines, an automaker would be unprofitable; if all subsystems were common, its cars would be so bland that they would fail to create interest or excitement in any particular market segment. Thus, a thoughtful balance must be sought between the common and the unique. Excellence in those two areas is essential in pleasing both shareholders and customers, and the Element team pursued them.

With a business plan approval in its pocket, the team pushed through product line and platform development, Phase 2 of our management framework for new market applications (figure 2.2). This involved:

1. Solidifying the product concept, going from the Brain Cage shown in chapter 6 to a more pragmatic vehicle that looks like the Element we see on the street today;
2. Finalizing exterior styling—the overall shape, the b-pillarless frame, the skylight, the clamshell tailgate, exterior panels, colors, bumpers, and so forth;
3. Finalizing the interior styling—flexible seating configurations, driver controls, interior materials, and colors.

Stylists drew sketches for various exterior and interior components. From these, designers created quarter-size clay models and, after successive iterations, full-size prototypes. The most senior directors of the company then convened to review these designs and prototypes and approved movement to the next phase. These senior management reviews were critical, not just for getting to the next development phase but also for the positive impact that the executives had on the vehicle's ultimate form and function.

User-centered design practices did not stop with business plan approval. In fact, these activities intensified. During 1999, the team formed a user group of

30 men between the ages of 19 and 29. All lived near Honda's Torrance, California, design center. The center's stylists met periodically with this group to show them a series of sketches, followed by prototypes for segments of the exterior and interior design. Step by step, user by user, the team transformed the abstract Brain Cage into something very real that these young men found compelling.

The user group was kept together until mass production commenced in December 2003. Establishing a user group of this nature and actively engaging it during the design phase was a first for Honda R&D. A user group seemed logical because the Gen Y men were not Honda's traditional customers. Today, Honda considers this approach best practice and uses it for many different types of projects.

The Element team concentrated its design efforts on four key subsystems: the exterior, interior, chassis, and power train. Honda executives reviewed each subsystem design at appropriate times. Most of the team's choices proceeded without impediment because senior management was anxious to get this new vehicle to market in record time. On occasion, however, executive review had an impact on the project that affected the design and the timetable. For example, as the team moved to a rugged exterior styling, one executive liked what he saw but thought the tires were too small to suit a rugged vehicle; he favored larger tires. Accommodating that change would require a wider underlying chassis—30 millimeters wider than the CR-V chassis on which the team had based its design. It would also require more steel and add weight, which, in turn, would require new tooling and some structural alterations in the East Liberty production plant. Despite these costs, the larger tires were deemed essential. In the words of one SED team member, "We all knew that this was the thing to do, and we also knew that it would be a lot of work. Rather than worry about it, we decided to get started."

### The Exterior

In the auto business, the exterior body is a major subsystem. Its subsidiary subsystems include the vehicle frame, body panels, bumpers, windshield, sunroof, and tailgate. For the Element, the styling for many of these subsystems was unique—the b-pillarless frame in particular. That design made it much easier to move cargo, sports gear, and other "guy toys" into and out of the vehicle. The overall styling and colorization was also distinctive relative to Honda's existing product line: the boxy appearance, the stub-nosed front, and substantial amounts of glass provided a unique appearance and best-in-class cargo-carrying capacity.

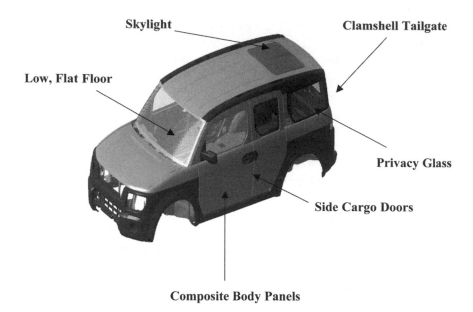

**FIGURE 8.1** The Body and Exterior Concept (Honda Motor Company. Reproduced with permission)

Figure 8.1 shows the exterior design concept that evolved from the earlier vision. Each design concept was developed for a compelling need on the part of the Gen Y user, such as the scratch-resistant body panels and privacy glass.

Differentiation, tailored to Gen Y needs, is apparent in many other exterior subsystems. Consider the doors. Unlike other SUVs, the Element's b-pillarless doors made it possible to offer "side-gating," facilitating greater easy of entry and exit for cargo and making the vehicle a better platform for tailgate parties. The clamshell tailgate system did the same.

Once design concepts are turned into subsystem features, Honda as a matter of practice benchmarks its implementations against the products of competitive offerings, and it did so in this case. For example, figure 8.2 shows the opening aperture of the Element's tailgate subsystem compared with those of two competing vehicles (at the time of launch).

Figure 8.3 shows a similar design strategy for the exterior shell. Knowing that target users would be moving large pieces of gear and furniture, Honda's engineers wanted an exterior material that was more dent and scratch resistant than competitors' shells. Working with suppliers, they developed a new composite material that provided superior durability for the Element's snap-on exterior panels. The skylight was another important aspect of this exterior

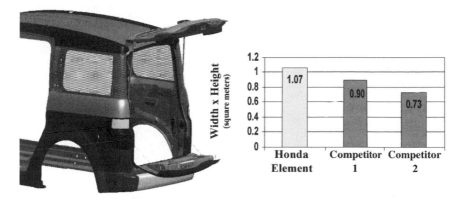

FIGURE 8.2 Clamshell Tailgate Design Benchmarked (Honda Motor Company. Reproduced with permission)

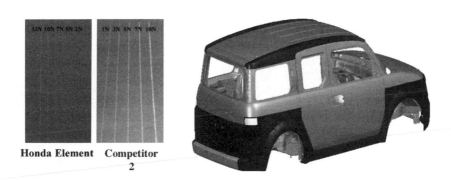

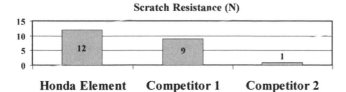

FIGURE 8.3 Scratch-Resistant Body Panels (Honda Motor Company. Reproduced with permission)

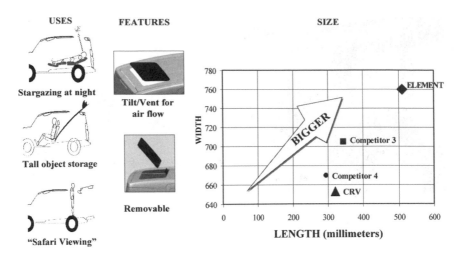

FIGURE 8.4  The Skylight Design

subsystem. Its concept and comparison to competing vehicles is shown in figure 8.4.

## The Interior

As with the exterior subsystem, development of the Element's interior proceeded rapidly. Guided by the concept of an interior Freedom Zone that had emerged from user studies and early consumer-centered design, this interior placed a premium on cargo space and flexibility in using it. They aimed to give the Element unsurpassed flexibility in handling many different use scenarios. Consider the seating subsystem. All four seats were designed so that they could be easily reconfigured into different positions—to provide maximum cargo space, sleeping platforms, or standard passenger conveyance. Whereas typical seats would either pull out or pull into the floor, the SED team concept opted for a flat floor. Seats could either be folded up against the sidewalls and out of the way or removed entirely for still more storage space. Figure 8.5 shows the results of these efforts. Flexibile interior seating and cargo space has become a competence and design feature across many Honda vehicle products, such as the Ridgeline pickup truck.

In the end, a low, flat floor made it easy to place bicycles and furniture in the cargo area. The flooring itself was a urethane-coated material with drainage channels. This design allowed users to use a brush or wet sponge to sweep out

FIGURE 8.5 The Freedom Zone Comes to Life (Honda Motor Company. Reproduced with permission)

beach sand and clean off mud from mountain bike tires after a weekend trek. Critical electronics were placed above the floor, and electronics below the floor were encapsulated in waterproof barriers as an added precaution. Seating fabric was also waterproof.

And then there was the sound system. A Gen Y man won't walk to the corner store without a music player attached somewhere to his body, and the music has to been LOUD. A robust music system was deemed a must. Further, the bass in the standard Element sound system was specified to be eight times louder than the one used in the CR-V and to have multimedia audio.

This attention to interior detail was pervasive. Instead of a standard coffee cup holder, Honda's engineers designed a system for holding typical fast-food french fries and soft drinks, complete with little tabs to hold items in place on bouncy rides. Bungee cords on seat backs, a rear cargo tray, and privacy shades on windows and the skylights were similar features designed to the requirements of the Endless Summer.

## The Suspension

The design concept for the Element's suspension aimed to provide a highly maneuverable, stable, but enjoyable ride. That translated into greater firmness and sportiness than the CR-V suspension. A combination of subsystems achieved this end, and some of these were shared with other products in the Honda lineup. First, the Element used the same basic chassis as the CR-V (rear wheel wishbone suspension and front wheel struts), but with some 0.44 meters greater width and 0.25 meters closer to the ground. The Element also used the power steering gearbox common to the CR-V, the MDX, and the Pilot. Added to this were 16-inch versus 15-inch tires. This arrangement created a firm ride. In sum, the CR-V suspension subsystem was adapted as a product platform for the Element.

## Power Train

As described earlier, the Element team designed most of the exterior and interior subsystems to meet the needs of the young male user. The suspension, on the other hand, was largely adopted from the CR-V and tuned for sportier ride performance. The team approached the power train in similar fashion. If a team can leverage one of the leading—if not *the* leading—engine platform in the industry, why not use it?

When it comes to the development of new market applications, Honda's engine technology and its prowess in user-centered design are its two greatest assets. The former provides leverage; the latter provides the differentiation needed to create point specific solutions. Honda's 2.4-liter, VTEC (variable valve timing and emissions control) engine, the one adopted for the Element, provided a maximum of 160 horsepower at 5,500 RPMs. It also achieved 25 miles per gallon in highway driving while meeting stringent California LEV II emission standards. Honda's power train group in Japan had several years earlier released this engine to various SED teams around the world who were working on other new vehicle developments. Different versions of the engine had found their way into both passenger cars and SUVs.

Honda engine development is centrally controlled by the company's R&D center in Tochigi, Japan, where hundreds of engineers work on a range of engine technologies and create specific engine designs for cars and trucks. The

Tochigi facility has impressive R&D assets for experimentation, prototyping, and testing. Staff in the power train group also work with the manufacturing plants that produce Honda's engines. Subsidiary engine development groups in other regions of the world supply SED teams with engine specialists.

Honda's power train engineers focus on three key goals for each next-generation engine:

— Make engines more powerful—that is, provide greater horsepower per liter of combustion chamber.
— Make engines more energy efficient. Honda takes this goal very seriously, both for its conventional and hybrid engines and for its zero-emission fuel-cell power trains.
— Reduce engine emissions.

Beneath these goals is the broader business objective of creating engines that can be used across multiple product lines when appropriate. The engine dictates a substantial portion of the customer's driving experience and total cost of ownership. It also contributes between 20 percent and 30 percent of the manufacturer's overall cost for each vehicle. Getting the engine right makes many other things work for users and for the business.

Honda's car and light truck SED teams are not authorized to design entirely new engine or power train requirements. Instead, the central power train group publishes a detailed engine roadmap that shows current and next-generation engine developments and delivery dates. In the case of the Element, the new 2.4-liter engine was designed in Japan, manufactured in Ohio, and transported to the Element manufacturing line for assembly. One of the benefits of the new engine is that it provided substantial torque at high-end speed intervals, the type of performance needed, for example, for passing on highways—a feature designed to please Gen Y men.

Figure 8.6 shows the engine roadmap serving Honda's automotive products at the time of the Element's market introduction. Arrayed by power range, the figure shows the various gasoline combustion engines, as well as low-emission engines (hybrid gasoline/electric), and zero-emission power trains. For readers working in centralized R&D groups, this is the type of technology roadmap to which one should aspire. For those involved in the financial matters of an enterprise, this same roadmap helps achieve a high return on capital assets resulting from shared product platforms and manufacturing processes.

The 2.4-liter VTEC engine with intelligent valve control was first delivered to the 2002 CR-V and Acura RSX SED teams. Soon thereafter, the same design was delivered to SED teams working on the 2003 Accord and the 2004 Element. Thus, a single new engine development supported four product applications.

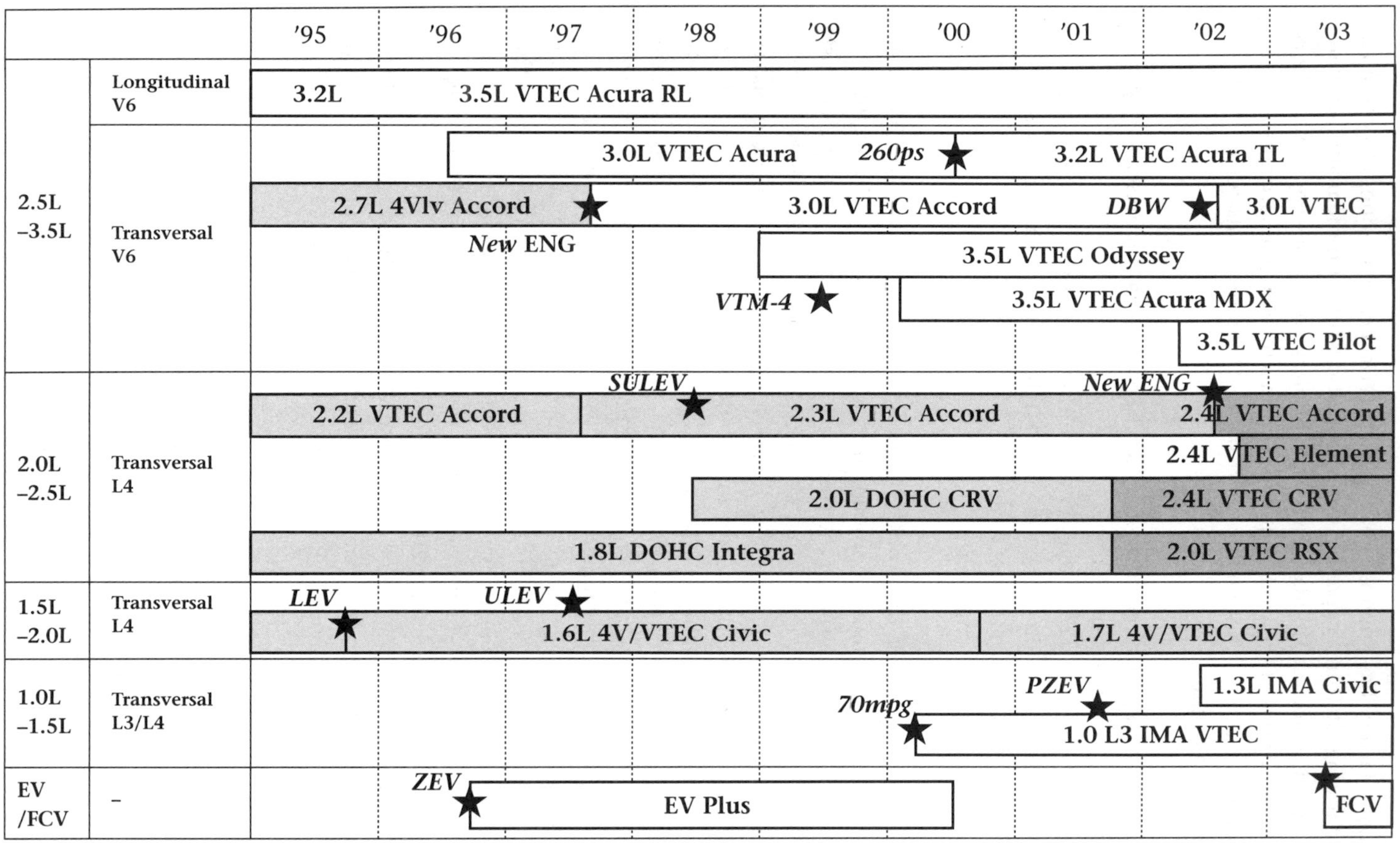

**FIGURE 8.6** Honda's Power Train Roadmap (Honda Motor Company. Reproduced with permission)

| | | '95 | '96 | '97 | '98 | '99 | '00 | '01 | '02 | '03 |
|---|---|---|---|---|---|---|---|---|---|---|
| Longitudinal V6 | 2.5L–3.5L | 3.2L | 3.5L VTEC Acura RL | 3.0L VTEC Acura | | 260ps ★ | 3.2L VTEC Acura TL | | DBW ★ / 3.0L VTEC | |
| Transversal V6 | 2.5L–3.5L | | 2.7L 4Vlv Accord / New ENG | 3.0L VTEC Accord | VTM-4 ★ | 3.5L VTEC Odyssey | New ENG | 3.5L VTEC Acura MDX | 3.5L VTEC Pilot |
| Transversal L4 | 2.0L–2.5L | 2.2L VTEC Accord | | SULEV ★ | 2.3L VTEC Accord / 1.8L DOHC Integra | | 2.0L DOHC CRV | 2.4L VTEC Accord / 2.4L VTEC CRV / 2.0L VTEC RSX | 2.4L VTEC Element |
| Transversal L4 | 1.5L–2.0L | LEV ★ | | ULEV ★ / 1.6L 4V/VTEC Civic | 1.8L 4V/VTEC Civic | | | 1.7L 4V/VTEC Civic | |
| Transversal L3/L4 | 1.0L–1.5L | | | | | | 70mpg ★ / 1.0 L3 IMA VTEC | PZEV ★ | 1.3L IMA Civic | |
| – | EV/FCV | | ZEV ★ | EV Plus | | | | | | FCV ★ |

- The Engine was '03 Accord common
- The Water Tank and Water Pump for Element unique
- All else was '02 CR-V common

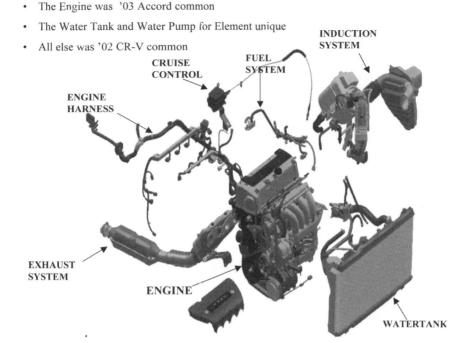

FIGURE 8.7 Power Train Commonality for the Element
(Honda Motor Company. Reproduced with permission)

The figure also shows how a larger engine design serves Acura sedan and larger SUVs, such as the MDX, Pilot, and Odyssey minivan.

Thus, any major advance by the power train group benefits several product lines. For 2005 models, for instance, Honda deployed its next-generation hybrid engines, delivering the performance of the V6 with fuel economy equivalent to a—cylinder Civic.[2] This approach provides a reasonable expectation that these new hybrid engines will be made available across Honda product lines.

Figure 8.7 indicates how much the Element power train shared common platform technology with other Honda products. The engine, as just described, is shared across the Accord, the Element, the CR-V, and the Acura RSX. The Element's exhaust system was a modified version of the CR-V's exhaust system. Only the water tank was designed uniquely for the Element because of the vehicle's special front-end body styling.

This is a powerful strategy, but one that works only if the corporation makes superb common subsystems. Honda assures this by investing generously in the central power train group's capabilities. Honda's long tradition of leveraging subsystems may be a legacy of its origin as a small, upstart firm that had to compete head-to-head with larger, better financed rivals. That strategy has continued as a pervasive engineering philosophy, embedded in the fabric of new product development, even though the company has grown. Honda's engineers like to say that they "build cars to drive the engines." Other manufacturers speak of platforms and internally publish roadmaps, but few take the concept as seriously and implement it as rigorously as Honda. Some automobile companies design vehicles with unique power trains, producing dozens of distinct engines.

## Manufacturing Process Development

As described in chapter 6, Honda executives decided to assemble the Element at the East Liberty Plant, which was then making the Civic, a smaller and much lighter vehicle. Producing the new SUV on that same line would require substantial reengineering.

Traditionally, all of Honda's automotive manufacturing projects had been guided by the philosophy of "tool and go." Tool and go means preparation of tools and equipment in order to "go" with manufacture of those items. Achieving tool and go requires a tremendous amount of preproduction testing and many test runs. It also requires close coordination between Honda and its various machine and component suppliers. The Element involved more than 200 Tier 1 suppliers with many Tier 2 and Tier 3 suppliers working through them. The SUV's specialized seating, for instance, required more than 150 individual parts in the driver's seat alone; these were produced by many different suppliers, some new to Honda. With so many suppliers involved in the East Liberty operation, a high level of coordination was essential. The SED team conveyed its requirements to its Tier 1 suppliers, which then coordinated and delivered an integrated set of equipment and component specifications from their own respective suppliers back to Honda. Honda tested these specifications for concept fit, quality, and cost. The SED team also made commitments for the tooling and materials required to make parts in the preproduction runs needed to assemble test units.

The production line in East Liberty had about 50 sophisticated pieces of automated equipment, some for putting on tires, other for filling liquids such as antifreeze, and so forth. There were hundreds of other tools on the assembly line. Engineers had to "teach" these various pieces of equipment—which recognized data points for the Civic sedan—how to work with the data points unique to the Element. Further, plant engineers had to modify much

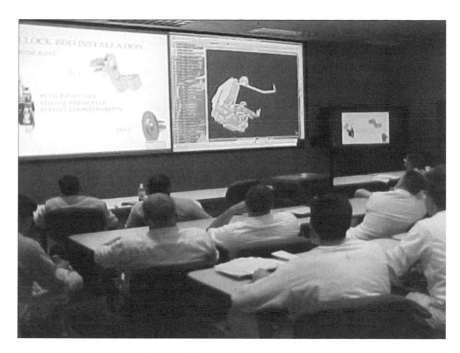

FIGURE 8.8 The One-Floor Room (Honda Motor Company.
Reproduced with permission)

of the equipment to work on a vehicle that was higher and wider than the
Civic.

### The Virtues of Co-Location

Concurrent engineering was nothing new to Honda, and it was, indeed, one of
the driving rationales for the SED team structure. For the Element, this meant
that manufacturing staff from Ohio had been involved since the earliest
phases of concept and business plan development. Once executives moved the
concept into full-scale development, team leaders decided that R&D, Tier 1
suppliers, and manufacturing engineering personnel would have to co-locate.

With that in mind, R&D set aside a very large workroom in its Raymond,
Ohio, facility. This workspace—dubbed the One-Floor Room (figure 8.8)—
was to be shared by R&D's engineers and by personnel from the East Liberty
plant five miles away. The workroom was located near R&D's model shop so

that team members could easily see quarter-size and full-size molds for new component designs. Once the project passed through its final product design specification stage, the One-Floor Room was moved to the East Liberty plant. This made sense because the emphasis of the project had shifted to designing, installing, and testing new machines. This co-location was a first for Honda, but has become a company standard practice for new vehicle development.

### New Equipment

Co-location enhanced the Element team's effectiveness. So, too, did its approach to ordering, installing, and testing new capital equipment. Prior to this project, company practice followed this routine:

1. Complete all component and machine specifications
2. Have suppliers produce them in test mode
3. Test components and machines
4. Gear up for mass production

This "tool and go" approach required that specifications for components, and for the machines that make them, be finalized and approved before any new equipment was installed. That approach would not have met the Element's planned launch date of December 2002. East Liberty plant engineers had to design, tool, and install all equipment faster than ever.

Working on such a short timeline, the Element team did not have sufficient time to wait for *all specifications for all equipment and materials* to be completed before ordering and testing equipment or for all tests to be completed before gearing up for mass production. Rather, specification, purchasing, and testing would have to be staged for the manufacturing processes associated with the Element's major parts. As each subsystem design was completed, production tooling for that subsystem was ordered right away. When the machines came in from suppliers, they were immediately tested.

Suppliers were authorized to purchase equipment and buy necessary materials (such as steel) to start testing the equipment. The risk of this approach, of course, was that the team had to work twice as hard to plan and control integration, both for vehicle components and for the machines being readied for the assembly line. This represented a substantial change in work processes for Honda's R&D and manufacturing engineers. However, without co-location and true partnership with its suppliers, Honda could not have brought concurrent engineering to the level it achieved with the Element.

FIGURE 8.9 An Element Following a Civic at East Liberty
(Honda Motor Company. Reproduced with permission)

The net result of all this work was a single production line that could switch over between Civic and Element models—the first Honda line with that flexibility. Figure 8.9 is the proof of this remarkable accomplishment. Just as Honda used the Element to enlarge its approach to user-centered design, the manufacturing effort was a proving ground for a new level of flexible manufacturing. Once achieved, it had beneficial implications for asset utilization in Honda's other plants around the world.

East Liberty planned to make 360 Elements daily. According to the business plan approved by senior management, the SED team targeted annual production of 50,000 units. This would consume about a third of the plant's annual capacity. In the automotive business, the first-year production rate of a new model tends to be the highest for that model, followed by incremental declines over the course of five or so years, at the end of which manufacturers introduce a new model to reinvigorate sales. In the back of its collective mind, however, the team suspected in addition to Gen Y men, many 30-something and 40-something men would also want an Element for its pragmatic function and flexibility. Management would have to count on manufacturing's proven ability to scale production if demand exceeded forecast.

## Market Launch—and Some Elemental Surprises!

The concept development team also explored go-to-market strategies for its new vehicle. It observed that the Gen Y man was averse to traditional automobile advertising; word of mouth and recommendations from trusted authorities and peers were much likelier to create interest. Honda's communications around the new SUV would reflect this insight in a marketing campaign that was very different from anything used for other Honda SUVs.

Innovative products require innovative marketing. It was clear that decisions regarding the Element's marketing would be as important as decisions regarding its design and manufacturing, so the company established a special brand and advertising team to work on the new vehicle. Naming it was one of its tasks. Consumer product naming is a tricky business. It must be right the first time; there's no turning back once the choice is made. In many cases, market researchers test several potential brand names to learn which best suits the product concept and evokes a positive response. Once the name is chosen, consumer-focused companies spend royally on advertising and other forms of promotion to launch and develop their new brands. Some of the largest consumer product companies estimate that $250 million is needed to create and sustain a global brand. Brand development for nonconsumer products can be equally important and expensive. As mentioned in the first chapter, IBM spent well over a billion dollars to create awareness for its e-business and e-server brand names.

In Honda's case, Element was just one of many potential names. These names were presented to a panel of Gen Y men for comments and feedback. The short list of names that pleased the panel was tested with a panel of potential buyers. The name "Element" emerged at the top of the list. Using that name, a separate marketing group then developed a range of communication strategies for the launch.

The product had to support the brand with real substance. Marketing claims on its behalf had to be believable, authentic, and confirmed every time the owner sat behind the steering wheel. The Element had to deliver the goods it promised. It had to be highly utilitarian, provide space for many different activities, and still meet the Honda reputation for reliability and driving performance—and at a price within reach of the target market. This was a tall order, but the SED team was confident that its product would deliver on all fronts.

The Element brand also had to be clearly and crisply communicated to target users. Toward this end, the SED team focused on the Gen Y lifestyle and how the Element fit into it. The first commercials for the Element celebrated new young male users and their friends—a coming out party of sorts. One commercial depicted four young men taking a road trip, going to the beach, and then to a party, clearly having a lot of fun. Their Element was an integral part of the experience.

Because research had shown that Gen Y audiences do not respond well to direct, aggressive advertising, the SED team used its resources to create buzz around the vehicle at auto shows and promotions on college campuses, at beaches, and at sporting events. Early reviews in automotive magazines and newspaper columns fueled prelaunch publicity. For example, in 2003, *Automobile Magazine* named the Element the best new small SUV of the year. Honda sponsored surfing events and tailgate parties at universities, both of which were unique to the business.

Honda did its initial preproduction runs of the Element in the summer of 2002, even as the marketing rollout was underway. East Liberty delivered some units to the sales force for training purposes and other units to the test track. Some six months later, delivery of the Element to dealers began.

Two model versions of the Element were made available: the LX and the EX. Honda has used these labels to convey a sense of "good, better, best" to consumers for its sedans and SUVs. During the first year, both the LX and EX Elements versions came with four power train options: a front two-wheel drive manual transmission, a two-wheel drive automatic transmission, a four-wheel drive manual transmission, and a four-wheel drive automatic transmission. The EX offered a more powerful sound system, anti-lock braking, alloy wheels, optional side air bags, and extra interior features, such as a driver's armrest.

### Look Who's Buying

Elements began arriving in dealers' showrooms at the end of 2002. The initial target buyer was a man up to age 26 (or his parents). This group represented 10 percent of the U.S. automotive buying market. As data trickled in from newly registered car owners and dealers, management realized that its concept—focused like a laser on the Gen Y man—appealed to a much broader market. In fact, only 20 percent of first-year Element sales were to Gen Y men; another 40 percent were purchased by Gen Xers in their mid-30s, and drivers in their mid-40s purchased most of the rest. Element buyers were generally but not exclusively male. Whatever their ages, these buyers were physically active, with some type of sport being their favorite leisure activity. In fact, 68 percent of Element buyers sampled during 2004 saw themselves as highly active, compared with 58 percent of new Civic buyers. Even older Element buyers, when asked what they liked about the SUV, often responded, "I like the fact that it is for younger people."

The SUV that Honda had focused so totally on young male buyers also appealed to older users who were active in sports and young at heart. Weekend warriors in their 30s and Boomers with active lifestyles loved the SUV for its character and multiuse flexibility. Attraction to the Element was not a matter of age, per se, but of attitude, psychographics, and utilitarian needs. This was both a surprise and a great learning experience for the Element SED team who continued to manage the project throughout its first year of launch.

Upon reflection, these managers continue to feel that *staying true* to the vision of Endless Summer had been the right course. Had the team tried to make a car for all men in their 20s, 30s, and 40s, the product would have come out as mush. By focusing on Gen Y male car buyers, the team had made a car for other buyers with similar attitudes, expectations, and needs. Management knew that beyond just making a richly functional product, the Element was a unique "experience" for the user, just like Starbuck's coffee or Apple's iPod.

The Element's surprising broader appeal had a clear upside. By the end of 2004, production reached 75,000 units, 50 percent over the original projection. It also gave credence to the saying that "you can sell a young person's car to someone who is older, but *never, never* try the other way around."

As this case demonstrates, great companies do more than just one thing right. The Element SED team fired on multiple cylinders: target marketing and product positioning, user research, subsystem designs, leveraging power train platforms, and some very clever marketing.

By any measure, the Element is a fascinating story of innovation for enterprise growth, rich with concepts and methods from which readers can draw valuable lessons. Honda makes a determined effort to leverage its competence in user-centered design and its major product platforms in the pursuit of new market applications. That Honda's R&D has its own marketing, business, and technical staff to create new concepts and business plans for those concepts is telling. It is also notable that a multifunctional team from sales, manufacturing, and engineering was tasked to see the project all the way through to completion. Co-location in the One-Floor Room took collaboration to the next level. And driving everything was a senior management team that was totally devoted to internally generated growth and willing to invest heavily in it.

We are now ready to take the next step in our journey. There are no reader exercises here, just my wish that readers reflect on what the Honda experience means for *their* companies.

## Notes

1. This is also true at IBM, as it was for the MathWorks venture into financial services modeling. Successful new market applications development teams typically reported up to senior executives, providing the air cover needed for innovation in both marketing and technology, as well as access to key resources.

2. Fuel-efficiency and low-emission technologies have been hard-won competencies within Honda. As the Civic and Accord were taking hold in the United States, Honda achieved a number of firsts with its engine technology. It won all the major fuel-efficiency awards with its CVCC engine in the early Civics and Accords. Honda then brought to market the first mass production VTEC engine (variable timing emissions control), the first LEV engine (low emissions vehicle) in its hybrids, and the first ZLEV engine (the zero emissions, hydrogen fuel cell engines now installed in Civic). Honda's LEV vehicles, the Insight and the Civic Hybrid, accounted for more than half of all U.S. hybrid sales in 2003 (according to R. L. Polk vehicle registration data).

# CHAPTER NINE

# Business Model Innovation

*A definition—Key business model decisions—Different types
of business models—Examples of business model
innovation—A template for planning the business model—
Reader exercises.*

In our journey toward new product line and service development, we have examined a number of concepts and methods:

— Segmenting markets for growth and creating new product or service strategies
— Performing user research
— Developing use case scenarios to formulate design drivers for new products and services
— Creating design concepts that meet user needs and focusing those concepts on major subsystems
— Defining architecture and subsystems that can be deployed across multiple products or service lines

This chapter explores business model innovation, which can be as essential to enterprise growth as anything discussed to this point. Within the context of the management framework shown in chapter 2 (figure 2.2) business model innovation must occur early on in parallel with user-centered design and prototype development. After the market test is completed, a team may then find it necessary to fine tune or, in some cases, fundamentally revise its business model.

The importance of using new market applications to take a fresh look at a company's conventional business model can be seen in the successes of eBay, Dell, Amazon, and Southwest Airlines. Yes, they all provided improved products or services relative to established competitors, but they also figured out how to make money—often in new ways—through those products and services. An innovative business model can be a clear point of competitive differentiation, providing value to both customers and shareholders.

Changing an established business model is often necessary if one aims to capture the full benefits of a new market application. Yet business model innovation is something that many innovation teams fail to consider. And for executives, this can be particularly challenging, given the many years they have spent growing the established business. Seeing *the prototype* is one thing; visualizing *the business* behind that prototype is something else. An innovation team must help executives make that connection.

## Defining Business Model Innovation

To understand business model innovation, we must first define it and understand some of the forms it can take. Simply put, a business *model* describes how a company plans to make money. It is not *what* you do, but how you *make money* doing what you do. Business model *innovation* is, then, an important change to a company's existing business model.

Andrew Hargadon and Robert Sutton have described how breakthroughs can occur when a company occupies a unique position within an industry network, combining existing technologies, processes, and people to form winning solutions.[1] Consider Apple's iPod/iTunes business, a wonderful example of business model innovation. It combines new channel development, third-party developers and suppliers, a premium price for the music player, and a recurring revenue model for the digital music. Apple isn't simply selling equipment; its selling an ongoing relationship with buyers and users of its equipment. The $300 iPod is simply a platform on top of which users can download 15,000 songs (at $1 per song) and other types of entertainment software. The iPod would not have reached its potential without of the treasure chest of downloadable music made available to users through iTunes and Apple's licensing agreements with music suppliers. The result is that Apple is making money not just on one-time sales of its music player (the hardware) but also on those downloads (the software). This business model eclipses the traditional music paradigm, which includes portable music players like the Sony Walkman, traditional retail channels for CDs, and the old music pricing model. Five years after the iPod was launched in 2001, Apple's revenues had almost tripled, and its share price had increased tenfold!

The potential impact of business model innovation on a company's fortunes is demonstrated by Automated Data Processing (ADP), a leader in payroll processing, whose past president shared this story with me. During the 1980s, ADP undertook a major transition: from selling time-shared software to providing turnkey payroll services. As part of that transition, ADP's business model shifted from generating revenue on software usage to collecting and depositing payroll deductions on behalf of employers with federal, state, and local taxing agencies. From a strategic perspective, ADP was no longer competing against potential software entrants; it now had direct service relationships with customers. ADP's new business model changed its mechanism for generating revenue. Suddenly, ADP was making money on the "float" obtained in the transfer of money. Revenues grew tenfold, and the income statement and balance sheet of the company were radically transformed.

Web services technology architectures (such as IBM's Services Oriented Architecture) are enabling a transformation of the traditional business model of the software industry. Most companies still sell software licenses based on the number of servers upon which the software will operate. An emerging business model is to sell software as a service, whereby customers access software through the Web and pay a usage charge, as opposed to licensing the software on a per server basis. "Pay as you go" fits nicely with Web services architecture.[2] One example is salesforce.com, a contact and relationships management software company. Instead of charging a per server license, salesforce.com charges on a per user or per group basis, with variations either by month or by year. This yields a far lower initial charge relative to the traditional software licensing model for enterprise customer relationship management systems. That lower charge is not only good for customers but it also produces recurring revenue for salesforce.com. By the close of 2005, salesforce.com had more than 20,000 corporate customers and almost 400,000 subscribers, and it had surpassed $300 million in annual revenue. The company's integration of a software product rich in function withwith a new business model highly attractive to users put more traditional competitors on notice and forced them to respond.[3] It seems just as clear that as Google and other Web-media companies introduce spreadsheets and word processors that are HTML-based and thus, software delivered as a service, Microsoft's traditional business model for its Office suite—its cash cow—will be similarly threatened and the company will be forced to respond.

My students typically come to class thinking that that financial statements and the business model are synonymous. This is incorrect. Financial statements are a reflection of a business model, but they are *not* the business model itself. Rather, they are the outcomes of a business model and the many decisions needed to create the business model.

Rushing to build a profit-and-loss statement too quickly might prevent a team from thinking behind the numbers. Teams that develop new market applications must not assume that the firm's traditional business model is the best one for the new product or service line. The price level may well be different. Channels might be different. Support services might also be different. In short, the new target customers might simply prefer to do business in an entirely different way relative to a firm's traditional customers: services versus products; on-line versus retail; a turnkey solution as opposed to bits and bites.

## Where to Begin?

To build a business model, a team should think about the key economic components of every business: demand and supply. Start with the demand side of the equation:

— Who will be our customers? For consumers, do they represent a new use in the same demographic or an entirely different demographic? For business customers, do they work in a different area of the same type of company, at a different level in that company? Might they be working in an entirely different type of organization, a systems integrator, for example, as opposed to a traditional end-user corporation?
— How will our new product satisfy customer needs relative to competing products or services?
— How will our customers value the product? Putting aside for a moment how they value our current products or services, if we make something possible that was never possible before, might not our customers see this as unique and therefore deserving of a high price?
— Are there new, unexploited opportunities to sell customers a stream of value-added enhancements, plug-ins, or complementary services, all of which can be priced separately and constitute a rich source of recurring revenue?
— What do we know about the cycle of customer learning, ordering, fulfillment, and payment?

Then the team must think about the supply side: Will we make the product ourselves or use contract manufacturers? Will we use internal or external R&D? How might these decisions affect our cost of goods or capital expense and our operating margins?

When, and only when, demand and supply questions have been satisfactorily answered can the team move on to projections of revenues, expenses, and capital requirements and to the development of pro forma financial statements. We will address these issues in greater detail in the next chapter.

## Strategic Business Model Decisions

What are the major strategic decisions that drive the business models for new market applications that I observed in the companies studied for this book?

The transition from products to services is clearly one of these. Successful new products, for example, often have explosive revenue growth, as the introduction of Apple's iPod clearly demonstrated. Successful services, on the other hand, generally produce a more gradual ramp-up. (The rapid revenue growth of Google is a striking exception.) The product versus service decision also determines the nature and magnitude of R&D expenses, both before and after launch. Products typically require heavier R&D investments than services. As one goes through other aspects of business financials—the cost of production and delivery, capital asset and marketing investments—it is clear that services are a completely different animal in terms of conceiving and executing a business model.

There were others fundamental types of business model innovations that accompanied new market applications:

— *Premiumization.* Another important type of business model innovation I observed was, to take liberties with a term, *premiumization*, or repositioning products or services on the price-performance spectrum. Teams that adopted this business model were motivated to escape the profit margin stranglehold of commoditization.
— *Plug-in modules.* The adopter of a *plug-in reseller strategy* creates modular interfaces in the product line architecture that readily accommodate the addition of other modules and accessories. The plug-in modules and accessories might be made by the company itself or sourced through business partners. Plug-ins provide new incremental streams of revenue on top of the base product or service.
— *New channel choice.* This important business model decision affects the amount of revenue and size of margins provided (or not provided) to intermediaries. Selecting or developing a new channel outside the company's traditional area of competence is an important form of business model innovation.

— *Manufacturing and supply.* Innovation in a firm's traditional *manufacturing and supply* strategy can have a dramatic effect on financial outcomes by affecting gross margins, asset intensity, and operational expenses. Some very large manufacturers in my sample wrestled with supply issues. They debated whether to process raw materials themselves or purchase them from suppliers. The first option would have enormous financial consequences from increased capital intensity and perhaps a higher cost structure for materials. Nevertheless, some companies felt that vertical integration provided distinct advantages in terms of proprietary know-how. Nonmanufacturing firms, particularly those in financial services, took a different position; they were aggressive in outsourcing key functions to reduce operational expense. (The quality implications of their choices have yet to be fully understood.)

Each of these strategies is a type of business model innovation that can be focused on a new product line or service development. At least half of the several dozen companies found themselves undertaking business model innovation in the context of new market applications. It is only by looking at a few of these firms that we can fully appreciate the scope and impact of business model change.

### Modular Pricing for IBM's e-Business Processors

The modularity of products, systems, and, increasingly, services has allowed many firms to offer plug-in capabilities for their base-level products and thereby revisit their pricing models.

For example, IBM has applied an important business model change to its "mainframe" servers for open systems computing—a new hybrid pricing model. IBM has one pricing structure for the use of a mainframe server for traditional online transactions processing and another pricing model when the same machine is used to process Linux and Java applications—the coins of the realm for e-business.

The traditional pricing model was based on "measured service units" (MSUs). The purchased capacity for a particular machine was listed as a certain number of MSUs. Each MSU corresponds to a set number of MIPS (millions of instructions per second) per processor and the number of processor configurations for each new mainframe model. Rather than have a single price list for its various mainframes, IBM worked with customers to determine their peak load requirements, which necessitated a certain number of MSUs (just like horsepower in an engine). Then, pricing was set based on that number.

The zSeries architecture (now called System z) offered the flexibility to keep the MSU pricing scheme but then to add something else. The zSeries still ran the transactions processing application, but it also ran Linux and Java applications—all on the same physical server. This technology made something possible that was never possible before: to combine the throughput power of a mainframe with open systems computing capability. For the Linux and Java programs, IBM developed special-purpose processing engines. This has led to a new "engine-based" pricing model.

Each new specialized processing engine is priced at $125,000 per unit (at the time of this writing), regardless of function. A Linux processing engine (for running open systems software) is priced at $125,000, as is a special Java processing engine (IBM's ZAAP processor). The typical customer today orders a large mainframe server with different combinations of all three processing engines. This is a better deal for the customer because all three engines—OLTP, Linux, and Java—can then share data I/O and networking adapters. This makes the entire system very modular, scalable, and cost effective for high-volume users. A customer who wishes to upgrade can then purchase new engines or activate whichever engine type is needed. The new business model is in keeping with the inherent modularity and flexibility of IBM's thrust into open systems computing with its Services Oriented Architecture that spans both hardware and software.

## From Selling Bricks and Mortar to Selling Ad Space

Street furniture is a small but rapidly growing segment of the $6 billion outdoor advertising industry.[4] Its products include bus shelters, subway and bus line map displays, and yes, even public toilets. Under the traditional business model, manufacturers design and assemble their furniture, install it, and invoice municipal customers at a reasonable markup over cost.

Wall USA has taken a different approach. It agrees to build, install, and maintain street furniture *at no cost* in return for the lion's share of advertising rights. Figure 9.1 shows one of the company's installations, which is located near my office in Boston. Revenue from advertising pays for the work and provides incremental revenue to the municipality—a win-win situation for the vendor and its customer. Wall USA even takes responsibility for finding willing advertisers. After five years, a bus stop is revenue positive and effectively becomes a money machine for Wall and the municipality.

In this case of business model innovation, building and selling bricks and mortar—a one-time event—has given way to creating a conduit for recurring revenue. This makes for a totally different business, however: selling partnerships with cities and towns on the front end and selling advertising and collecting fees thereafter.

FIGURE 9.1   Where Is the Money Being Made? Not from the Bricks and Mortar
(Wall, USA. Reproduced with permission)

## Business Model Innovation in Financial Services:
## The Invention of Quota Share

During the 1990s, a life reinsurer developed a particularly interesting example of business model innovation coupled with service design innovation.[5] This company (then called LincolnRe) was the largest life reinsurer in the United States. It had approximately $6 billion in annual revenues and more than $130 billion in assets under management. As a reinsurer, LincolnRe provided insurance to insurance companies. Here's how it works. A direct insurer such as Pacific Life sets a retention level on the face value of individual policies. When the dollar amount of an insurance policy exceeds that retention amount, the remainder is passed on to reinsurers, who, for a premium, bear that additional risk.

LincolnRe had great competence in assessing the risk of life insurance policy applications. It could develop accurate risk profiles and life expectancy predictions from applicants' medical conditions, family histories, and information on vocations and hobbies. LincolnRe's dedicated multifunctional team of physicians, underwriters, actuaries, and expert system developers could also tell insurers which insurance applications not to accept or how much more those applicants should be charged to cover their additional risk.

During the 1990s, many large financial companies entered the life reinsurance market. These global corporations began to take market share by discounting anything that LincolnRe offered. They were turning reinsurance into a commodity business. As the largest domestic reinsurer, LincolnRe could survive this pressure, though its fate would be "profitless prosperity." To remedy the situation, senior management chartered its underwriting and actuarial experts to create a new reinsurance offering that would change the terms of competition.

LincolnRe decided to target an area where its customers were having trouble making money: inexpensive "term" life insurance. A number of banks were moving into the insurance arena, and they were having real profit difficulties in this part of the market. LincolnRe applied its best minds to develop an expert system that could analyze the demographics of an insurer's target population and design term insurance programs (pricing, durations, and conditions) that would make money for the insurers.

In this case, LincolnRe demonstrated the wisdom of reassessing one's business model in conjunction with new technology. It was designing successful products for its customers: the insurers. This was special, unique within the industry. Rather than the traditional fee of a certain cost per thousand dollars reinsured, LincolnRe successfully requested that insurers pay it a percentage (say, 25 percent) of actual premium revenue.

This new business model altered the industry and allowed LincolnRe to escape the commoditization trap. Not only did this change produce substantially more revenue but also it placed LincolnRe in a direct partnership with its customers. LincolnRe's innovation, called "quota share," soon became the envy of the industry, and all other major life reinsurers tried to emulate it. The largest of these, SwissRe, decided that the easiest and surest path to competing with LincolnRe was to acquire it, which it did at the turn of the millennium. In the larger perspective, LincolnRe had won by providing "design services" in addition to its traditional products; in doing so, it fundamentally changed its value proposition to customers.

## A Pharmaceutical Supplies Company Moves beyond Rats and Mice

Charles River Laboratories (CRL) has become the largest global provider of outsourced drug discovery services. It got to this point through an aggressive strategy of internal development and strategic acquisitions—and through a fundamental change in its business model.

CRL was founded in Boston in 1948 as a breeder of rats used for medical research in hospitals, universities, and pharmaceutical companies, primarily along the Northeast corridor. For many years, the company was small and privately held. Its founder, Henry Foster, a veterinarian, correctly anticipated that research institutions would seek an alternative to breeding their own test animals owing to space, labor, and time constraints. The company grew by adding a new "product": mice. In medical research, rats are the heavy lifters of toxicology (drug safety) studies. Mice are more often used in earlier-stage discovery experiments that seek answers to specific biological questions.

For customers, CRL's mice and rats represented cost-efficient, consistent, and accurate components of medical research, and they contributed immeasurably to medical progress. If you have taken an antibiotic lately, there is a very good chance that the drug was first proven on a CRL "research model."

The product development history is fascinating; yet for decades, it was based on a single business model of charging a certain price for a research model/animal. CRL's initial products were "general purpose"—that is, the same mouse or rat could be used for any type of drug research. They were also "outbred," meaning that any female mouse would be bred with any male mouse in the general population. The firm's ability to charge for these general-purpose mice, however, was limited; until the 1990s, the price was less than $20 per healthy mouse.

During the early 1970s, random breeding was replaced by breeding within familial lines. This yielded animals with more specific traits and characteristics, as well as consistency not found in random genetics. These "inbred" standardized animals improved the productivity of research customers by ensuring predictable, accurate, and repeatable outcomes. (CRL acquired inbreds from public sources, such as the National Institutes of Health, without restrictions or licensing.) The company's rats and mice were further upgraded and differentiated by eliminating many of the contaminants (viruses and bacteria) that typically infect rodents. The research community recognized the absence of contaminants as a major advance in quality and reliability.

Thanks to its improved products, the company continued to grow. By 1984, CRL had annual revenues of $50 million, derived mostly from the sale of mice and rats. Foster continued to drive the company forward on a path of internal development.

"Mutants," the company's third-generation platform, were developed during the late 1970s and early 1980s. Mutants are animals carefully selected from inbred litters that demonstrate very specific genetic outcomes; they are even more targeted than inbred animals. By using mutant mice, researchers can be far more effective in studying analogous mutation in humans. A fourth-generation platform then appeared during the mid-1980s: induced mutations.

These animals included the "nude" mouse, a rodent with a severely compromised immune system that was popular among customers studying infectious diseases and cancer. With induced mutations, the company's products had come a long way—from general-purpose mice and rats to highly specific research models that targeted specific human medical conditions. It was toward these specific conditions that academics and drug companies were increasingly focusing their research. As demand for outbred rats and mice declined during the 1990s, these ever-improving animal research models provided management with the ability to preserve revenue and charge higher prices.

All the while, the company's business model remained the same: per animal pricing. Development of fifth-generation products began in the late 1980s; that work focused on the genetic engineering of mice with certain diseases. An evolution of staged mutations, this application of genetic engineering was called "transgenics." The first and most notable transgenic model was the patented OncoMouse, a mouse with cancer that was genetically engineered by researchers at Harvard in the late 1980s. OncoMouse was a proprietary model owned by Harvard and its commercial sponsor, DuPont. CRL and laboratory researchers could use OncoMouse, but only under very restrictive licensing terms. Those terms made it difficult for CRL to grow a viable product line. Although some "open source" or unrestricted transgenic models were available, few reached a level of utilization adequate to support a CRL product line.

Rather than give up on the technology, CRL thought of a new way to leverage it through a different a new business model: it would offer genetic engineering services to research laboratories using "open source" transgenic mice. Genetic research in mice was expensive, labor intensive, space consuming, and highly specialized. CRL executives concluded that if they could provide this capability, researchers in hospitals and pharmaceutical companies would be eager to procure their services. CRL went to market with this new service in 1987, marking a watershed in the company's business.

CRL's shift from products to services accelerated during the mid-1990s. Instead of delivering rats and mice, it was delivering the results of experiments and studies. By the early 2000s, CRL was providing expertise in the areas of genomics and proteomics as applied to animal models, emerging fields of drug discovery. As service volumes grew, the company recruited more and more scientists with advanced degrees—veterinarians with postdoctoral training and laboratory science certification, molecular biologists, microbiologists, and medical doctors.

CRL's migration into more profitable areas of the value chain continued. From drug discovery services, it moved into preclinical drug testing in a variety of animal research models. That required expertise in toxicology, pharmacology, pathology, and other specialties. Each of these moves involved a substantial investment.

To support its move into services, CRL made a series of selective acquisitions, buying niche service providers in drug discovery and development areas. It also expanded its global reach through a deal with Scotland's Inveresk Research Group, a provider of preclinical and clinical services. This was the final step in the progression to human clinical trials management, from Phase I (a small number of healthy patients in a hospitallike facility) to Phases II and III (large numbers of health and sick patients). CRL could then claim to be a provider of all significant nonproprietary steps that a potential drug candidate must take toward to final federal Food and Drug Administration approval. Today, CRL has its own Phase I facility—a "mini-hospital" for human patient testing. It also designs and manages clinical trials conducted at hospitals, clinics, and doctors' offices on behalf of biotech and pharmaceutical clients.

By 2006, CRL's business model had truly changed. Annual revenues exceeded $1 billion, of which rat and mouse products—the old business—represented only about 25 percent. Preclinical and clinical services dominated the revenue mix. Both areas were highly profitable, and these endeavors had a healthy effect on the company's stock price, which rose from $16 at CRL's initial public offering in 2000 to over $50 in 2005. Jim Foster, the founder's son, and chairman and CEO for the previous decade, was named CEO of the year by *Fortune* magazine. Clearly, for CRL business model innovation had proved a powerful engine for enterprise growth.

### Moving from a Capital-Intensive Business Model to a Services Model

Commoditization is one of the most powerful motivators of business model change. We observed that in the case of LincolnRe, whose market was invaded by rivals eager to compete with standard products on price alone. Commoditization was also a rationale for Charles River Labs to move upstream from generic rodents to more specialized versions—and eventually into highly technical services. Commoditization inevitably leads to a pricing slugfest among traditional competitors. Thin margins, if not outright losses, are the usual result.

One way to escape this situation is to move elsewhere in the value chain. In some cases, that means moving into some service capacity. In the right circumstances, that move can improve profit margins and give a company an opportunity to step away from capital-intensive operations. A supply management company I studied, which we will call Synergtx, provides an example.

Synergtx was driven to change its business model by commoditization. Many readers may find their companies facing similar pressures in maturing markets. This company opted out of a fairly standard printing business in favor of a strategy for linking suppliers, manufacturers, and customers with a host of global supply chain management solutions.

The company started as a capital-intensive, high-volume printer of manuals for the computer and electronics industries. It owned printing and duplication plants in North America, Europe, and Asia. Companies such as Microsoft, Adobe, and Apple outsourced their printing and CD duplication activities to Synergtx. The launch of Microsoft Office in 1995, which came with many user manuals, created a huge volume of business.

Because companies like Microsoft sold their software through computer hardware manufacturers (OEMs), Synergtx not only kitted the manuals and CDs but also shipped the finished product directly to the OEMs. The OEM channel created additional needs. Microsoft, for example, had to know the exact number of copies of its software sold through these OEMs on a quarterly basis so that it could correctly invoice each one. This was hard to do well. Synergtx stepped in and developed a computer system that maintained a precise accounting of licenses sold through to various OEMs and reported the data back to customers such as Microsoft. This made Synergtx much more than a supplier and more like a business partner with its customers; its information was an important part of the revenue-generation process. In fact, this service was so successful that by the turn of the millennium Synergtx was doing about a billion dollars in annual revenue.

During the mid-1990s, however, offshore contract manufacturers surfaced in great numbers and heavily discounted their work in order to build volume. The result: Gross margins slumped to less than 20 percent of their high-water mark. Synergtx's management knew it had to do something different or live with the same type of profitless prosperity that LincolnRE had faced.

Management created a vision to become an outsourced supply chain management services provider. The vision was to be the "first to touch" to "last to touch" for "clients" such as Adobe or Microsoft and their own end-user or corporate customers. This meant developing capabilities in order taking, fulfillment, support, accounting, and even customer returns. This entire spectrum was branded as an e-fulfillment service. Synergtx changed its business model to one of transactions-based services. Management also sold off its existing printing, CD duplication, and kitting plants to low-cost suppliers, thereby dramatically changing its balance sheet and producing a much more attractive return on capital for equivalent amounts of revenue.

The transition did not come for free. Management invested heavily in the development of processes and computer systems for a suite of services such as program management for new product launches, Web design, online payment processing, inventory and sales reporting, demand planning, shipment and fulfillment, software license administration, and product returns handling. It was a dramatic value chain migration, as so aptly described by James Quinn in the *Intelligent Enterprise*.[6] Solution centers were established around the world. The company also provided telephone customer support for the end users of its customers' software and electronics, and even began handling the messy business of customer purchase returns—all for a fee.

Thus, a highly capital-intensive, high-volume business model—one suffering margin erosion—was transitioned to a service model, with high levels of recurring revenue and a much more intimate relationship with key customers. The differences between the two business models can be seen in figure 9.2, a summary P&L for the company during its transition from the old printing business to the new supply chain management business. The costs of materials for the new business were about half those of the printing business as a percentage of revenue, and gross margins (39 percent) were twice those of the old business— even after staffing customer service centers around the world. The new service

| | Product | Service | Total |
|---|---|---|---|
| **Revenue** (in $millions) | 450 | 110 | 560 |
| **Cost of Materials** | 250 | 32 | 281 |
| **Margin after Materials Purchases** | 200 | 78 | 279 |
| *% of Sales* | **44%** | **71%** | **50%** |
| **Cost of Production** | 121 | 36 | 157 |
| **Margin after Production** | 79 | 43 | 122 |
| *% of Sales* | **18%** | **39%** | **22%** |
| **SGA Expenses** | 59 | 30 | 88 |
| *% of Sales* | **13%** | **27%** | **16%** |
| **EBITDA** | 21 | 13 | 34 |
| *% of Sales* | **5%** | **12%** | **6%** |

FIGURE 9.2  A Business Model in Transition

business model required heavy administrative costs in labor and computer systems, but even then, profitability (EBITDA, earnings before income taxes, depreciation, and amortization) was twice that of the old model.

## A Template for Framing Business Model Conversations

The business model innovations described here are just a handful of the many I uncovered in my study of enterprise growth. Other companies pursued channel innovations, such as the Web or network marketing (home shopping parties). I once encountered a Web startup that searched through four very different business model transitions: from specialty online exchange, to superstore online exchange, to B2B software infrastructure provider, to software tools vendor. At one point, it had a market capitalization of over $8 billion; a few years later, it was gasping as part of the "living dead."[7]

If changing from one business model to another is difficult, so is selling the idea of business model change to senior management. Like most people, executives are less comfortable with the new and uncertain than with the old and familiar; they are inclined to view new ideas through lenses suited to older ways of doing business. In large, mature corporations, executives instinctively think of a new venture as already being a $100 million to $200 million business. They assess new opportunities with the same financial measures (internal rate of return, return on invested assets, and so forth) they apply to the company's established businesses. They forget that today's mighty oak trees were yesterday's puny saplings, whose growth required years of tender loving care. In these cases, one of the innovation team's challenges is to get its senior executives to look at their new business model with fresh eyes.

To help communicate business model change, I show the concepts in figures 9.3, 9.4, and 9.5, which can collectively be considered a business model planning template.

— Figure 9.3: The first figure positions the business model as the link between the business strategy and the projected financial outcomes of the venture. The key strategic decisions are enumerated. Business strategy: the target market, target users or positioning of the new product line or service, the types of products and services to be provided, and the best channel for reaching users. The desired financial outcomes are best expressed in conventional financial statements, such as a projected P&L, a cash flow statement leading to net present value, and a capital plan

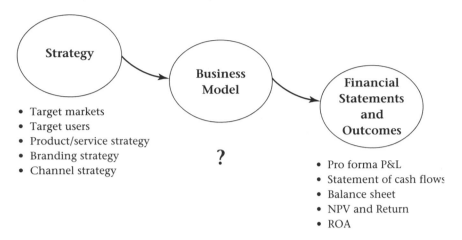

- Target markets
- Target users
- Product/service strategy
- Branding strategy
- Channel strategy

?

- Pro forma P&L
- Statement of cash flows
- Balance sheet
- NPV and Return
- ROA

FIGURE 9.3  Thinking about Your Business Model as the
Link between Strategy and Financial Outcomes

that, when linked with the P&L, provided measures of projected return
on assets.

— Figure 9.4: This second figure lists key questions with respect to defining the business model. Many of these are straightforward; others are
subtler. The answers to these questions might well show that you have
defined a business strategy that is financially either unattractive or un-
feasible. At the very least, most executives will want you to consider
how to build recurring revenue into your business model and show a
path to profitability that does not require a herculean investment in
assets or other forms of infrastructure.

— Figure 9.5: This last figure simply recasts the prior two figures into a
planning process. Project financial statements can easily a lead a team
to reshape its business model, and changes to a business model can dramatically affect a firm's strategy, to whom it sells, what it sells, and its
branding.

Business model decisions—the answers to the questions in figure 9.4—can have
an enormous impact on an innovation's need for capital and on the operating
outcomes from commercializing the new product or service. These factors then
lead to the basic profitability characteristics of the business: time to market,
profit, how profits ramp with revenues, and whether the business is going to be
a high-margin, low-volume business or a low-margin, high-volume business.
These decisions cannot be made lightly or by defaulting to what the business
has always done in the past. Rather, figures 9.3, 9.4, and 9.5 should be the basis

- Are we selling just products, services, or a combination of both?

- Can we get recurring revenue from the same users? How much is it?

- What are our streams of incremental or add-on revenue? Can we resell third-party products?

- Is there a production requirement, and what do we do in-house versus outside?

- What is the best channel to achieve market penetration and learning? What are the incentive structures needed to make that channel dynamic?

- How much is it going to cost to execute our brand strategy? Are we building a new brand?

- How many smart people do I need to engineer the product or systems? Do I need any?

- What is our time to first dollar? How quickly can we get to market?

- What is our path to profitability? How much do we have to invest (how large do we have to scale and how much variety does our product line have to offer) in order to achieve profitability?

- How does the business scale in terms of production and selling? Who will it take to scale it?

- At the end of the day, does this leave us as capital intensive, or nonintensive, business? Do we have reasonable access to the capital required?

FIGURE 9.4 Questions Driving Business Model Design

of intensive discussions between the innovation team and its executive sponsors and, perhaps just as important, run by key prospective customers and suppliers.

## Reader Exercises

This set of reader exercises aims to help you become more facile in planning innovative business models.

**Exercise 1** To get started, try your hand on Apple, Inc. Work the iPod example described early in the chapter through the figure 9.4 template. What is the target market and just how big is it? Describe the primary target users and their

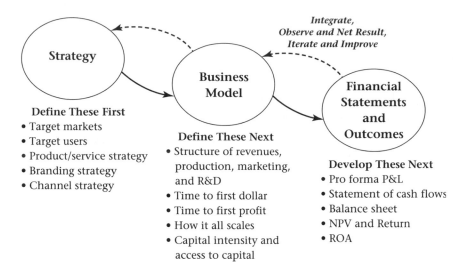

FIGURE 9.5  The Business Model Planning Process

appetite for new and varied music. What are the products (manufactured), what are the services (the music), and how is each priced and distributed (channels)? Accessories sold by Apple and third parties are yet another important revenue stream associated with this business. Do a Google search on Apple's iPod sales, apply a traditional 40 percent manufacturing cost to the business and royalties of 5 percent to music supplier, and you will see the model unfold. Then compare it to the traditional norm of a music player manufacturer. A comparison of the two very different business models should be telling.

**Exercise 2** Take a successful product line or service innovation in your industry—one whose traditional business model was tweaked or transformed. Apply the template once again, first to the traditional business model and next to that of the successful innovation.

**Exercise 3** The ultimate challenge, of course, is to apply the template (figure 9.4) to your own new market application. Once again, take the business model template and apply it to the new product line or service that you are considering. What is the conventional product positioning for offerings in your company? How might your new idea be different? What are the traditional cost structures within established businesses, and how might yours be different? Does it make sense to use an external manufacturer, and if so, what are the implications of that for the business model? How are other product lines or services marketed? What might you do that is different, and what are the implications of that for initial launch and subsequent scale? This applies not just to channels but also for promotion and communications.

As you tackle these tough questions, do not be too quick in projecting revenues or profits; instead, think broadly and try to integrate across the three columns of the template.

We will soon turn to more detailed methods of creating elements in the template's third column: projected financial statements and measures of financial performance. But first, let's turn to a number of new market applications launched by one of the world's largest snack and pet foods manufacturers: Mars. Each represents a departure from that company's tradition business model. As you read about these innovative new product lines, notice how attention to new users and new uses helped Mars create higher margin, premium-value businesses.

## Notes

1. Andrew Hargadon and Robert Sutton, "Building an Innovation Factory," *Harvard Business Review*, 2000. 78(3): 157–66.

2. I consider the architecture of Web-centric software as the generation of dynamic HTML Web pages from diverse media sources. It provides a great, thin-client interaction between software vendor and user. The emerging Web architecture, referred to as Web 2.0, is a much more interactive, participatory framework in which software is a service, loosely coupled with many other software services, and constantly refreshed and enriched by those using these services. For me, Web 2.0 is an implementation of the thinking of Kevin Kelly's communities of software developers and users. See Kevin Kelly, *Out of Control* (Reading, MA: Addison-Wesley, 1994).

3. Siebel, the market leader in enterprise CRM and now part of Oracle, developed and launched its own "on demand" version. At the time of this writing, however, it remained behind the newer entrant, salesforce.com, in terms of market penetration in the Web services space for CRM.

4. See www.oaaa.org/outdoor/facts/, accessed January 18, 2006.

5. Marc H. Meyer and Arthur DeTore, "Creating Platform-Based Approaches to New Services Development," *Journal of Product Innovation Management*, 2001, 18: 188–204.

6. James Brian Quinn, *The Intelligent Enterprise* (New York: Free Press, 1991).

7. Marc H. Meyer, Neil de Crescenzo, and Bruce Russell, "In Search of a Viable Business Model," *International Journal of Entrepreneurship Education*, 2004, 2(2): 31–43.

CHAPTER TEN

# New Brand and Product Line
# Development at Mars

*The challenge of enterprise growth for mature corporations—
The history of Mars—Personalized candy in My M&M'S—A
new type of energy bar in Snickers Marathon—Whole Meals,
a complete pet meal in an extruded bone—CocoaVia, a heart-
healthy bar—ethel's, a new retail concept for women—
Lessons for management—The sources of innovation—New
market applications do not usually fit with the established
business process—Breaking the tensions in positioning new
concepts—Leveraging product and process platforms.*

Many large consumer products goods companies find themselves pressed by
the forces of commoditization. Despite being lean on the production side,
their margins are squeezed by mass merchandisers with enormous bargaining
power. Aggressive competitors are vying for the same shelf space. This chapter
describes how one such firm—Mars, Incorporated—has become a leader in innovating new product concepts. In fact, we will see how teams inside the company synthesized many of the methods described in this book: segmenting
markets for growth, diving deep into user needs, defining new product line architectures to incorporate modular platforms and flexible manufacturing processes, and combining all these factors into business models different from the
company's standard fare.

This chapter also suggests how new market applications can change the
way a company thinks about itself as a business—not just what it makes, but
how it sells and how it makes money. This chapter, then, provides instructive
examples for the business model chapter before and the financial modeling
and business process chapters to follow.

211

Mars is a consumer products powerhouse. At the time of this writing, it is the largest confectionery company in the world. It is also the largest global pet food manufacturer. It also remains privately held.

The company has a proud history of developing major consumer product brands. These include M&M's and Snickers brands.[1] And this tradition continues; in recent years, innovation teams within the company's U.S. operations have developed and brought to market five new product lines targeting new market applications:

— My M&M's Chocolate Candies—a personalized product that allows users to customize messages printed on their choice of colorful candies;
— Snickers Marathon Energy Bar—a great-tasting energy bar, with several varieties for men and women;
— Whole Meals Food for Dogs—a new type of pet food format that provides a nutritionally complete and balanced meal *and* complements a dog's natural eating behavior;
— Cocoavia Heart Healthy Snacks—a patented product that combines real chocolate with plant sterols with breakthroughs in the benefits of cocoa flavanols to promote heart health; and
— ethel's Chocolate Lounges—a new retail concept that involves the consumer in a new chocolate experience.

Each of these products is a new concept in its industry, and each has been introduced to the market over the past few years. Each has become the basis of a multivariant product line, and each has shown steady sales growth in the year after launch. Collectively, they represent the potential for hundreds of millions of dollars in new annual revenue for Mars. Perhaps more important is that each of these takes the corporation into premium markets and higher margins and, in many ways, represents what the company has come to call the "premiumization" of its products and, in most cases, a new business model for the company.

Many inside the company would agree that understanding these new business models, and then implementing them, has been a greater challenge than designing and manufacturing the products themselves—products that are richly innovative and bold forays into the future.

## Mars, Incorporated—A Capsule History

Mars, Incorporated now has more than 50 business units around the world in 65 countries around the globe. The company owns of some of the world's most popular brands. M&M's, Snickers, Milky Way, 3Musketeers, Dove chocolate and ice cream bars, Kudos granola bars, Skittles candies, and Uncle Ben's Rice are parts of the portfolio. Mars pet products include Pedigree food for dogs, Whiskas food for cats, and Royal Canin, a highly successful premium brand in Europe expanding in North America. The Mars experience in snack food retailing also led it to develop Flavia packet-based single-serve brewing systems for coffee and teas, a rapidly growing business-to-business and direct-to-consumer hot drink system.

The beginnings of the company can be found around the turn of the last century in the kitchen of Frank Mars and his mother in Tacoma, Washington, where they produced a small line of locally marketed gift chocolates. In 1920, Frank Mars moved to Minneapolis to grow the business. There, after visiting a local drugstore, Mars got the idea for a chocolate malted-milk snack that could be enjoyed anywhere. The result was the Milky Way bar—an immediate success. Snickers, a bar filled with peanuts, followed, as did 3Musketeers. Even during the Great Depression, Frank Mars continued to expand his business. Forrest Mars, Frank's son, joined the family business and established the company in Europe.

Forrest established the first Mars manufacturing plant in Slough, outside of London, England. He also renamed the Milky Way the Mars Bar and, perhaps most important, used an acquisition to launch the company into the pet food business. The key was to combine modern, high-volume manufacturing with advances in nutrition science. Today, the world's leading center for pet care nutrition is the Waltham Center for Pet Nutrition, located in England and owned by Mars, Incorporated.

As Forrest traveled in Europe in the 1930s, he saw products being made in Spain, at that time caught in civil war. Forrest saw chocolate pieces with a sugar coating, where the sugar provided not only a barrier but also special taste. This was the "aha!" that led to the now ubiquitous M&M's candies, a panned chocolate product coated with a colorful candy shell so that the chocolate does not melt in your hands. M&M's gained much of their early popularity when they were supplied to soldiers on the battlefield in World War II. The company developed a peanut-filled version in 1954.

Forrest's vision remained constant: to provide a great-tasting chocolate, at a value, to families. Operating efficiency and producing high-quality products efficiently became core values of the business and remain so to this day.

Strategic focus on food and snacks for humans and pets is also an important part of the Mars culture. Forrest acquired the patent for parboiled rice, with the vision of bringing convenience to the kitchen, a huge, untapped market opportunity. Uncle Ben's soon became one of America's top-selling brands of packaged long-grain rice.

Through the years, the company developed and still retains an egalitarian culture and relatively flat organizational structures. There are still no private offices in any of the company's plants or offices. Executive desks are mixed with those of staff but formed in an executive ring with the president of business unit and the various vice presidents of the business functions: marketing, sales, manufacturing, HR, supply, R&D, communications, and finance. Associates can easily access senior management working at their desks, and vice versa. Despite the present size of Mars, people still know other people around the globe to a remarkable extent and interact with counterparts in other Mars business units. Everyone, including the president, still punches a time clock, with incentives (a 10 percent punctuality bonus) given for showing up on time. Some outsiders might call the Mars culture "old fashioned," and others "quirky." Others, I among them, think the environment is well suited for the type of teamwork, executive sponsorship, and hard work that leads to growth.

Efficiency is a key operating principle of the company, which aims to produce maximum revenue using minimum operating assets. This has led to an emphasis on manufacturing engineering and carefully managed supply chains. R&D has always been important but not the lead player in a business where high volumes, low prices, and distribution to grocery stores, mass merchants, and convenience channels are king. Cost of goods and conversion costs, measured by the tonne, remain an important part of any business plan seeking senior management approval. The reader can imagine how fledgling small businesses, with initially low volumes, might have a tough time getting traction in a "tonnes are us" culture.

The Mars formula for success has produced decades of continued growth. However, the environment began to change in the early 2000s, especially in the snack food division, given the rising rate of obesity and the low-carbohydrate and low-fat diets exploding in popularity. Both trends presented a challenge to most food manufacturers. For growth to continue, the company would have to provide new value to customers. This would not be easy. For decades, the company had focused on not making mistakes. As one senior executive put it, "All of us were brought up on making no mistakes, trained on methods to insure no mistakes, and made decisions that were clearly risk management." How could such a company develop new businesses that were riskier, that needed a "launch and learn" approach?

## My M&M's: A New Business That Started from Process R&D

This first new product line involves printing on individual M&M's candies. This venture—My M&M's—shows how an idea can evolve from a promising technology to a great product line and then to a highly profitable business. An example

FIGURE 10.1 My M&M's (Mars, Inc. Reproduced with permission)

of the new product is shown in Figure 10.1. Personalization for gifting and celebrations is the essence of the concept.

Personalization of confectionery products was potentially at odds with the company's business model of low-cost, high-volume snacks, made on large capital assets and sold through broad retail channels. Although management in other mature corporations might have dismissed such a radical change as "far-fetched," Mars managers sensed an opportunity to extend their brand to a new market well beyond grocery shoppers.

There were precedents for M&M's brand extensions. Colorworks was a current, albeit small, service where people could select colors from a much broader palette than standard M&M's. But My M&M's represented a higher order of customization: individually defined messages. The enabling technology was developed in a central R&D group based at the Hackettstown, New Jersey, plant. This small group had created a number of process breakthroughs for the company. Mars has always prided itself on world-class quality in manufacturing at high volumes, so it is fitting that one of its hottest new businesses came from the process R&D group.

That group worked hard on different technologies for printing on various types of candies. However, it also developed a strategy and product roadmap for the technology it was inventing. The process R&D manager created a chart much like those presented in our chapter on modular platforms and product strategy. On one dimension, he showed increasingly higher levels of technical capability (one-sided printing, dual-sided printing, rotogravure, and ink-jet), and a second showed uses and occasions, the most advanced being personalization. The vision represented in this chart was refined with the general manager of the snack division, a strong champion for My M&M's who is now president of the North American business unit of Mars.

In 2000, the process R&D group began printing images on the blank side of the M&M's pieces. Their initial trials led to a special-edition candy with the likeness of the green M&M's brand character on the back. Both the traditional "m" and the test images were transferred to each candy piece through a printing process using an edible ink. This process was cost effective for large batches of candy but unsuitable for a business based on hundreds and, later on, thousands of unique personalized orders coming in each and every day.

Experimentation eventually indicated that another printing process was the best approach to economically produce small orders. My M&M's could provide the best of both worlds: personalized printing on one side of standard M&M's candies and leverage the company's other printing assets for the other. Engineers in the company had previously developed a capability to print high-resolution photographic images on chocolate bars. As the team progressed, it initiated a portfolio of patent applications across product and process. Once senior management endorsed the general concept of customized M&M's, product development proceeded rapidly. Prototypes were created and used to obtain consumer feedback. Before long, the team could demonstrate the process of printing on the M&M's curved surface and was taking limited orders from associates over a special intranet site. This last measure had come about in early 2003 as part of a broader internal corporate initiative called "Pioneer Week."

Pioneer Week was intended to supercharge innovation. A number of R&D teams were given 90 days to create a trial production line for their new product lines. The culmination of that three-month period was a series of new internal product introductions.

That deadline forced the My M&M's team to pick a few basic options without the customary extensive consumer research. The team reasoned that after implementation, it could improve all dimensions with real user feedback. Rapid launch and learn became the team's mantra, no matter how different it was from standard company procedures, where even small changes to established brands were extensively tested.

There were many challenges to this internal launch: some necessary equipment had lead times of more than 90 days. It was difficult to get dedicated resources for the project. The team also needed to determine what was acceptable to print on the candy and develop filters to screen out undesirable messages. Even getting space to locate the production line was a challenge. However, the team was encouraged by an "innovation charter" signed by the entire senior management team, which confirmed that the custom printing project was a priority. Team members referred to the charter shown in figure 10.2 as their "get out of jail free card."

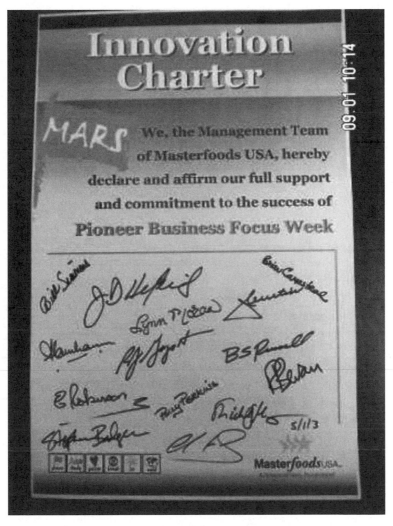

FIGURE 10.2 The Innovation Charter for My M&M's (Mars, Inc. Reproduced with permission)

In June 2003, the team began offering company associates its new product, at the time called M&M's Colorworks Print Shop Milk Chocolate Candies—a mouthful of a name created by the R&D staff! Orders for 800 pounds of custom-printed candy were received on the first day, and product deliveries began the next day. There had been skepticism in the business about the viability of the product. Many associates weren't sure they would ever get their orders, let alone the day after placing them. Making Mars associates actual product users made them true believers.

The original option was for a four-pound order of candies with printed personalized messages. The My M&M's team received feedback from its internal customers that smaller minimum order sizes, colored candy (not just white), and "party favor" packaging options were needed. The team responded to all these needs with a new release of the product line.

With an improving technology and a product that not only looked good but also tasted great, the team now had to learn how to create a successful business proposition. The first step was to create a business plan. No one on the team had ever planned a new venture. Management asked a trusted outsider to help. The team proceeded to develop a product line market strategy, a Web channel plan, and a business model. Its product-market strategy is shown in figure 10.3. Notice the contrast between the focus of standard M&M's and the many possible use occasions for My M&M's.

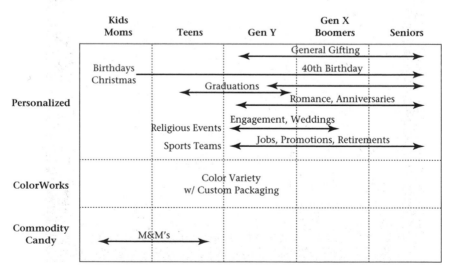

FIGURE 10.3 Segmenting Markets by Occasion
(Mars, Inc. Reproduced with permission)

Another important decision for the team was the brand name. M&M's Colorworks Print Shop clearly would not do; the product needed an emotional brand name. A discussion of the emotional meaning of personalization quickly led to My M&M's, and the name stuck. It was a classic subbrand that would leverage an existing core brand and add new value to it. This was also quite different from conventional practice, which heavily involved outside advertising agencies in naming.

How to price the candy was the source of further discussion. Value to the consumer, high volumes, and operating efficiency were the company religion. At the start of the project, the central process R&D manager felt strongly that personalization candies could command a substantial price premium over standard M&M's—enough to more than carry the additional costs and complexity of the new business. For the internal launch, the team had arbitrarily set the price at $12 per pound—$4 per pound higher than the retail price of standard M&M's. But some team members wanted to charge more per pound. A higher price, they reasoned, would improve the projected financials and create an aura of uniqueness or scarcity around the product.

Rather than base its pricing decision on instinct, the team initiated a conjoint study to determine consumer preferences for My M&M's.[2] Using some of the methods described in chapter 5, respondents were asked to make trade-offs between product features, packaging features, and price. Some results of this initial conjoint study are shown in figure 10.4. The study not only supported a higher price but also showed the most preferred size and packaging for the product. It also showed a very high level of "trial." All of these findings have proven true in subsequent market experience. One of the fascinating side notes of My M&M's is that Mars' traditional users had always been female household shoppers; this new product line reached out to men as well as women. The figure shows one slice of the gender data.

Order taking, fulfillment, and logistics for the new product were also entirely different than for conventional M&M's. My M&M's would involve small, discrete orders shipped directly to consumers—the opposite of traditional M&M's transactions, which were shipped in large quantities to retailers. The company's manufacturing systems were entirely geared for mass production, not small batches. It would also have to turn to new partners to assist in Web site development, call center services, fulfillment, and shipping.

My M&M's were officially offered online to the public in March 2004. Mars had not done any promotion for the customized product other than a splash on the M&M's site, where a link to My M&M's appeared. The link itself was hardly prominent, and the ordering Web site itself was initially cumbersome. Nonetheless, traffic through the Web site overloaded supply capacity within just four hours! Orders continued to pour in at such a furious rate that production

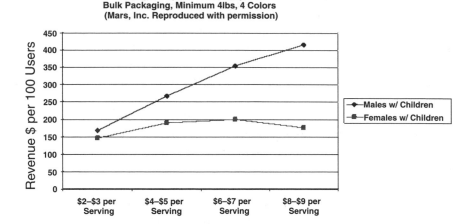

FIGURE 10.4  Market Simulation (Mars, Inc.
Reproduced with permission)

could not keep pace. More machines were needed. The team raised the price per pound in an effort to reduce demand, but that only served to enhance the special quality of the offering, and *orders accelerated*! Consumers literally had to be asked to come back later. Meanwhile, the team was working hard to double the number of M&M's candies running down the line.

Within five months of the public launch, more than 30,000 pounds of custom-printed My M&M's had been sold. Soon, sales had surpassed $10 million, and continued to accelerate. Just as the product-market strategy grid had predicted, users were buying personalized M&M's for anniversaries, graduations, birthday parties, and weddings. The reader is encouraged to visit the My M&M's Web site (try a simple Google search) to see how the team has structured navigation in the site itself to reflect this market segmentation by users and uses.

Without the standard formal marketing campaign, during 2005 the product showed a viral marketing effect. People who encountered My M&M's at a party wanted the product for their own parties. By late 2005, the team was busy working on product enhancement, production efficiencies, and new buzz through the Web. An extensive public relations campaign was initiated, resulting in product profiles and celebrity usage in leading television shows and other mass media outlets. My M&M's also received a "50 Best New Product" award from *Business Week* at the end of the year. The new business was well on its way toward great success.

## Snickers Marathon: Strategy-Driven Brand Extension

Whereas My M&M's was a process-driven innovation, the Snickers Marathon energy bar was strategy-driven. In this case, senior management reasoned that the company's formidable manufacturing assets and know-how should be leveraged into an emerging new market. It was a clear example of using existing competencies to serve a new set of users with a different product.

The product's lineage can be traced to a concept called Snickers Sport, an energy bar idea hatched in 1992, when the energy bar category was in its infancy. Snickers Sport aimed to provide energy to high school and college athletes during endurance competitions. It was never launched because management deemed the market too small to justify the expected investment. Several years later, the Sport concept was reborn under a new name, VO2Max.[3] The target, again, was the athlete. By this time, more users had entered the energy bar market, and the financial projections were beginning to look attractive. Also, independent players, such as Powerbar (later acquired by Nestle) were showing signs of ramp and scale. VO2Max had the added twist of incorporating antioxidants to help speed recovery for muscle soreness. Mars launched the product in 1994, exploring new channels relative to its traditional grocery focus. Bike shops and mail order were new channels with which the company had little experience. Within a year, the sales volumes were seen as simply too low to continue, and the product was withdrawn.

The VO2Max failure taught management an important lesson: The company had to differentiate in terms of the target market application for the energy bar segment. As long as the primary target users were athletes, any new entrant would face an "arms race" with current competitors such as Powerbar in terms of triglycerides, carbohydrates, and antioxidants. What was needed, instead, was a clear *point of difference*. This, as it turned out, was *taste*, an area where the company has always excelled. At the same time, VO2Max was to serve Mars just as the Lisa computer served Apple as the predecessor to the Macintosh. The learnings from "failures" are often foundations of subsequent success.

The turn of the millennium came. Like many breakthrough ideas in large corporations, the energy bar idea had been floating around Mars as a high-potential idea waiting for the emergence of the more mainstream market needed to justify the large capital expense for manufacturing and a new brand launch. New consumer research was performed. This time, the study showed that taste was a major barrier for broader market acceptance of energy bars. The research indicated 20 percent annual growth in the energy/health bar segment. But despite that growth, only 13 percent of U.S. households were consumers of products in this category. The challenge was to attract the remaining 87 percent. Executives took these data as the time to move forward to actual launch. Thinking strictly in terms of athletes unnecessarily narrowed the market, so management's market thinking shifted from truly sports-active buyers to time-constrained, nutrition-conscious individuals, including busy weekend warriors who needed a nutritious snack and, sometimes, a meal replacement.

A seminal moment in the birth of Snickers Marathon was when the vice president of R&D gathered together strong technical players in the division for a two-day review of how to best achieve high protein and great taste. Several strategically important patents emerged from this work. A new multifunctional team was formed around this expanded market view and the notion of better taste. That team included a Snickers marketing manager, two dedicated food scientists, and one dedicated process development scientist. It also had priority support from the market research department. A dedicated process engineer who worked between the team and the manufacturing site in Albany, Georgia, was added as the product entered the implementation phase. The team established a consumer research program featuring focus groups, prototypes, and continuous feedback and refinement. This work began in 2001, initially in energy bar–intensive markets, such as Boston and Seattle. "Durability" became another important design driver. Target users were active, time-pressured, and looking for a bar that they could take anywhere and that could used as a snack or a meal replacement.

Focus group panels brought together users and nonusers. Users included anyone who had purchased an existing brand. Nonusers were of two types: those who would not try energy bars because of what they had heard about bad taste and others who had tried energy bars but had (for any reason) rejected them. Company R&D and marketing associates attended all focus group sessions; they were looking for consumers' beliefs, values, and current product uses.

Based on this user research, the team created a product concept and developed and tested prototypes at the Mars Hackettstown facility. The concept was a go-anywhere, durable (no melt), tasty energy bar with good health attributes. The concept bar was shown to the focus groups and later placed into a concept market study against competitive brands. It scored higher than all competitors by a considerable margin. A full-scale volumetric market study to estimate sales was then performed. This study confirmed the sales potential, particularly amongst traditional nonusers in the energy bar category.

This user research also generated specific design attributes—as much as for the exterior and interior subsystems of the Honda Element—for the recipe subsystem in this particular product line architecture.

— Great taste was necessary to reach the mainstream user. This had to be provided with Mars chocolate, peanut, and grain recipes.
— The product needed high levels of protein to play in the energy bar market.
— Too much fat would be a negative in the health-conscious bar market.

The Snickers Marathon taste would be the "point of difference" and motivate high levels of consumer trials. The product had to be genuine and use wholesome, healthy ingredients because target users were skeptical of false claims for wellness products in an increasingly noisy marketplace. Also, instead of just featuring athletes in the promotion, Mars wanted to show firefighters, truck drivers, doctors, and other individuals with demanding lifestyles.

To meet the requirements determined through user research—and still win the taste war—scientists on the team formulated a trademarked high-quality, good-tasting protein blend called Quadratein: a blend of peanut, soy, whey, and casein proteins. In the months to follow, the team developed the first two varieties that would go to market in 2003: the chocolate-chewy peanut and the multigrain crunch. The product prototypes showed visible chunks of peanuts and grains and featured 10 grams of protein, which satisfied the energy requirement and delivered an acceptable level of fat.

Once the product was launched, further user segmentation was conducted. Focusing on low carbohydrate, high protein, and women's needs, the team developed several additional varieties. These new varieties were further differentiated by the coloring and graphics on their flow-wrap package.

While this product development work proceeded in earnest during 2002 through 2005, the team actively debated business issues such as the brand name, the price, and sales channels. Each of these was a challenge because the product was reaching into a new market application.

What should Mars call the product? When the product concept had been a straightforward energy bar, the wisdom of introducing a new brand name seemed obvious, hence VO2Max. But by now the market had expanded to include nonathletes for whom taste and wholesomeness were as important as energy. Thus, a subbrand under the Snickers flag had distinct possibilities.[4]

Given its combination of proteins and complex carbohydrates, costlier ingredients, and great taste, a premium price over the standard Snickers products was justified. But how much higher? After price studies and much internal discussion, Snickers Marathon was priced at parity with mainstream energy bar competitors. That price would help identify the brand as a serious energy/health bar entry and not a revamped candy bar. That put it at a retail price of $1.50—twice the price of a standard Snickers bar. This premiumization of the Snickers business model was a first step in expanding beyond the company's value-pricing culture.

Upon launch, the product went to food stores, drug stores, mass merchandisers, and convenience stores. Figure 10.5 shows some of these varieties. Distribution was a new challenge for a sales force accustomed to selling products to confectionery buyers. Snickers Marathon demanded special focus on the health/energy aisle of specialty, grocery, mass merchant, and convenience stores. It takes time for any company to develop new sales competence. Therefore, it was not a surprise to many that initial sales of Snickers Marathon were less than those projected initially for the first year. Nevertheless, management would not let go of the idea. It tackled distribution problems head-on and then redirected its marketing campaign to reach out to mainstream users. This is an as important lesson as any for a management team seeking enterprise growth through new market applications.

Second-year sales began to approach sales targets. The level of trial was incredibly high relative to competitors. In 2005, industry research groups reported that Snickers Marathon bars were the first and second highest selling items in the energy bar segment in the stores where the new product appeared. This meant a high "repeat purchase" rate. Once consumers tried Snickers

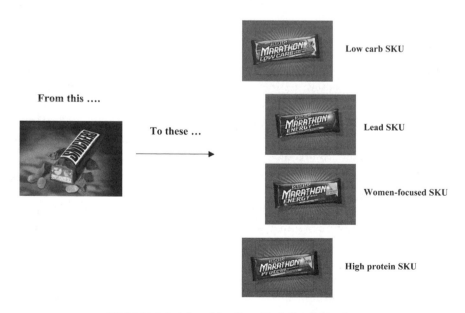

FIGURE 10.5  Snickers Marathon Varieties (Mars, Inc.
Reproduced with permission)

Marathon, they wanted more. Men in particular were adopting the new bar as a mid-morning or mid-afternoon snack; for some, it was a lunch meal replacement. The challenge was to get the product into more stores.

True, the new Snickers Marathon bar had been something of a marathon in its own development. Yet, this privately held business, with a rich tradition of internally generated growth, understood the virtue of patience—to wait for markets to develop and to formulate a winning combination of product ingredients, branding, and marketing. In the end, patience and persistence paid off. In-market performance suggests that Snickers Marathon is on its way to changing the energy bar category.

## Whole Meals: User-Centered Design for People and Pets

We turn to the next new product line, Whole Meals (initially called Mealbone). My M&M's had its origins in new process technology, and Snickers Marathon from a market-driven strategy, but this third venture came from an idea to bring a new feeding format to the mature pet food industry. Its origins are in the user-centered design methods described in earlier chapters. In this case, some of the users have four legs!

Dog food formats have been static for decades. Main meals for dogs have been marketed primarily in only two ways: as dry, bagged kibble, which has dental hygiene benefits and is easy to serve, and as the wet, canned food that dogs generally prefer because of its moist texture and taste. Dogs and dog owners could have the benefits of the one only at the expense of the other.

Mars R&D associates wanted to use a new feeding format to disrupt this long-standing market. Combining the satisfaction of "wet" with the dental health and convenience of "dry" was a key design driver—much like Hewlett Packard created its all-in-one desktop printer-fax-scanner-copiers. More important, the Mars team wanted to appeal to the natural, innate instincts of dogs—to chew and use their paws.

Early efforts had centered on an extruded "bone" concept, a product with bonelike interior and meaty exterior. In parallel, the team reversed the subsystems, creating prototypes with a hard, bonelike exterior and a meaty, marrowlike center. This second design was developed and launched in 2002 as the Jumbone snack for dogs. Sales of Jumbone steadily grew, confirming the desirability of manufactured bonelike products. Now, the challenge was to make this form a carrier for higher levels of nutrition. Then it would be a fully nutritious meal and still offer a level of dog enjoyment far in excess of traditional kibble.

A dedicated business innovation team was formed in the fall of 2003 to pursue the venture. A senior marketing manager with extensive brand-launching experience was assigned to the project. He knew a tremendous amount about sales channels and advertising approaches. R&D also assigned a savvy food developer, an equally strong market researcher (human and animal), and a process engineer. Others with backgrounds in manufacturing, materials purchasing, sales, and advertising were assigned to the project on a part-time basis. An independent project manager was recruited to shepherd the product toward launch in 15 months.

Fifteen months was a short time line for this type of product. The team had to deliver scientifically sound levels of nutrition, a texture consistent with high dental health performance, and manufacturing costs that would support a competitive price.

Manufacturing was also a challenge. Achieving efficient production on extrusion machines took numerous trial runs, including some all-nighters. The resulting know-how and patents from that hard work, however, would provide formidable barriers to entry.

Even as process problems were being attacked, other team members were testing the product concept on dogs and their owners. How did two-legged shoppers buy dog food? How much would they pay? Would dogs like it or turn up their noses? Extensive observational research watched how users purchased food, fed their pets, and played with their pets. Then the team wrestled with the question of the type and amount of empirical market research that it needed prior to launch. An initial concept attractiveness test was conducted.

More important was an in-home test with panels of small, medium, and large dogs and their owners As described earlier in chapter 5 (as a method to validate user-centered designs), participants were provided with new versions of the product for a week; their feedback was then aggregated and assessed through standard statistical methods. One week, the size of the "bone" would be tested; another week, the hardness and texture of the outer bone would be the subject of interest; yet another week, pet owners would respond to the ratio of the outside of the bone to the inside "marrow." At the end of each week, each owner was then asked to rank various prototypes on a 1 to 5 scale of preference. Such a fast turnaround time for getting new versions of the product would not have been possible without a pilot extrusion line available for the team's use. Fortunately, Mars had placed this pilot line in the same facility as the R&D prototyping "kitchen." By the end of testing, the team knew with confidence what owners of different sizes of dogs preferred, and those insights translated into the number, bone count, and packaging of the Whole Meals product.

Channels were another challenge for initial launch. Mars pet food lines were sold primarily through three nationwide channels: grocery chains, mass mer-

FIGURE 10.6 Whole Meals (originally launched as Mealbone)
(Mars, Inc. Reproduced with permission)

chandisers, and pet specialty retailers. Although most of its sales volume came from grocery stores, Mars knew that sales in pet specialty stores such as Petsmart were growing much faster, year over year, than any other pet food channel.

Given the price and uniqueness of Whole Meals, however, it made more sense to design a regional launch through a pet specialty partner that could be expanded later on. This approach also had important implications for projected sales, as well as for size, type, and scope of initial advertising and promotion activities. In March 2005, Whole Meals was launched regionally through Petsmart. This included innovative packaging and marketing, as shown in figure 10.6.

The Whole Meals team continued working in launch and learn mode. Team members frequently visited the Petsmart stores, and others were busy prototyping new variants of the product as well as different packaging concepts. Meanwhile, reports back from Petsmart were showing the repeat usage rate for initial Whole Meals purchasers running at twice the team's forecast and far higher than typical new products in the pet food category. This was an indicator of strong product performance. As sales continued to grow week over week, it was clear that methods for user-centered design—now brought to the world of pet food—had once again played an important role in developing a new market application within a mature business.

## Cocoavia: Science Driving Enterprise Growth

Our fourth Mars venture is just as creative and interesting from an organic growth perspective as the previous ones—but in a very different way. This venture, Cocoavia, was based on truly disruptive technology. It was a new product line of heart-healthy chocolate snacks whose roots lie in deep scientific research.

Starting in the early 1990s, the company's analytical science department had been trying to isolate the compounds found in cocoa to study their bioactive qualities. One of the cocoa compounds studied was flavanols, a subset of cocoa polyphenols. Management focused research on the cardiovascular benefits of these flavanols. Research was also conducted to understand how to preserve the power of these bioactive agents after the cocoa was processed into a finished product.

Meanwhile, scientists were studying an indigenous population—the Kuna Amerinds—living on a chain of islands off the coast of Central America.[5] The Kuna showed no tendency for the expected rise in blood pressure with age, despite a high-salt diet. These people had excellent cardiovascular health and a much lower incidence of hypertension than either Kuna Indians living in Panama City or the general population of that city. Field research found that Kuna Indians consumed copious amounts of cocoa—typically up to five cups per day of cocoa beverages. The prominence of these cocoa beverages led researchers to speculate that perhaps something in the cocoa itself contributed to the Kuna's healthy blood pressure levels. The particular cocoa powder used in these traditional beverages was found to be a rich source of flavanols.

Laboratory work by partner university research groups pointed toward the possibility that cocoa may improve cardiovascular circulation, or blood flow. Researchers were finding that "flow mediation dilation," a measure of vascular relaxation that correlated with improved circulation, seemed to improve with concentrated amounts of cocoa flavanols. The flavanols seemed to increase the production of nitric oxide in the blood, which modulates blood platelets by decreasing their clotting tendency. When platelets become "active," they tend to clot and adhere to blood vessel walls, which, over time, can lead to heart disease. A major clot can induce a heart attack or stroke by creating a blockage. Compared with other natural ingredients, cocoa flavanols seemed to exhibit a potentially powerful effect.[6] Recent clinical studies have likened the effects of cocoa flavanols on platelets as similar to those of aspirin.[7] Mars has been awarded many patents to protect, among other things, its flavanol application and processing.

Management was determined to leverage its flavanol science into a commercially viable product. It took the first steps in that direction in 2002. The goal was to develop a heart-healthy chocolate snack in tasty, convenient formats. Management assembled a dedicated, multifunctional team representing marketing, market research, R&D, and finance to do the job, using the brand name Cocoavia. The flavanol patent family that emerged from all this work is a rich example of how a team can manage its intellectual property for a new market application, and it also represents a sizable commitment by a company to pursue patent initiatives early on.

The team began a series of consumer tests. These tests registered high interest in Cocoavia among "bar purchasers" and a high repeat rate after initial trial. Initial product prototypes included a solid chocolate bar, chocolate with various inclusions, and bars with lower fat chocolate, all highly portable and great tasting. They also had to have fewer than 100 calories and register low on the glycemic index (which means slow conversion of carbohydrates into blood sugar). Nutritional negatives such as high sodium and transfats were off-limits. All these products were made with the company's proprietary flavanol-rich cocoas processed from specific or specially selected beans that were roasted, ground, and blended with proprietary methods. Prototypes were tested through a repeated series of consumer research run in various parts of the country. Many were seen as "winners" by target consumers.

The team then looked at the manufacturing side of the business, where they found internal manufacturing capacity. That equipment was then making the Kudos bar. The Cocoavia product design was compatible with that of Kudos; leveraging the line as a process "platform" made sense because it saved the team tens of millions of dollars in what would have been new capital expense, as well as all the time needed to purchase, install, and test that equipment.

The team listened carefully to consumers and worked with leading nutritional and cardiovascular experts to design the product line to be a great-tasting and portable chocolate snack for health-conscious individuals. It would also be a rich source of cocoa flavanols to promote healthy cardiovascular circulation and natural plant extracts (soy sterols) that help reduce LDL cholesterol. Based on a clinical study, the Cocoavia Snack Bar significantly lowered bad cholesterol. The bar was also fortified with heart-healthy B vitamins and antioxidants and contained three grams of fat or less.

Cocoavia was first launched in 2003 with four varieties: chocolate, blueberry, almond, and cherry snack bars. Products had to be developed with flavanol-rich cocoa powder to achieve the minimum 100 mg of flavanols per serving. Cocoa powder is very bitter, making the goal of great taste a substantial challenge. In addition, the process of alkalization, which enhances the functionality and flavor of cocoa powder and chocolate, could not be used because it destroys flavanols. Finally, standard factory manufacturing practices had to be altered and new processes developed to ensure that the flavanols were not destroyed in making the finished product. These obstacles were overcome, and taste tests demonstrated that consumers highly preferred Cocoavia snack bars.

Distribution was another challenge. The team planned a one-year direct-to-consumer (DTC) online test market to get in-market learning, after which the product would be distributed through selected retailers. The market test involved advertising in choice magazines such as Cooking Light and Smithsonian to direct consumers to the Cocoavia Web site or to a toll free phone number to order product. After this market test, the team launched its retail strategy—and the business began to grow. In 2005, the group was reorganized into a new health and nutrition products business unit within Mars. With an extensive public relations campaign touting the product's breakthrough science, as well as its great taste, sales began to ramp up. Also, within a year of that change, the company launched an expanded set of products, a sign of Mars' growing appetite to develop and market products that combined the benefits of taste and health.

## ethel's Chocolate Lounge: Applying the Principles of User-Centered Design to Create an Entirely New Retail Concept

This, the last of our Mars ventures, is also entirely different from those preceding it. It is also equally innovative, if not more so!

Mars' strength was in grocery stores and mass merchandisers. However, the company also had its Ethel M unit focused on premium gift chocolates. (Ethel Mars was the wife of the company founder.) In 2003, Ethel M had 15 retail chocolate shops, all located in Las Vegas. It also had a direct mail business featuring the Ethel M brand of boxed gift chocolates.

These gift chocolates were excellent and packaged in stylish silver boxes. Most pieces had chocolate-coated fillings. Among these was the signature Almond-Butter-Krunch that year after year won culinary awards in the premium category. Store locations, decor, and the packaging suggested that Ethel M chocolates were for special occasions, as opposed to everyday consumption. Tourists to Las Vegas purchased Ethel M chocolates in these stores, and many reordered once they returned home.

In 2004, however, management took a fresh look at the business. Mars hired a successful retail executive who had developed national chains. The new president of Ethel M first set out to improve the existing Las Vegas business. A team was formed for this purpose, and success was swift in coming. Ethel M's retail business in Las Vegas grew substantially, even though some of the original stores were closed. Several new outlets were then opened elsewhere.

The larger challenge, however, was to create a new growth strategy, to which the new president assigned an experienced staff. That team quickly determined that the company's gift chocolates lacked a clear point of difference. As the team studied its own stores and those of competitors, both were found wanting. Except for a few independent vendors, everyone approached the retail experience in much the same way. Boxes of chocolate were dressed for the appropriate season or holiday, stacked up on shelves, and minimum-wage sales associates stood behind the sales counter. Customers went into a shop, bought an entire box of chocolates, and quickly left. Few stores made the purchase of chocolate anything more than "shop and buy."

The Ethel M team aimed to make the first premium chocolate for everyday use, as opposed to special occasions. The experience of chains such as Starbucks, Panera, and Aveda showed that women were willing to treat themselves on a daily basis. For these women, these stores were themselves powerful brands.

The primary consumer was to be the adult female with a higher household income who wanted to engage her passion for chocolate with close friends. Creating an environment for small groups of women to socialize also offered the promise of more frequent visits and multiple purchases.

Eschewing the large sample research traditionally used in other parts of the business, the innovation team leaned entirely on empathetic, observational research. Focus group sessions conducted in three different cities over the course of six months indicated that women had to search for the chocolate varieties they liked through trial and error. Customers viewed the vast majority of stores as formal and cold. The overall message of packaging and pricing was that premium chocolate was for special occasions only. Other important insights were that:

— Everyday chocolate occasions meant simpler, more basic, wholesome flavors, particularly when compared with the "mystery" fillings of traditional gift chocolate.
— The silver packaging used by Ethel M connoted a special occasion. Warm, rich colors would convey a more contemporary everyday occasion.
— The shopping experience should allow women to share special moments with friends, even to the point of sitting down in a manner similar to Starbuck's to have coffee or tea and to sample their chocolate purchases.
— The store environment should be warm and friendly.

Based on these findings, the team created several potential positioning concepts for the business. A second round of focus groups helped to refine these into a central concept: everyday, approachable premium chocolate. A third set of focus groups helped the team with the communications, packaging, and retail store

FIGURE 10.7 The ethel's Retail Concept (Mars, Inc.
Reproduced with permission)

environment that would serve as that central concept. Several retail configurations were then tested, with the winner shown in the figure 10.7, the ethel's chocolate lounge.

Instead of trying to outdo competitors' stores, ethel's chocolate lounge sought to change the terms of competition by offering customer-pleasing products in a cozy environment of couches, coffee tables, rugs and tapestries, and muted lighting. Messaging and communications were also important. For example, the new ethel's product line would feature what Mars called Warm-Blended chocolate, with chocolate swirls as supporting imagery. The focus groups had shown that these words and imagery had special meaning for target consumers in terms of how they related to chocolate. The team also adopted the language of "no mystery middles," which the focus groups had shown to be a major frustration of women with current competitive offerings.

Execution of the concept into products and retail environment was all-important. To simplify customer choice, themes were created around different types of assortments. There was an American pop collection, a cocktail assortment (made with real alcohol), a fruit assortment, nuts and caramel, and truffles. Within these were various flavors. Further, messaging had to be on target, conveying the very special way that women relate to chocolate.

The new retail business was launched in Chicago, where the team purchased, remodeled, and renamed an independent chocolate store with many of the physical features it desired. Within a year of launch, Mars had opened 10 more ethel's chocolate lounges, with plans to expand in the future.

## Lessons for Management

The sheer diversity of origins of enterprise growth in just these five projects is inspiring. So often, managers and consultants point to formal strategic planning processes as the source of all growth. Not so—at least in the cases presented here. My M&M's emerged from a central process R&D group, Whole Meals and ethel's from observational research and user-centered design, and Cocoavia from deep science. Only Snickers Marathon can be fairly said to have had its origins and sustenance from proactive strategic planning. Like most corporations, Mars has well-structured planning and resource allocation processes; but I suspect—also like most corporations—its best ideas for enterprise growth often emerge from outside that process. I also suspect that this occurs most frequently when a corporation has confidence in the inherent strengths and capabilities of its people and a culture of listening to their ideas and aspirations.

The five new market applications described here leveraged company know-how (amplified by product and customer research) to serve new users or uses. That know-how included a deep knowledge of chocolate (and other confections), manufacturing, packaging, and shipping. It also included a growing confidence to step outside traditional empirical market research—which rarely provides breakthrough insights—and instead apply the observational and user-centered design methods described throughout this book to learn about what customers want and how they want to be served.

Even with these strengths, Mars—like any company—went through the ups and downs of transforming great new insights into robust businesses. What it has learned in that process can be boiled down into three important lessons.

### Lesson 1: New Market Applications Do Not Usually Fit within the Established Business Process

The Mars experience suggests that companies that want to break out of their current business processes with new market applications should be prepared to rethink their approaches to development organization, business models, new branding, and how they reach the market. These factors are the "business innovation" dimension of enterprise growth and may, in fact, be an even greater challenge than the technological dimension. This is the reason for implementing a business process designed specifically for creating new market applications such as that shown in chapter 2 (figure 2.2).

Figure 10.8 is part of a scorecard for these new market applications, indicating degrees of newness and other factors on key business dimensions. It shows

| | New Target User Relative to Core Business | New Target User Relative to Core Business | New Channel Relative to Core Business | New Branding | New Business Model Relative to Core Business |
|---|---|---|---|---|---|
| **MY M&M's** | Yes (New occasions) (B2B) | Yes (Customized) | Yes (Web) | New Subbrand | Low volume High margin |
| **SNICKERS MARATHON** | Yes (Older) | Yes (Health/energy) | Yes (New part of store) | New Subbrand | Low volume High margin |
| **WHOLEMEALS** | Yes (Premium Pet) | Yes (Bone that's a meal) | Yes (Specialty retailers) | New Brand | Low volume High margin |
| **COCOAVIA** | Yes (Older) | Yes (Cardiohealth) | Yes (Web, direct) | New Brand | Low volume High margin |
| **ethel's** | Yes (Affluent women) | Yes (Everyday premium chocolate) | Yes (New store concept) | New Brand | Low volume High Margin |

FIGURE 10.8  Mars Business Innovation Scorecard
(Marc H. Meyer and Mars, Inc. Reproduced with permission)

clearly that each venture had fundamental business questions to resolve in parallel with product development: understanding new target users or uses, developing new channels, new branding issues, and a very different approach to volume and margins relative to the company's core business. These are wonderful examples of the business model innovation we described in the previous chapter and that we also revisit in the next.

This "newness" requires a company to carefully think things through. Management must understand the different parts of each new business and the interfaces between them. It must understand how decisions made in one area of a new venture affect others. Call it "multidimensional" business planning. Any fundamental change to Mars' traditional business model—be it from a new brand position, a premium price, a new channel focus, or a different source of materials or conversion—had a dramatic impact on the financials of the business. And as team members indicated time and time again, business model innovation can be a lot harder to accomplish than new product, process, or packaging development. Visualizing the new business behind a prototype takes time, patience, and careful articulation. Our business model templates from the prior chapter (figure 9.3, 9.4, and 9.5) can certainly help.

## Lesson 2: Find Opportunities to Create Excitement in Mature Markets

In chapters 3 and 4, we talked about segmenting markets for growth and then understanding user needs and frustrations to help form winning product or service concepts. There are no finer examples of how to create distinctive positioning—even in seemingly mature markets—than the cases described here. They were grounded in an understanding of the deeper role and meaning of these brands, existing norms, and constraints with their respective product categories. Only with this understanding could the management teams develop a clear vision of where their brands might grow and how to expand the expectations of consumers. Those means might be through product development, channel development, or both.

Existing brands are often constrained by traditional perceptions on positioning products or services. ethel's confronted this constraint. Tradition limited purchases of fancy chocolates to holidays and special occasions; ethel's broke through by associating its product with socialization among upscale women—an everyday event. With ethel's, these women did not need a special event or holiday to enjoy chocolate.

Positioning a brand or subbrand in a way that will break through a marketplace constraint is always a challenge and has been a focus of much creative

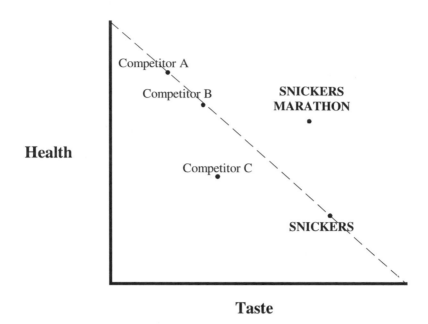

FIGURE 10.9 Breaking the Tension between Health and Taste
(Masterfoods, USA. Reproduced with permission)

thinking within Mars as it ventures forward. Traditional positioning for new products in mature markets is to charge less, provide more functionality, or offer some combination of both—that is, provide more for less. Mars has pursued all three positioning strategies across its core brands on numerous occasions. It has also found that each one, whether it's leadership in price, functionality, or value, is pursued rapidly by competitors, nullifying its early advantage.

Another approach to positioning a new product or service is to *break what-ever tension* limits user choice or satisfaction. Whenever consumers are faced with an either-or trade-off of qualities or functions they value, companies should look for opportunities. Breaking a tension can create ownership of a new market space. Snickers Marathon broke the tensions between good health and good taste. Whole Meals broke the tension between good nutrition and dog enjoyment. Cocoavia broke the tension between heart-healthy food sup-plements and good-tasting snacks. Figure 10.9 maps the tensions that the Snickers Marathon team used to help management understand the product positioning. Breaking the tensions is an example of the *hybrid positioning* that many of the firms in my research pursued for their new market applications, be it IBM's positioning of its servers as *fast* and *open* or Honda's Element having equal amounts of *attitude* and cargo carrying *flexibility*.

## Lesson 3: Leverage Current Product and Process Platforms

Platform thinking and the methods for planning the development and application of platforms described in chapter 7 are clearly part of the Mars DNA. It has product platforms, such as cocoa and peanut, and it has process platforms, the specific processes and equipment used to create and combine these ingredients into finished products. The ventures featured in this chapter are masterful examples of leveraging proven product and process platforms to new market applications: My M&M's leveraged M&M's pieces; Snickers Marathon leveraged a brand name; Cocoavia leveraged the company's cocoa science and existing manufacturing assets.

This leveraging of existing assets and know-how produced savings in time to market, R&D expense, and capital costs. Perhaps more important, it allowed these teams to focus on areas of the growth venture that were truly different and new. We also saw earlier how IBM leverages its microprocessors in various servers, as does Honda its engines. Platforms, when they are robust, are ever so powerful!

Many of the new product line developments described in this chapter presented Mars managers with the challenge of understanding new business models. The goal of the next chapter is to provide methods for framing business model innovation in financial terms and, from those terms, to make an effective business case for a new market application. After that chapter, we will consider the business processes executives can use to turn good ideas into profitable new businesses.

### Notes

1. KUDOS® Brand, SNICKERS® Brand, M&M'S® Brand, MY M&M'S® Chocolate Candies, UNCLE BEN'S® Ready Rice, Whole MEALS® Food for Dogs, JUMBONE® Snack Food for Dogs, ethel's®, COCOAVIA® Brand, SNICKERS® MARATHON® Energy Bar, COLORWORKS®, V02 MAX®, PEDIGREE®, WHISKAS®, Royal Canin®, MILKY WAY®, 3MUSKETEERS®, SKITTLES®, DOVE® CHOCOLATE, Almond-Butter-Krunch®, Warm-Blended™ Chocolate, and FLAVIA are all registered trademarks of Mars, Incorporated. POWERBAR® is a registered trademark of Nestle.

2. The team turned to MBA students at a major university, who used industry-leading conjoint survey and analysis software. These data proved highly useful in pricing discussions. Mars also learned that you did not need a $500,000 "perfect answer" market research program if the business approach is one of "launch and learn."

3. VO2Max stands for the volume of oxygen that can be consumed by the human body and used for physical activity.

4. Want to learn more about branding? Read David Aaker, "Should You Take Your Brand to Where the Action Is?" *Harvard Business Review*, 1997, September–October, 135–43.

5. N. K. Hollenberg, et al. "Aging, Acculturation, Salt Intake, and Hypertension in the Kuna of Panama," *Hypertension*, 1997, 29(1): 171–76; K. A. Chevaux, et al. "Proximate Mineral and Procyanidin Content of Certain Foods and Beverages Consumed by the Kuna Amerinds of Panama," *Journal of Food Composition Analysis*, 2001, 14: 553–63.

6. Red wine is another product in the press lately for its beneficial effect on cardiovascular health. Red wine can range from 45 milligrams of flavanols per 100 grams of volume; Cocoavia provides a minimum of 420 milligrams of flavanols per 100 grams of volume. See N. Hollenberg, H. Schmitz, I. Macdonald, and N. Poulter, "Cocoa, Flavanols, and Cardiovascular Risk," *Clinical Pharmacology*, 2004, 8(13): 379–86; D. Rein, T. Paglieroni, T. Wun, D. Pearson, H. Schmitz, R. Gosselin, and C. Keen, "Cocoa Inhibits Platelet Activation and Function," *American Journal of Clinical Nutrition*, 2000, 72(1): 30–35.

7. D. A. Pearson, T. G. Paglieroni, D. Rein, T. Wun, D. D. Schramm, J. F. Wang, R. R. Holt, R. Gosselin, H. H. Schmitz, and C. L. Keen, "The Effects of Flavanol-Rich Cocoa and Aspirin on Ex Vivo Platelet Function," *Thrombosis Research*, 2002, 106: 191–97.

# CHAPTER ELEVEN

# Making the Business Case

*Storyboard the business case—Financial statements and
metrics—Projecting revenue—Different types of customers—
Setting prices—Sales cycles—Derivative products and
services—Hunting for recurring revenue—Projecting costs,
operating profit, and cash flow—Unfair taxation for new
ventures—Metrics that make the business case—The
manufacturing ramp-up challenge—Compare the revenue and
margins for new product lines with existing ones—Defending
revenue projections—The human side of financial
statement development.*

A business *model* explains the mechanisms for making money. A business *plan*
goes a step further, explaining the strategies and actions that will put the
model to work. A business plan also contains detailed financial statements that
project the required investments and financial outcomes for those actions
at various stages of launch and ramp-up. Strategy, actions, investments, and
outcomes—these are the essence of business plan development and execution.

A good business plan is detailed, capturing team decisions on target markets, users, product models and services, pricing, distribution channels, and
market communications. The financial statements with the plan should be
equally detailed, with revenues, manufacturing costs, selling costs, and operating profit tuned to the team's volume expectations. For manufacturing operations, the business plan contains a detailed capital plan for scaling production
capacity.

Effective business plans gain senior management's respect and stimulate
discussion. Sloppy plans hurt a team's effort as much as a poorly conceived

design concept. So take the time to do this right and to do it well. And begin early. If a team lacks business planning and financial modeling expertise, it must get that expertise on board during the early phase of the project. "Making the business case" is a parallel activity with user-centered design within our framework for new market applications development—and of equal importance.

## The First Step: Storyboard the End Result

A number of the teams I studied used a mechanism similar to the template shown in figure 11.1 to create a prototype of their business plan, just as they created sketches of product or service concepts. I call this *business plan storyboarding*. The major categories of the storyboard template contain the key sections of a solid business plan: market, technology and products, channel, supply (which includes manufacturing and logistics), financial projections, and organization. Note the icons on the template.

Storyboarding is best accomplished in a large conference room with a very large whiteboard. The templates, sketches, user profiles, photos, and videos described earlier for user-centered design should be visibly present in the room to serve as constant reminders of the team's initial vision.

Team members should progress through each part of the template and devote as much time as needed to understanding how its different parts fit together and how conflict between parts can be resolved. For example, the target market for a new piece of software might be so far outside the firm's area of expertise that several years will be need to develop a sales force or find channel partners to distribute it effectively. Here, the team would brainstorm the impact of that problem on the time of launch and on projected revenues and costs. Alternative solutions to the problem would also be considered.

Once the team is satisfied with its storyboard, it should ask trusted colleagues for feedback. That feedback will generate more questions: "Is the design concept strong enough to justify the price premium we need to make this business profitable?" "Do we need to add other target users to get the unit sales we need to be successful?" "Should the product be manufactured internally, or should we look for a contract manufacturer?"

Storyboarding is an effective tool for executive involvement. Every successful team studied had one or two highly involved and supportive executives. After internal debate and the input of helpful colleagues, an innovation team should bring these executives into a similar interaction with the story-

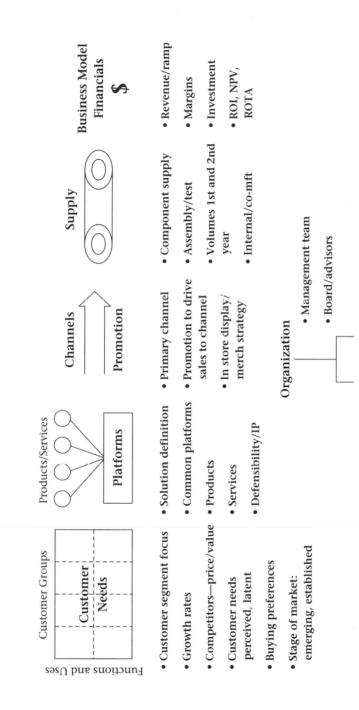

FIGURE 11.1  The Business Plan Storyboard Template

board. It should support the storyboard with the results of its market research: use case scenarios, personas, and sketches of design concepts for various parts of the new product line or service. Storyboard participation gives executives an opportunity to familiarize themselves with the plan without having to read 30-page documents or stay awake through lengthy PowerPoint presentations.

Of the companies most closely profiled in these pages, all had executives who took advantage of opportunities to gain direct customer knowledge. These executives peered into the world of users and understood their needs and fears. Honda executives spent a weekend on a California beach with Element team members and potential buyers. IBM executives visited customers to better understand the competition and user needs for new applications. At Mars, senior executives helped their innovation teams achieve breakthroughs for new business models and channel partners. At Charles River Laboratories, the senior management team spent countless hours visiting research laboratories, the smaller firms that provided drug development and testing services, as well as the pharmaceutical firms that would become the customers for its new services.

A passion for new products and technologies among executives is obviously a key to enterprise growth. Demonstration of that passion, however, is what matters. Will an executive visit a new target user with the team? Will that executive test-drive a prototype? Many executives I met during my studies could quickly grasp the connections between markets, business models, and new product or service concepts. Their contributions to business model innovation and business planning were substantial. But not all executives fit this description. An executive who is primarily focused on cutting costs and squeezing profits out of current business is unlikely to visit new customers and help sell new channel partners. Consequently, innovation teams must pick their sponsors wisely.

## Making the Business Case with Financial Statements and Metrics

In making a business case to management, teams must translate market opportunity into realistic financial results. This is typically accomplished through financial statements and performance measures. The financial statements of interest here are the income statement, otherwise known as the "P&L" (profit and loss) statement, and the capital plan. Clear and detailed financials are essential

---

**A Business Planning Guide and Financial Templates**

My Web site (www.fastpathmanagement.com) contains a business planning guide that has been used to good effect by teams over the past decade, and readers can go there to download updated versions of this guide for distribution to team members. That Web site also provides financial templates for different types of products and services.

Although this chapter focuses on developing financial projections, a business plan typically accompanies such projections. As you read the business planning guide, pay particular attention to the questions in each section that are highlighted in italics. Make sure that your plan answers these questions!

Many of the planning templates in this book will fit nicely into each section of that business planning guide, particularly the market segmentation grid, the user case scenario, the product strategy map, and the product line architecture.

Try to keep your business plans shorter than 30 pages. As noted well by William Strunk and E. B. White, "Vigorous writing is concise."[1] Concise financial statements—the P&L, cash flow, and capital plan—are preferred. However, your company may require more elaborate spreadsheet formats for R&D, marketing, and capital expense approvals.

---

when the new market application occurs outside the corporation's established product lines and customer markets.

For example, in the My M&M's case described in the previous chapter, the team knew that it needed a direct-to-consumer Web channel—something largely new to Mars—and a fulfillment process that was very different from the company's warehouse distribution system for retailers. The My M&M's team also wanted to charge three to four times more than the price of standard M&M's candies. Because management's acceptance of "nonstandard" product lines like this eventually turns on "the numbers," the team should offer detailed and realistic financial analysis.

A team can use its pro forma P&L and capital plan to produce key business case metrics. The metrics used most widely by the companies studied were the net present value of discounted cash flows (which include project investments) and the return on operating assets used to produce revenue. Many teams also estimated "time to first dollar" and "time to first profit."

Figure 11.2 shows how a team might project revenues and operating profit for a new product line or service. Figure 11.3 projects capital requirements, cash flow adjustments, and important measures of financial attractiveness. These two spreadsheets constitute a template for financial planning. They, too, are available as a single spreadsheet on my Web site, as are examples taken from software and services businesses.

Having all this information modeling on a single worksheet helps a team think through the integration of different business components such as unit sales, margins, and capital investments. The details underlying these projections should follow in secondary worksheets that are linked to the higher level worksheet shown in figures 11.2 and 11.3.

These figures were taken (and disguised) from a new product line development in one of the companies. A manufacturing engineer, whom we will call George, manned the keyboard as team members from sales, R&D, and finance contributed data and their expectations for the new product line. Interestingly, although George had substantial experience developing manufacturing cost models in spreadsheets, financial modeling was new to him. So, if George can do it, so can you!

George's team worked closely with the finance department to refine calculations with more precise cost estimates for manufacturing and logistics. They also dealt with knotty issues such as corporate overhead, the "tax" most new product and service lines must pay once revenues begin flowing. The result of their interaction with the finance department was a number of complex worksheets, which were eventually linked to the top worksheet. Team members agreed that starting with that complexity would have been a bad idea; doing so would have confused everyone and detracted from discussions on strategy, business models, and desired financial outcomes. Thus, George's initial pro forma—like a product prototype—served as a foundation for subsequent discussion, learning, and refinement.

An innovation team must own its numbers. It cannot delegate their development to a central finance department, which cannot possibly have an intimate knowledge of the markets, technology, and supply factors associated with the new product line or service. Instead, the team must control its numbers and seek *participation* from finance staff. That way, team members will fully grasp the financial consequences of their decisions on product or service positioning, functionality, the number of SKUs or models to be offered, how those models are priced, distribution, and packaging. Allowing central finance to dictate the numbers leads to "we want this" but "you can't have it" conflicts. Collaboration with finance, on the other hand, leads to more realistic numbers and better decisions.

| | Price / unit | $22.50 | Units/Shift | 350 |
| --- | --- | --- | --- | --- |
| | | | Shifts/year | 576 |
| | | | Units per machine per year | 201,600 |
| | | | Cost per machine | 350,000 |

| | Development | Year 1 | Year 2 | Year 3 | Year 4 | Year 5 |
| --- | --- | --- | --- | --- | --- | --- |
| **Volume Projections** | | | | | | |
| **Orders/day Channel 1** | | 50 | 75 | 100 | 125 | 150 |
| **Orders/day Channel 2** | | 200 | 600 | 1,000 | 1,500 | 2,000 |
| **Total Orders/Day** | | 250 | 675 | 1,100 | 1,625 | 2,150 |
| **Avg units per order** | | 4.00 | 4.00 | 4.00 | 4.00 | 4.00 |
| **Units per Year** | | 360,000 | 972,000 | 1,584,000 | 2,340,000 | 3,096,000 |
| | | | | | | |
| **P&L Projections** | | | | | | |
| **Gross Sales** | | **8,100,000** | **21,870,000** | **35,640,000** | **52,650,000** | **69,660,000** |
| **Manufacturing Cost per Unit** | | 6.00 | 5.70 | 5.42 | 5.14 | 4.89 |
| **Total Conversion** | | 2,160,000 | 5,540,400 | 8,577,360 | 12,037,545 | 15,130,268 |
| **Shipping (per unit)** | | 4.50 | 4.28 | 4.06 | 3.86 | 3.67 |
| **Shipping** | | 1,620,000 | 4,155,300 | 6,433,020 | 9,028,159 | 11,347,701 |
| **Gross Margin** | | **53%** | **56%** | **58%** | **60%** | **62%** |
| **Advertising and Web Dev** | 250,000 | 1,000,000 | 1,100,000 | 1,210,000 | 1,331,000 | 1,464,100 |
| **R&D** | 1,500,000 | 750,000 | 750,000 | 750,000 | 750,000 | 750,000 |
| **G&A** | 200,000 | 810,000 | 2,187,000 | 3,564,000 | 5,265,000 | 6,966,000 |
| **Operating Profit** | **−1,950,000** | **1,760,000** | **8,137,300** | **15,105,620** | **24,238,296** | **34,001,931** |
| **% Gross Sales** | | **22%** | **37%** | **42%** | **46%** | **49%** |

FIGURE 11.2  A Financial Template for a Manufactured Product (Marc H. Meyer)

**CAPITAL INFUSIONS FOR OPERATING ASSETS**

| | 1 | 2 | 5 | 8 | 12 | 16 |
|---|---|---|---|---|---|---|
| **New machines needed** | | | | | | |
| **New capital invested** | 350,000 | 700,000 | 1,750,000 | 2,800,000 | 4,200,200 | 5,600,000 |
| **Fixed Asset Total** | **350,000** | **1,050,000** | **2,800,000** | **5,600,000** | **9,800,000** | **15,400,000** |
| | | | | | | |
| | | | | | | |
| **BUSINESS METRICS** | | | | | | |
| **EBIT/operating profit** | –1,950,000 | 1,760,000 | 8,137,300 | 15,105,620 | 24,238,296 | 34,001,931 |
| **Adjustments (A/R, A/P, working capital)** | | –88,000 | –406,865 | –755,281 | –1,211,915 | –1,700,097 |
| **Cash flow** | –1,950,000 | 1,672,000 | 7,730,435 | 14,350,339 | 23,026,381 | 32,301,834 |
| **NPV of Cash flows** | 38,269,515 | *Discount rate: 15%, 10% WACC plus high-risk factor of 5%* | | | | |
| **FATR** | | 11.57 | 11.36 | 8.49 | 6.84 | 5.53 |
| **ROA** | | 251% | 423% | 360% | 315% | 270% |

FIGURE 11.3  Capital Plan and Performance Metrics (Marc H. Meyer)

## Projecting Volumes and Revenue

Let's now concentrate on the financial template described in figure 11.2. We'll begin with assumptions.

### Assumptions

In the figure 11.2 template, basic assumptions are stated at the very top. Here, assumptions focus on price per unit and the cost of each new production machine. Always state your assumptions for the benefit of the executive reviewers. In this case, the project has a highly modular production process in which new machines can be added in an incremental way to meet new levels of output. Each machine is projected to cost about $350,000. Had George's team required a single machine costing, say, $10 million to begin production, the return on operating assets metric shown in figure 11.3 would have been far less attractive at the level of sales anticipated during the first several years after launch. The team might have been forced to seek a contract manufacturer and, as a consequence, worry about intellectual property protection.

Price is another assumption. The unit price at the top of the figure can be changed to facilitate different "what if" scenarios—one of the great advantages of spreadsheets. The impact of any price change is dynamically linked to other values in the spreadsheet. In this particular case, the innovation team conducted price tests with target users. The results of those tests were plugged back into the spreadsheet, providing immediate feedback between marketing and finance.

### Volume Projections

User research can give you a good sense of what the individuals you interview will pay for a new market application and how *many* they will buy at a given price within a particular time frame. Extrapolating individual customer demand to the wider universe of potential buyers is more difficult, yet it is extremely critical. Future demand projections can make or break a business plan. Most executives understand this. Having been disappointed if not burned in the past by rosy demand projections, many of the executives in the companies I studied preferred conservative volume forecasts. In some cases, a *worst case* scenario and *likely case* scenario for volume projections were presented in parallel.

Unit sales projections can, in some cases, be benchmarked against other successful products in the same or similar categories—products that already have a record of sales. For example, an enterprise software development company might look at the sales trajectories of similar products it has launched as a starting point for estimating quarter-to-quarter or year-to-year unit sales of its new product. However, such volumetric studies tend to be benchmarks of a new product concept against "like" products already on the marketplace. If the new product concept is fundamentally different, those benchmarks will be meaningless.

Figure 11.2 shows a projection of annual unit demand through two different channels. For a consumer product company, those two channels might be retail sales and direct sales through an e-commerce site or a mail order catalogue. For a business-to-business supplier, the two channels might be direct orders through the company sales force and online sales. In the vast majority of companies studied, however, there was a single channel targeted for distribution. This helps to focus effort and reduce complexity. Managing one channel well is hard enough; managing two often proves too much and introduces the risk of conflict between the firm and its channel partners.

However you format this section of the spreadsheet, be sure to have a credible response when an executive asks, "How did you come up with these volume projections?" We will now look at different methods for projecting revenues.


### Revenue Projections

Once assumptions are set and annual unit sales are projected, the spreadsheet can calculate annual gross sales (revenues). Gross sales is the "top line" that is then reduced by manufacturing, shipping, and other costs in reaching operating profits—or profits before income taxes and interest expenses (although some companies in my study included the tax effect). Those "other costs" include expenses for marketing, R&D, and administration.

Some new businesses generate multiple streams of revenue. While the figure 11.2 shows these as emerging from two distinct channels, multiple streams of revenue can flow within the same channel. For example, a new software product line might produce licensing revenue, customer support fees, and additional sales from plug-ins or add-on modules. Other streams of revenue might include systems integration services; in some large software companies, these account for upward of 40 percent of gross revenue. Similarly, a Web-based business produces transaction revenues, advertising fees, and subscription fees.

Revenue from the licensing of intellectual property is not usually considered by new market application teams. This can be a mistake. Of IBM's approximate $91 billion in annual revenue (2005), for example, more than a billion dollars came from the licensing, sale, or custom development of IBM's own intellectual property. That figure should grow as IBM is granted more patents—it obtained almost 3,000 *new* patents in 2005 alone!

## Additional Factors Affecting Revenue Projections

Projecting volumes and revenues in a detailed, granular way is important. They drive everything else on the spreadsheet; consequently, projections should be as realistic and fact-based as possible. One way to do that is to create a separate worksheet that breaks down revenue projections by specific components. The results of this worksheet can then be tied back into the top line (gross sales) of the projected P&L. Let's now consider factors that a team should take into consideration as its projects revenues.

### Different Types of Customers

Customer "type" is important. If the customer is an OEM (original equipment manufacturer), then the revenues can be projected on volumes anticipated from each OEM, the price per unit and discounts associated with those volumes, and the number of new OEM customers that the team thinks it can sign up quarter by quarter. If, on the other hand, the customer is a distributor, you need to find the target distributor's current unit sales of like products, and use that figure as the basis for revenue forecasts.

Selling to retailers directly requires a different approach: The team needs to consider which *type* of retailer its products are most suited for (be it specialty, grocery or department store, convenience, mass merchandiser or club) and then estimate how many retail partners can be enlisted at launch and afterward, as well as average unit sales per retail partner.

If the customer is an end user, such as a consumer reached through the Web, a team will have to consider the advertising expenditures needed to generate market awareness and purchases. If, on the other hand, the end user is a corporation that, for example, will buy software, then consider lead user corporations, server licenses, or even site licenses.

Each one of these customer *types* therefore represents a different revenue model.

### Setting Prices Too High or Too Low

The price attached to the new product or service must be carefully determined. But what is the right price? In many instances, the current market will suggest a suitable pricing structure. A team starts with a product strategy that leads to a certain positioning for its new products or services along a continuum of "good, better, best" and, in some cases, specific offerings that hit various points of price/performance. Then it can observe the current prices charged by existing players in its new target market. When combined with strategy and positioning for the new venture with respect to premium, mid-range, or "value" offerings, this benchmarking tells the team the appropriate pricing for its products or services.

Price is not often so easily determined, and it is often hotly debated. The only way to resolve such debates prior to launch is to perform market research with target end users, using the conjoint type and market testing techniques described in chapter 5. The McKinsey consulting firm provided insight on this, showing in one of its own studies: "Companies consistently undercharge for products despite spending millions or even billions of dollars to develop or acquire them. The incremental approach often underestimates the value of new products for customers."[2] By using an existing product as a primary reference point, a company undervalues a revolutionary product. "With every new product, companies feel tempted to build market share quickly through aggressively low prices—a tactic known as penetration pricing. But a fixation on volume usually sacrifices profitability and may ignite a price war. As a result, it is generally better to keep upward pressure on prices and to promote good industry pricing behavior."

Despite McKinsey's warning, penetration pricing may not be entirely wrongheaded for a unique new product. For example, a number of the software companies I encountered take this to an extreme by "giving away" base-level versions and hoping to lure paying customers for professional versions. The goal here is to try to gain market leadership through a broad base of installed users. At the same time, even the most externally successful new product line or service will be reviewed harshly if it continuously fails to make money for the corporation.

### A Lengthy Sales Cycle

A team must also ask itself about the sales cycle for a new product line or service. They cannot assume that the cycle is the same one experienced by the company's core product lines. A sales cycle is the period between the first exposure of a product to customers and receipt of orders. During that period, the product's features and benefits must be communicated and customers must make decisions. For impulse consumer products, the customer decision process may be very brief. For expensive goods, specialty goods, and industrial goods, the decision process may be many months; buyer committees are often involved. IBM's products, for example, are very complex, and their sales cycle can extend over many months. A new high-end server, with its many software and storage management devices and integration support services, can be a multimillion-dollar investment requiring the education and agreement of many decision makers. This applies to intermediaries as well. For example, a convenience store chain may be a much quicker sale than a grocery store or mass merchandiser.

The sales cycle must be factored into sales projections. It is especially critical in the period following launch, when the product is new and unfamiliar to targeted customers. The companies I studied often discovered a substantial difference between their theoretical projections of user demand and the time required to obtain orders: "$10 million may sound reasonable, but if the sales cycle is nine months (as it would be for a complex computer system), do you really want to bet that everything will come in as expected in the last quarter?" The sales cycle is only one of the good reasons to have a person with sales experience on the team—if only on a part-time basis.

## Creating Derivatives Products and Services

In projecting revenue over a multiyear period, consider possible derivative products possible with a modular product line architecture. Each derivative product or service can produce its own revenue stream and costs. For example, a pet food manufacturer such as Mars has specific formulations for the life stage of the pet, as well as snacks developed to supplement main meals.

Think carefully about related product developments and the opportunity to create supplemental revenues. However, if these are shown arriving in the first year of launch, senior management may rightfully be skeptical. Years 2 and 3 are another matter. The goal here is to create a fully featured product line or service, based on common product and process platforms.

### Hunting for Recurring Revenue

Recurring revenue is the holy grail of entrepreneurs and corporate intrapreneurs alike. Once customers are won, repeat purchases fuel revenue growth—and at much lower sales costs. The customer has already bought into the brand and its value proposition; now, many will want more features and greater functionality. That need can be served with modular products and services that either upgrade or work in conjunction with initial purchases.

Among manufacturers, Hewlett Packard ink-jet printer line generates a continuing stream of revenue from the sale of ink cartridges. Both the price per unit and the frequency of cartridge repurchases have increased during recent years (in part because of digital photography) to the benefit of HP's revenue stream.

Software companies expect a significant portion of their revenues—say, 20 percent—to come from customers who upgrade to newer and better versions. Or new revenue is gained from the sale of complementary software. Adobe Photoshop, for example, is a leading image-editing package. In addition to Photoshop, Adobe also offers at extra cost Adobe Photoshop Elements (to quickly fix, edit, and add text to digital photographs) and Adobe Photoshop Album (to create, organize, and share albums, calendars, and the like). IBM gains recurring revenue through the development and sales of system upgrades, software enhancements, new networking adapters, and faster processors. Customers expect these new product releases and are often willing to pay for the new functionality they offer. Annual maintenance fees, training services, and custom application development services are another source of recurring revenue from the same users. Services themselves are rarely single use, and the essential nature of the most successful ones is recurring use and the revenue associated with it. That is why so many software companies are using technology to reposition their licensed software as software services.

A team that shows no recurring revenue from current customers in outlying years *had better find ways to generate it.*


### Costs, Operating Profit, and Cash Flow

Once revenues have been projected, the next step is to estimate the costs and expenses associated with the new business. Once you subtract these from projected revenues, you'll have an estimate of operating profit (or loss).

Expense estimates can often be gathered from similar types of products (in terms of material content, conversion costs, and logistics or shipping) already offered by the firm. Similarly, because one of the goals of a new market application is to leverage existing product and manufacturing platforms, a team should have a good understanding of its likely R&D costs and the retooling needed to produce the product. From this foundation, the most effective teams in my study carefully established product, platform, and process roadmaps and earmarked R&D and capital costs to each improvement, year by year, both prior to launch and after. Teams also had members visit the manufacturing line or comanufacturers to develop detailed models for manufacturing costs per unit—and how costs would decrease as volume increased in postlaunch years.

These costs, together with administrative and selling expenses, become the basis of projecting operating profit. As shown in the template, a stream of operating profits and losses spanning the development period and the first and subsequent years of postlaunch operation is the end result of the team's projections.

A team should also revisit its spreadsheets to adjust for cash flow issues. The time between when a company books a sale and actually receives payment—known as the accounts receivable collection period—will *reduce* cash flow. A team needs to consider this if the collection period is greater than, say, 45 days. The speed with which a company pays its vendors for raw materials and supplies may be another factor. Again, if that payables period averages more than 30 days, project cash flow should *increase*. Last, new product line manufacturing seldom qualifies as *lean* manufacturing, at least initially. Consequently, manufacturing can tie up cash in the form of materials inventory. If inventory will be a large factor, the team might have to *decrease* its projected cash flow. Even better, it should plan on tight inventory controls. Commercial procurement, manufacturing, and supply professionals who join teams often bring along a mind-set attuned to efficiency.

### Unfair Taxation: Capital Charges, Corporate Overheads, and Hidden Charges

Once the elements of the financials are in place, it's a good idea to go back and fine-tune the spreadsheet to accommodate the company's particular approach to items such as equipment depreciation and overhead. Collaboration between the innovation team and the finance staff will facilitate this fine-tuning.

Depreciation is an economic and accounting convention that recognizes the using up of capital assets, such as plant and equipment. Though it is a non-cash expense, its application reduces profitability. If depreciation is appropriate, the finance department can give the team the right charge to apply to its capital assets.

Corporate overhead, often called "burden" (or for some British readers, "oncost"), is another charge against revenues that the new product line may be required to accept as a matter of company policy. Overhead is a method companies use to allocate the cost of heat, rent, insurance, staff compensation, upkeep of corporate jets, and other expenses to the product lines that benefit fit from them, either directly or indirectly. As CFOs are fond of saying, "Somebody has to pay for these things." Every company has its own particular and often mysterious way of dealing with corporate overhead. They want all product lines to carry some portion of overhead, whether or not they benefit from all of it.

Capital charges and corporate overheads place an added burden on the market application's financials, making it more difficult for the team to make its case and win approval. Some corporations provide waivers on these "taxes" until after the first two full years of revenues or until profitability is achieved.

A product line should bear only the new incremental costs that it incurs in areas such as manufacturing or marketing. *This is a critical consideration for venture teams and the executives sponsoring them.* For example, in my study, some teams found that their per unit costs for manufacturing were overblown because plant managers were bundling in the fixed cost of existing assets as a variable cost quoted to the teams. These are "hidden" charges that forced teams to turn to outside manufacturers to achieve the necessary profitability. However, this also placed a team's proprietary process know-how into the hands of outsiders—contract manufacturers who eventually could apply that know-how to help a firm's competitors. That is a shame, because those same in-house machines that teams wanted to use but which were deemed as too costly for production were not being used to full capacity. New product line production on those assets should have been encouraged, not discouraged.

## Metrics That Make the Business Case

Once projections of sales, net income, and cash flow are made (figure 11.2), the team can derive key measures of business attractiveness (figure 11.3). The first and perhaps most important of these is net present value (NPV). This method discounts projected cash flows from the project by the company's cost of capital or by some percentage "hurdle rate" approved by the CFO. Other things being equal, a project with a high NPV is better financially than one with a lower NPV. NPV recognizes the company's cost of capital and the time value of money. Cash flows received sooner in time have a greater value per dollar than equal cash flows received later. Cash flow is the net of incoming and outgoing cash during a period of time.

Cash flow is not the same as operating earnings, or even net income. Investors typically look to operating earnings, which are earnings *before* interest, taxation, depreciation, and amortization—all of which are subject to machinations by the company's accounting department. Looking at operating earnings is important for teams. However, it is also important to make further adjustments such as those that any new business would make; a new product line or service is, after all, like a new business.

In figure 11.3, cash flows, positive and negative, for all the years in the planning horizon are discounted back into current dollars and accumulated to derive the projected net present value of the project—in this case a new, manufactured product line. The discount rate used in this example is the firm's cost

### Terminal Value

One of the challenges of calculating NPV is determining the "terminal value" of the cash flows associated with a new product line or service. Terminal value is, in effect, part of the final year's cash flow modeled on the spreadsheet, say, Year 5, and discounted back into current dollars.

There are several ways to estimate terminal value: liquidation value for the assets, a multiple of earnings or revenues in the last year modeled, or an assumption that cash flows grow at a constant rate forever after that last year modeled. The most professional way is the last method. Here's the equation[4]:

$$TV_{Year\ 5} = [CF_{Year\ 5} * (1+g)]/(r-g)$$

where:

$TV_{Year\ 5}$ = the terminal value at Year 5, where that could actually be any final year that the team has modeled

$CF_{Year\ 5}$ = the projected cash flow in period t

$g$ = the estimated future growth rate of the cash flows beyond t

$r$ = the firm's cost (of borrowing capital)

This is particularly important for new products developed in the biotech industry, for example, where the typical new drug takes 10 or more years to reach market.

of capital (10 percent) plus a risk factor (5 percent) to represent the uncertainty of the new market application relative to established product lines. Each team needs to think about what its own risk factor should be. Five percent is just the example used here![3]

For manufacturers, equally important performance measures include turnover ratios based on the relationship between sales and the capital spent to either create a new product line or upgrade the current ones. One of these measures is the *fixed asset turnover ratio* (FATR), the year's sales divided by the average assets used to generate those sales. FATR tells a firm how many sales are generated for each dollar of investment in manufacturing assets.

$$FATR = Sales/Average\ assets$$

Return on assets (ROA) is another important metric for new market applications that are capital intensive. The simplest way to calculate ROA is to divide the operating earnings before interest and taxation by the value of average assets used to create those earnings during the time period under consideration.

$$ROA = EBIT/Average\ Assets$$

An equivalent method for calculating ROA, first developed by DuPont de Nemours in the 1930s and referred to as the DuPont model, is to multiply net profit margin times the FATR metric previously described.

$$ROA = (EBIT/Sales) \times (Sales/Average\ Assets)$$

Although the two sales numbers cancel one another out, computing and comparing year-by-year calculations of these two ratios helps a firm understand the key drivers behind ROA: the changes from year to year in the profitability ratio, on the one hand, and the changes in the asset turnover ratio on the other.[5]

ROA is typically calculated for an entire business. Here, we are applying it to the projected P&L and capital spending plan for a new product line or service only. The results are equally useful. Senior management can then compare the project ROA against its average cost of capital, perhaps adjusted for the riskiness of the new project, as well as against other mature product lines. Some teams may wish to calculate this on a year-by-year basis for their projected P&Ls and capital plans; they can just as easily discount the operating earnings and capital investments into current dollars by using the company's average weighted cost of capital (say, 12 percent), to derive a single project ROA across the planning horizon for the project.

Another approach to measuring manufacturing efficiency and asset utilization is to calculate inventory turnover. This is accomplished by dividing cost of goods within a given period by the average amount of materials and subassemblies maintained in inventory during I that period. The higher the turnover rate, the better. For example, a team I studied developed a new product line of fluorescent lighting fixtures and prided itself on achieving inventory turns of *60 times* on its new production line through the use of lean manufacturing techniques, whereas the rest of the corporation considered itself fortunate to achieve inventory turns of just *6 times* on its core business. Other companies that had successfully launched new manufactured product lines found that their internal processes, fine for the first year or two of volumes, literally broke down as the business scaled up. Lost orders, late shipments, and a higher percentage of returns were the telltale signs. Managers had to overhaul these ordering, production, and fulfillment operations in order to support increased demand.[6]

## The Manufacturing Ramp-Up Challenge: Projecting Capital Costs

For many of the companies studied, how to initiate production and scale it became more than a quality-of-manufacturing issue; it became a financial issue. In figure 11.3, for example, capital investments are needed for each new machine added to the factory. Each new machine produces a certain number of units at full capacity. As sales increase, so do the number of required machines. The experience curve, however, will certainly come into play for most businesses, and each new machine should be able to produce more units as the company learns better ways to manage output.

The company in this example can incrementally expand production by ordering $350,000 machines as demand increases. Not all manufacturers are so fortunate. Honda had to investment many millions of dollars to retool its Civic assembly line to accommodate the Element. Semiconductor makers also spend vast amounts for a new manufacturing line.

Only high levels of projected revenue can justify massive investments. The revenue versus capital relationship presents a challenge. If $20 million of productive assets are needed to get into the game, then one must achieve $80 million in annual revenue after two or three years to meet a fixed asset turnover ratio (FATR) of 4, a measure of operating efficiency for many manufacturers. Generating $80 million in revenues within several years is a high hurdle for any new venture. "But," one might ask, "who cares about operating efficiency for a new product line? The focus should be on market penetration. Efficiencies will come later." Unfortunately, executives in many of the corporations studied held new product lines to the same capital efficiency hurdle as their established product lines.

Figure 11.4 represents the challenge this poses to teams. Here we see a favorable sales-asset relationship when sales are $80 million and manufacturing assets are $20 million. If only $20 million of projected sales are generated, the team will have a hard time making a case. In that instance, the company will have little choice but to turn to contract manufacturers.

Corporations effectively use three basic manufacturing strategies in situations like those described in figure 11.4:

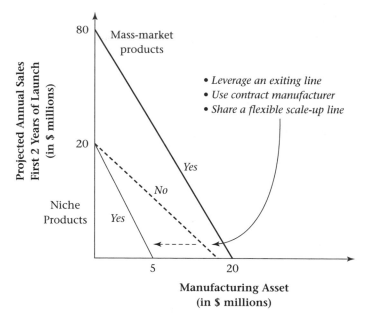

FIGURE 11.4  The Manufacturing Ramp-Up Challenge

1. Leverage existing assets.
2. Use contract manufacturers for the first several years of production until volumes reach the point where internal production make sense in terms of operating efficiency and asset utilization.
3. Develop specialized scale-up manufacturing facilities that are explicitly designed to accommodate different types of new product configurations, and even different materials.

Let's examine each of these strategies.

### Leverage Existing Assets

The first approach works in the area under the dotted line in the figure by designing the new product to take advantage of an existing manufacturing asset. As we saw in the previous chapter, Mars applied this approach to Cocoavia (its heart-healthy chocolate bar). Cocoavia was designed to a size that could be produced and packaged on the same line as the company's Kudos snack bar. This strategy eliminated the need to build a dedicated production line in the $20 million range. Absent that strategy, the "launch and learn" approach that is so essential for new market applications would have been cast aside for "place your bets and roll 'em."

### Use Contract Manufacturing

A second strategy for ramp-up manufacturing is to enlist a contract manufacturer. By doing so, the innovator can defer the cost of fixed asset investments until such time as the new market application has proven itself in the market and reached a revenue level sufficient to support operating efficiency. In my study, I observed examples of effective manufacturing outsourcing of new market applications in medical, computer, and consumer product companies. This strategy makes manufacturing cost largely variable. However, the company may have to pay the contract manufacturer an up-front fee to tool production for a new design.

Contract manufacturing, however, has a potential downside: Today's production partner may become tomorrow's competitor. You must exercise caution when using third parties for the initial production of noncommodity products. Part of the "secret sauce" in new products is often found at the intersection of product design and manufacturing. It's possible that the contract manufacturer will use its new know-how to enter the market as a rival or to form relationships with competitors to do the same, nondisclosure agreements notwithstanding. One practical defense mechanism is to control the truly proprietary aspects of manufacturing and outsource the rest. IBM has often taken this approach. It manufactures only those components that represent unique intellectual property (e.g., its microprocessors). The rest—electronics, cooling systems, cabinetry, and switches—are largely outsourced. Final assembly and testing of all System z servers, however, typically remains in an IBM facility, where they can be customized to buyers' preferences just prior to shipping.

Another approach to partnering with contract manufacturing is to take an equity position in the manufacturer. In the spring of 2006, Mars took this one step further by acquiring Doane Pet Food Enterprises, a billion-dollar private-label pet food manufacturer that at the time had 20 plants and two distribution centers in North America. The combination of Mars brands and new product line innovation with Doane's low-cost manufacturing and supply chain capabilities was clearly seen as a "win-win."

### Establish a Ramp-Up Manufacturing Facility

The third alternative to launch and scale is to build an agile manufacturing facility capable of rapid changeover between related products—a facility capable of serving several or more new product lines. Agile manufacturing is the ability to accomplish rapid changeover from producing one product to producing another. In assembly operations, rapid changeover is made possible through a combination of robots, flexible part feeders, modular grippers, modular conveyor systems, and software for managing and adjusting production.[7] Robert Hayes and Steven Wheelwright described this as "multiple products, low volume" with little standardization, which then transforms into higher volume, more focused operations.[8] An agile ramp-up manufacturing facility can be an incredibly powerful weapon. New product lines don't have to fight for time on the line, and test runs can be done with far less worry.

The cost of the agile asset can be amortized across many new product line launches. In our example (figure 11.4); if a dedicated production asset costs $20 million to install, and the fixed asset turnover ratio (annual sales to accumulated capital invested in plant and equipment) expected by the corporation is, say, four times, then the annual sales of the new product line must come to $80 million after several years to make the numbers in the business case work. A ramp-up facility changes this equation. Again, let's say the flexible manufacturing line can be installed for about $20 million. Let's further say that the firm is launching two new market applications a year. After three years, six new product lines will have been brought to market and scaled upward. The capital cost of the facility is divided equally into these new product lines, at least until each reaches the level of sales to justify a dedicated line or is deemed not successful and withdrawn from market. On average, then, each product line is being charged $3 million to $4 million, which means that each product line must achieve $12 to $20 million in sales—not $80 million. For most innovation teams, this is a much more feasible scenario.

For the corporation, the agile facility removes a major impediment to organic enterprise growth *without* having to "give away the goodies" to a contract manufacturer. Instead of rolling the dice, the company can launch and learn from every new market application. Agility typically comes at the cost of efficiency, as measured by cost per unit of production. It is not a focused factory in the traditional sense; rather, it is focused on handling the first several years of production for a series of similar new products.[9]

An agile ramp-up approach works only if the company (a) has a stream of new products in development and under trial launch and (b) transitions its most successful new launches to dedicated, highly efficient production lines capable of achieving maximum production. Nor does the ramp-up plant approach work in all industries. Car manufacturers, for example, typically see their highest new model sales in the first two years following launch. For them, high-volume manufacturing has to be achieved from the get-go.

**Anticipate Competitor Responses**

As your team makes its revenue projections, think about current competitors and how they are likely to respond when threatened. Unless those competitors are hopelessly asleep at the wheel, they will respond to your market entry. Some will try to mimic your new design, perhaps not the first year, but surely thereafter. A financially strong competitor may drop its prices, keep a number of customers from defecting, and perhaps force you to lower prices and kill the profitability of the fledgling new product line. What would a lower price do to both the unit volumes and revenues in your projected P&L? Also, if the new market space you open up is highly lucrative, others will notice and follow in hot pursuit.

## Ammunition for the Business Case: Compare the New Product Line to Established Ones

An innovation team's greatest competitors are not always the current players it hopes to displace but, rather, other business units in its own company. Because everyone wants resources, the managers of the company's established product lines may think, "What makes those new folks think they should get $2 million in R&D and $15 million for plant? I want those funds invested in the next generation of my product line! Their revenues are hypothetical; mine are real." Arguments like that can influence senior management. To counter them, compare your financial projections against those of the company's other product or service lines. If your new product line or service has an appealing business model, its financial profile—the sales growth, profit margin, and so forth—may be much more attractive than those of established lines of business also in line for precious resources. Many of the mature product lines may have high sales and high asset turnover but poor operating profitability. Intense competition in mature markets generally forces all participants to reduce prices. A product line that is truly new and that addresses customer needs can escape the pricing pressures of commoditization. And unlike mature products, for which demand is usually flat or declining, the new market application can rightfully point to rising unit sales.

Figure 11.5 shows how that story was told by one of the teams studied for this book. It mapped data obtained on the company's existing product lines and then projected (with a dashed line) the financial path for a newly

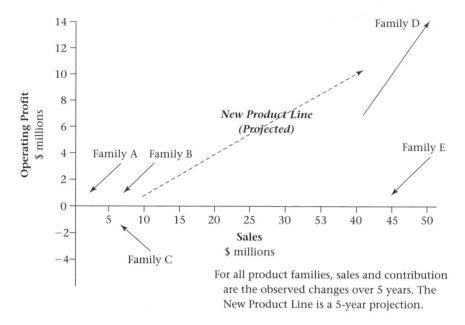

FIGURE 11.5  Product Line Profitability/Sales Map

proposed market application. Operating profitability is on the vertical axis, and sales are shown on the horizontal axis. In the figure, the beginning of each line is a start year; the end of the line marked with an arrow is a point three years in the future.

For all but one of this company's five product lines, the trend is headed in the wrong direction: lower sales, declining profitability. Family D, for example, has done well, growing from $30 million in sales to $50 million, and from $8 million to $14 million in operating profit. Families A, B, and C are sorry cases, small in revenue and marginally profitable. Family E had high sales at the beginning of the five-year period but has been marginally profitable ever since; its market position has eroded.

In contrast, the team's projected P&L shows increasing growth in sales and operating profit. The dashed line in the middle of the chart represents its three-year business case. When the company's executives realized that all five current product lines were essentially receiving the same amount of R&D money, their decision was to divert resources from the laggard lines into the new project. The figure made the urgency of the project apparent.

## Defending Revenue Projections

Once financial projections are made, the team must be prepared to defend its numbers. Several years ago, I was invited to observe a team's presentation to senior management. The team had prepared a detailed set of financial statements and was prepared to make its business case by explaining them page by page. That didn't happen. Instead, one executive grilled team members for over an hour on just Year 1 and Year 2 revenues.

This executive wanted to know the sources of those revenues, their lower and upper ranges, and which sources were greatest. Who would be their best customers? This executive showed little interest in market share expectations in outlying years. Instead, he drilled down on the details of the early years: "How many units do you expect to sell through each channel month by month?" he asked. "How does that compare to competitor's sales in the same category? How can we establish a beachhead with the best customers in your target market, make them reference accounts, and leverage out from there?" He understood that not all customers are equal. He also wanted to know about the team's proposed channel partners: "How will these partners give us more unit sales than those of current market leaders?" The executive was also curious about the impact of a higher price on sales projections: "A higher price might improve the profit margin, but its bound to reduce unit sales," he told them. "So, how many unit sales will a 10 percent price rise cost us, and how does that net out?"

His approach was bottom-up and fine-grained. Will the reader encounter an executive with the same level of detailed curiosity? The only safe way to proceed is to be prepared to answer questions that go to the heart of a team's projections—the assumptions, key customers, the most important drivers of both revenues and costs, and how the projections will change if those assumptions and drivers are altered.

As a team prepares to defend its financial projections, it must be unfailingly realistic. Revenue projections are often overoptimistic. Figure 11.6 shows one example taken from a company studied: It has two-year projected revenues and revenues actually realized for nine new product lines, where the revenue is disguised into a scale of 1 to 10. In most cases, the gap between projected and actual was substantial. This company was not alone in my sample. A rosy projection might sell a project to senior management but will disappoint everyone several years down the road. It can also lead to excessive capital expenditures at the beginning of a project—expenditures from which the new product line or service may never recover in terms of its return on capital.

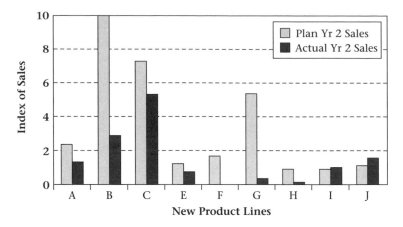

FIGURE 11.6 A History of Revenue Projections for New Market Applications
(Marc H. Meyer, data disguised from a sample member company)

Remember, even the best of a company's established product lines probably started small, and it is all right for new ones to do the same. The executives doing the grilling have been around long enough to recall the modest beginnings of today's cash cows. They expect and appreciate realistic numbers from you. *So don't oversell, and don't create unrealistic expectations* that will get everyone in hot water several years down the road.

Just as important, new market applications target new users and uses, for whom traditional business models might not apply. If a team has innovated upon the firm's traditional business model, then it makes no sense to force the new business to look like the old one. If executives view the new market application as "like" other company offerings, they may insist that it must use the same manufacturing facilities, sell through the same channels, and produce high rates of profitability and asset utilization from the beginning. If that were to happen, the new business would mostly likely be dead on arrival.

## The Human Side of Financial Statement Development

Developing financial projections can be as challenging as any other activity described in this book, yet it should not be delegated. Allowing someone who doesn't understand target users or the new business model, or who has no skin in the game, to make the projections is asking for problems.

In one company studied, the innovation team thought it owned its P&L. In reality, the marketing person on the team had gone the vice president of marketing, who set the numbers—improperly. Every analogous product in the market had done, for the purposes of this discussion, about $10 million in the first year of launch, and the best of these had grown to about $50 million after six or seven years. This team's product was special on several dimensions, so the team figured that it might come close to $15 million after year one, and scale up to $70 million over five years. That target would require about $5 million in advertising and other launch costs.

The marketing VP didn't see it that way. He set the venture's first-year revenue projection at $50 million. Where did he get that number? "All the products in my portfolio generate revenues between $50 and $100 million a year," he stated. "So, to be conservative, I'm pegging this one at the low end of the range." Team members were stunned. Each of the other products in the VP's portfolio had been on the market for *at least* five years, established markets at that. New market applications, they argued, followed a different pattern: They started small, attracting lead users, and then diffused to a broader set of adopters over time. The VP wasn't buying this reasoning; $50 million was the number. To support that higher revenue projection, the team would need an additional $10 million for first-year advertising and promotion. Team members knew that there was no way that first-year sales would exceed $15 million. And piling $15 million in sunk costs onto the P&L before the first dollar of revenue was earned would doom the venture to failure. It would probably never generate an attractive return, no matter how well sales grew in outlying years.

The lesson in this story is that a qualified person, a core member of the innovation team, should take the first crack at the numbers. The entire team should then discuss the outcome. Everyone, even the engineers, needs to understand the numbers and contribute to them. A diversity of skills and insights is helpful whenever forecasts are made. For teams creating new product lines or services, that diversity may be represented by people who may or may not be on the team, for example, a salesperson, a financial expert, a manufacturing manager, and someone with a distribution and logistical background. Their inputs lead to a realistic P&L and capital plan. Then, you've simply got to stick to your plan and try your best to stand up to unreasoned pressures from above.

With a financial plan in hand, and prototypes developed with the methods described earlier, a team should get its green light from senior management. It then enters the realm of organization and execution—the topics of our two remaining chapters.

### Reader Exercises

The reader exercises involve building a financial model for your new market application. These projected financial statements, together with product prototypes vetted with users, are where the rubber meets the road in our management framework from the second chapter (figure 2.2).Here, you are beginning to make commitments to how you see the business evolving, and this is the essence of making the business case. Use the templates of this chapter as a starting point, and then adjust them to your own type of business. Be forewarned, these exercises are by no means trivial tasks, be they undertaken by teams of practitioners or students. There is, however, so much to be learned in that effort. Too often, teams rest just with their product prototypes. These exercises are intended to reveal prototypes of the business—which at the end of day, *is the point.*

**Exercise 1** Storyboard the business plan for your new product line or service by using the template shown in figure 11.1. This requires that you have first thought through your business model (using the templates from chapter 9). Show the results to trusted colleagues. That figure will force you to discuss your new market application not just as the application of a technology but also as a business. Keep your presentation brief, even a series of bullet points within the template, written on a large whiteboard. As you change one particular set of bullet points, be sure to see the implications for strategies in other parts of the business plan storyboard. In many ways, you are designing a system—for a business in this case, as opposed to the products or services within it.

**Exercise 2** Next, take a first crack at volume and revenue projections for your new product line. Carry the numbers into a pro forma P&L following the template in figure 11.2. (If you are developing a service, go to www.fastpathlearning.com and download the services template.) Then, work through the cost of goods and the variable expenses associated with the business. Work toward a projection of operating profit.

**Exercise 3** Think about the capital investments needed to get your product or service line off the ground. Make adjustments to the operating earnings for cash flow. Then, use the template in figure 11.3 to take a first crack at measures of performance in terms of sales growth, operating profit, NPV, and capital utilization. Also show these results to trusted colleagues.

**Exercise 4** Next, obtain your company's official templates for financial planning, and understand what other data you need to complete them satisfactorily. You may find a few surprises, so leave yourself plenty of time. Try to find a finance colleague who will give you a guided tour through the company's own templates for P&L and capital planning.

Perhaps that finance colleague will also be able to show you financial projections developed for a new product line or service launched by your company sometime during the past five years. If you can do this, ask how that team made its projections, how those projected fared, the particular landmines that team encountered, and how it navigated through or around them. It would be unrealistic to think that you will not face many of the same issues.

## Notes

1. William Strunk, E. B. White, and Roger Angell, *The Elements of Style*, 4th ed. (Needham Heights, MA: Allyn and Bacon, 2000), 23.

2. "Pricing New Products," *The McKinsey Quarterly* (McKinsey & Co, New York), June 15, 2004.

3. For a brief overview of NPV calculations, see www.venturechoice.com/articles/valuation_methods.htm.

4. Source: www.venturechoice.com/articles/valuation_methods.htm.

5. Jeffery Cornwall, David Vang, and Jean Hartman, *Entrepreneurial Financial Management* (Upper Saddle River, NJ: Pearson, 2004), 120.

6. James Womack and Daniel Jones's book, *Lean Thinking*, remains a good guide for increasing operations efficiency (New York: Free Press, 2003).

7. R. Quinn, G. Causey, and F. Merat, "The Design of an Agile Manufacturing Workcell for Light Mechanical Operations," *Proceedings: IEEE Transactions on Design and Manufacturing*, 1997, 29(10): 901–9.

8. Robert Hayes and Steven Wheelwright, *Restoring Our Competitive Edge: Competing through Manufacturing* (New York: Wiley, 1984), 213.

9. Wickham Skinner, "The Focused Factory," *Harvard Business Review*, 1974, May–June, 113–21.

# CHAPTER TWELVE

# Executive Decision Making

*An executive board for new market applications*
*development—Staging investments—Pragmatic guideposts for*
*investment—Creating entrepreneurial teams within mature*
*companies—Whether to reintegrate new product lines back*
*into mainstream operations or create a new business unit.*

The framework for new market applications development highlighted in chapter 2 (and reprinted here for the reader's convenience in figure 12.1) serves as a new business development process. Every process, to be effective, requires an owner. In this case, the owners of the framework of figure 12.1 should be a few select executives who take personal responsibility and who are intellectually and emotionally committed to organic, enterprise growth. They comprise a special-purpose executive board. The new market applications development process and the projects flowing through it are their direct responsibility.

## A New Market Applications Board

Think of this executive body as owning the corporation's *new market applications* for internal, organically grown ventures. I will refer to it simply as "the Board" for the rest of this chapter. Your company may already have a structure that serves the purpose; most companies I studied did not. The Board defines strategic opportunities at the highest level (new product line or service opportunities that may exist in current or new market segments), launches teams

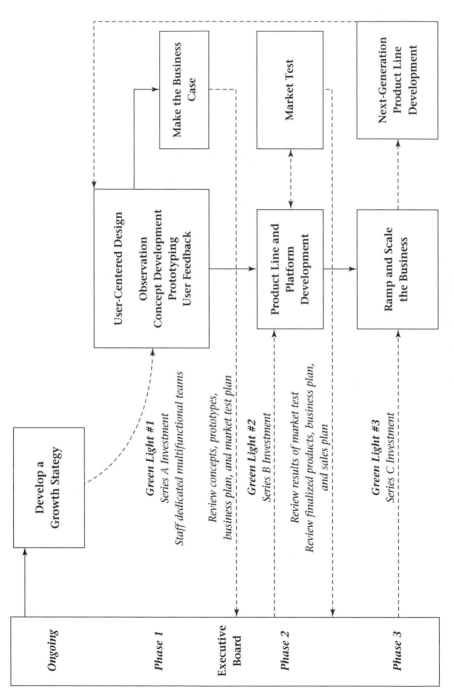

FIGURE 12.1 Executive Green Lights

and then responds to progress at key checkpoints in the development process, and provides the necessary funding to support the next phase of a team's growth.

Why form a special executive board for new market applications? Why not just run these projects through the company's existing business process for new product development and capital procurement? The answer is that a firm's efforts to leverage its technology to new market applications tend to be beaten down by traditional organizational structures and review and approval processes.[1]

Conversely, why not run new market application developments through a special *corporate venture capital* group? Henry Chesbrough has described how corporate venture capital units typically make investments in new companies, often in syndication with other venture capital firms, to achieve a return on investment and gain a window on new technology.[2] For the types of development projects described here, where the company's technology is leveraged to new users or new uses, a corporate venture capital approach can have its own problems. In the companies studied, innovation teams treated as external ventures found it difficult to access the R&D and manufacturing capabilities of their parent companies. They were treated as outsiders—and often resented.

If not a corporate venture capital group, then what? McKinsey & Company's "horizon" framework for distinguishing between different types of innovations provides a useful mechanism for linking management structure with the type of project at hand. First, McKinsey calls sustaining or incremental innovations Horizon 1 (H1) activities. These are incremental improvements to the company's existing product lines or services, sold to the same users for the same uses with the same business model and through the same channels. In many industries, H1 project decisions are often handled through the annual budget. Then, there are Horizon 2 (H2) initiatives. These tend to be the two- to three-year projects; the new market applications described in this book are examples of H2 activity. Finally, there are Horizon 3 (H3) projects. These are long-tailed disruptive technology developments, taking five years or longer to see the first real dollar of revenue.[3]

How should companies make high-level decisions, including funding, on H1, H2, and H3 projects? Generally, H1 projects—incremental innovations—are served best by an executive structure and process in which strategic business unit functional executives pass judgment on projects using traditional stage-gate methodology. H2 projects—our new market applications—require a focused executive structure and process, as shown in figure 12.1. I also believe that executive bodies governing new market applications should be formed for each major business unit in the corporation. If a company has three separate business units, each one should be trying to leverage its technology to new market applications to create new streams of revenue. This will further focus the Board's attention on a select few projects and help to make sure that each business unit is seeking to make its own contribution to organic, enterprise growth. Keeping such boards within SBU's keeps them close to adjacent markets and mindful of leveraging the in SBU's particular technology and that of the SBU's closest partners.

The H3 projects focus on technology breakthroughs—often a new generation of a mainstream technology or a total substitute for that technology. These can be approached in three ways:

1. Through long-term internal R&D. Once such technologies of these projects are functional, they can be transferred to new market application executive boards for application to the marketplace.
2. Through a corporate venture capital unit, as previously described, which makes early equity investments in entrepreneurial firms with promising technology.
3. By licensing that technology from a third party. Once the technology is proven, outright acquisition of the entrepreneurial supplier may be in order.

## Board Members and Their Responsibilities

Logically, the general manager of the business unit should chair the Board. If the business unit *is* the corporation, then the chair should be the CEO. In either case, this individual has responsibility for the good of the "whole" business and recognizes that a dollar spent here is a dollar that cannot be spent elsewhere. But "our CEO is far too busy to serve on this type of Board," you say. Well, if the leader of the corporation is not personally committed to enterprise growth, who is?

A marketing executive should also be on the Board to help identify and prioritize new market targets and channel decisions. To better assess technical feasibility and ensure robust product or service implementation, an R&D or IT executive should have a place at the table. Just as innovation teams require marketing, R&D, and financial expertise, so, too, the Board needs a balance of skills. These executives have specific responsibilities:

— Segmenting markets for growth at the highest level, a continuous process that should be crystallized into an annual review and perhaps a resetting of the company's growth agenda

— Identifying opportunities in which the company will invest
— Staffing innovation teams and choosing their leaders
— Deciding how many growth opportunities to pursue at one time
— Securing and staging funds for working teams
— Shielding infant new product lines from the business norms that apply better to established ones
— Deciding whether a successful new product line should stand on its own or merge into an existing business unit

These are difficult chores, and because they involve the company's future, they should command board members' full attention. That is easier said than done, because so much of every executive's attention is absorbed by the requirements of the ongoing business. That business cannot be ignored because it provides the month-to-month revenues that pay the bills and keep shareholders happy.

There is no question that keeping an existing business running smoothly is a full-time job. Michael Tushman and Charles O'Reilly have said that executives must be "ambidextrous," capable of partitioning their attention between the current business and the future business, but few in my study were able to give the latter its proper due.[4] New market applications are the crucibles of every company's future and deserve dedicated executive attention. They should be the clear responsibility of several key leaders and take a significant portion of their time, thought, and attention.

## Executive Involvement

Executive involvement in the new market application projects described in this book must be more intense than what we typically find in today's "best practice" for new product development: the stage-gate system. The stage-gate system features a series of development "stages" and review "gates" through which a new product concept must progress. The system aims to eliminate weak and technically unworkable ideas and move the best ideas more quickly to market. Executives use the review gates to make "go, no-go" decisions.[5] Projects that fail to pass through a review gate are either killed, placed in limbo, or sent back for more work until another review meeting can be scheduled, often many months later.

Given this arrangement, an executive's involvement with development projects is intermittent; he or she is not likely to feel the pulse of the project. Typical executives on a stage-gate committee review team documents shortly before the meeting and do so from the perspective of their own functions. There is simply insufficient time to take a holistic perspective. "Jump in" and "jump out" is the modus operandi.

The efficacy of stage gate systems has been demonstrated for incremental or sustaining innovations.[6] However, new market applications—McKinsey's H2 endeavors—require a different form of executive involvement. That is why many of the most successful new product lines or services in the companies I studied were created *outside* conventional review and resource allocation systems and entered back into it only upon "ramp up and scale."

In most companies, 95 percent of the typical executive's time is spent managing *the current business* and implementing incremental improvements to current products and services. Most of these executives were highly supportive of new market application developments but were simply too consumed with day-to-day issues to spend much time on them. *They deferred to a small set of executive colleagues who focused on that task and were held accountable for it.*

Of those executives who sat on boards focused on new product line and service development, the most effective viewed themselves as corporate venture capitalists. Indeed, building a new business within an established one requires a venture capital mind-set, and it provides a useful model for executive involvement. Consider what experienced venture capitalists (VCs) actually do. They:

— serve on the boards of the start-ups they finance;
— are viscerally engaged and meet regularly to discuss progress and problems in both strategic and tactical areas of concern;
— keep in contact with potential customers, suppliers, distributors, and outside technical experts;
— stage the financing of projects as they move from development to initial launch, and then toward market and product line expansion;
— assess the performance of key team members, replacing personnel when necessary; they understand that personalities suited for start-up are not necessarily suited for later growth; and
— pull the plug on projects that fail to meet reasonable milestones or simply fail to pass the test of either test marketing or financial return.

This is hardly hands-off behavior. No wise VC in a start-up would remain detached between major rounds of financing. Yet, that is what conventional product development review systems encourage executives to do. That behavior is all right for incremental or sustaining innovations whose market, technical, and financial uncertainties are largely resolved; for these, success is largely a matter of timely and effective execution. New market applications, however, are riddled with uncertainty in each of these areas, and a detached executive runs the risk of making uninformed and incorrect decisions.

## Green Lights for Phased Investment

Although a full-blown stage-gate system is not recommended for new market application projects, a set of major executive decision points is nevertheless needed. The reader might consider the following proposal a "modified" phase review process that uses the framework presented earlier in this book as the basis for reviews or "green lights" leading to further investment.

The first green light comes when the Board is sufficiently satisfied with the opportunities revealed by market segmentation. An innovation team is formed and set to its task at this point. The funds and time frame assigned to this phase are analogous to a venture capital firm's initial (Series A) investment; management approves the resources required for user research, concept development, and prototype development.

The second green light follows on positive results of those activities and leads to a larger investment. This is analogous to the venture capitalist's Series B round of financing. The resources approved at this point are for full-scale architecture, platform, and product line or service development, as well as for costs incurred in test-marketing or beta testing.

The successful conclusion of those activities results in the third green light. That approval triggers financing for increased production and intensive market development. This is analogous to the Series C investment of venture capital firms. For capital-intensive industries, this is the point at which requests for the purchase of machines and plant retooling are made. At the same time, an innovation team should have proposed both a strategy and resource plan required for next-generation development—essential activities for maintaining and capitalizing on its market lead.

These green light sessions are special meetings, focused on next-round funding appropriate for the next phase of growth for each project. As noted earlier, the involvement of the Board must be continuous so that when it enters these funding sessions, it is already well informed on all aspects of the emerging business. In most instances, the funding decision is known before the meeting, and the meeting itself is an opportunity for the Board to set future milestones for the project.

Once a reasonable degree of market penetration has been gained, the Board faces another key decision: whether the market application should be folded into an existing business unit or spun out as a distinct business unit. That decision point may mark an end point of a team's life in this special process, upon which it enters the corporation's standard business processes for planning and capital allocation. I think of this as "mainstreaming" success.

In summary, the market applications framework has three green lights, which respond to very basic questions at each major phase of the framework:

— Green Light 1: Do we have the right growth strategy and customer targets? Have we segmented our markets for growth, or are we simply working on the same old uses by our traditional target users? Positive answers lead to team staffing and the first level of funding.
— Green Light 2: Do we have a prototype that excites target users and a business plan that points to a viable business? Here, positive answers lead to the next level of investment—greater than the first—for full product and process specification and development, as well as reasonably fast market testing.
— Green Light 3: Has the team figured out how to produce the concept in high volume, and is investment in that capability justified by an actual market test? Positive answers lead to a much larger investment in tooling or outsourced manufacturing, as well as to channel development and aggressive marketing.

Figure 12.2 provides a summary of the issues and decisions at each step of the process. The executive board must also choose the appropriate organizational home for this ramp-up phase. Should it be placed under an existing brand or product line group, and report to the general manager of that group? Or should the fledgling product line or service become a new P&L center reporting directly to the general manager of the strategic business unit? Either way, it is at this point that a project may be ready to enter into the corporation's more standard business processes.

The Board must also have a careful eye on the team's proposal for next-generation R&D, for without it, market leadership cannot be sustained. Competitors will try to mimic a company's early success with a new market application, perhaps using their own existing scale of manufacturing and distribution to take back the market from the new entrant. The best way to fight them is with more product or service innovation, combined with a very focused and determined marketing effort.

| Funding Points | Information/Learnings Reviewed | Actions Taken | Elapsed Time |
|---|---|---|---|
| **Green Light # 1** | • Market segmentation<br>• Analysis of (new) competitors<br>• Find gaps and opportunities to leverage technology | • Launch innovation team(s)<br>• Joint work needed with R&D centers and other product/service teams | Continuous, leading to project start-up |
| **Green Light # 2** | • Review concepts, prototypes, and user feedback<br>• Business plan<br>• Market test plan | • Proceed to full product and process development, plus market test | 6 to 12 months |
| **Green Light # 3** | • Review improved product<br>• Market test results<br>• Revised business plan<br>• Sales—launch plan | • Go /no-go on launch.<br>• Capitalize and install assets or systems<br>• Organizational decision: spin into existing P&L, or create a new P&L (depends on product or service positioning and business model) | + 6 to 24 months (depends on industry) |

FIGURE 12.2 Executive Funding Points: Review and Action

Our management framework (figure 12.1) and its green lights give senior management a better handle on risk. Although the size of investments varies, their proportions follow a general pattern, with modest outlays at the beginning, followed by increasing outlays as the project moves forward.

## The Budget

The Board must have a dedicated budget for new market applications development. That budget should be large enough to handle two or three projects running parallel in each of the three phases of the new market applications business processs. (Remember, the first activity box, Develop a Growth Strategy, should be an ongoing process for the business unit as a whole, rather than a phase of development for each innovation team.) The reader can do a rough calculation of the general costs for the activities for the first two phases of the framework for his or her company, multiply those by three, and then sum the numbers. That number should be the executive board's budget, year after year. Phase 3, ramp up and scale, should be funded through an existing business unit or by new funds allocated to the product line or service's own business unit. Either way, those funds for ramp up and scale should be allocated through the corporation's standing budgeting process.

I have referred to the successive stages of investment in figure 12.1 as Series A, B, and C. This follows standard terminology for rounds of increased investment for start-ups from venture capital. In the world of start-ups, a syndicate of venture capitalists may invest $2 million to $4 million for Series A, $6 million to $12 million for Series B, and $12 million to $20 million or more for Series C. A blue-chip venture capital fund of $500 million will have between 10 and 20 firms in which its managers might be prepared to invest upward of $30 to $50 million in successive rounds of financing prior to exiting via a sale or initial public offering. Spreading the funding across that many start-ups gives them the diversification and risk management they need.

The numbers cited for the VC's Series A, B, and C investments are not unreasonable for a corporation developing a new market application: $2 million for market research and prototype development and $6 million for full product and process development. These sums fall under the Board's budget. And $12 million or more for higher volume manufacturing, channel development, and aggressive promotion is not unreasonable for a number of the industries studied. That investment falls under an existing business unit's budget or becomes the budget for a new business unit created to house the new product line or service.

Given the sums involved, it would be unrealistic for most companies to play the role of VC and have a portfolio of 10 to 20 new internal market applications in play at any given time. And it is not just a matter of money. An executive team focused on two or three projects—and examining them well—is more likely to produce success than a group whose attention is fragmented across 10 projects. Having two or three significant new market applications beginning to generate new revenue each year represents the high end in my study. When one of these enters the next phase of our framework, it is appropriate to have a new project enter the process. It is all about focus.

Every company must determine the magnitude of investment that makes sense, given the company's size, competitive position, and aspirations. Among the companies studied, IBM literally bet its future on its new market application: e-business. It spent approximately $1 billion for the scale and ramp-up of its e-business brand, as well as an undisclosed but certainly large amount on R&D for its new RISC processor, the microcode (for the multipoint switching in the intelligent resource director), and making Linux operate on these platforms in the product and process development phase. Honda's nine-month prototype and business plan development, performed by a small, focused team within its product planning group, was done at reasonable cost. However, the investments needed to retool the Civic line in Ohio to manufacture the Element were clearly large. Most of the other new market applications I studied, however, received much smaller investments.

Regardless of investment size, a phased approach to investing that matches the three phases of new market application development is a sensible way of managing risk under conditions of market, technical, and financial uncertainty. "We spent too much money too early—before we understood the distribution and financial implications of the new concept," complained one executive. The three-phase framework can help a company avoid that mistake. Investments to expand manufacturing and distribution are made only *after* many of the unknowns are clarified. Or, within the Phase 2 of the framework, heavy product refinements can be made after the results of test-marketing are in and the needs for product refinements are better understood. As another manager noted, "Once we've committed capital to a high-volume production line, that's pretty much it for major product changes, at least for a number of years." The approach shown in figure 12.1 makes it possible to "launch and learn" without having to be perfect in all respects.

Projects whose products or services require key technologies that are yet to be proven should be left to mature in R&D. Once these technologies have ripened to the point of being operational platforms, then the projects become good candidates to pass the first green light and, for example, be staffed with a multifunctional team.

---

**Practical Criteria for Launching New Projects**

---

Most companies have more opportunities than resources. The business executives with whom I worked in developing this book suggested the following criteria for new market application initiatives:

— Projects should leverage company technology—either product or process.
— Projects should target either new users relative to core business or new uses for products or services by current users. Projects operating within this framework should not be incremental product development activities that current business units should be doing already. Using this process to siphon resources from business and R&D managers in these groups for work that they should already be performing will only cause resentment and create barriers for reintegration later on.
— Every project should be assigned, at the beginning, an experienced full-time market professional and a full-time technical person. Consumer product or consumer durables manufacturers might find that they also need a manufacturing or supply professional right from the beginning as a full-time team member. Further staffing needs can then be determined as the project proceeds forward.
— No more than two or three projects should be chartered in any given year, even within a $1 billion-plus business unit. It is better to do a few things well than many things poorly. This is clearly different from a traditional venture capital portfolio management approach, where having many ongoing projects reduces overall risk. Here, a company places strategic bets on a few things. The risk profile of each effort is reduced, however, by the fact that the company is leveraging its technology—refining and applying it—to new users and uses. The risk is therefore that of understanding users, channels, and, potentially, new business models.

## Creating and Sustaining Teams: Rules of Engagement

Some companies have attempted to develop new product lines by placing development teams *outside* the organization—in distant skunk works. This approach is supposed to protect teams from forces within the company that would undermine them in hopes of protecting the status quo and from bureaucracies that would sap their time and innovative spirits. This might be okay for the H3-type projects described earlier, but it can be a fatal mistake for a new market applications team that needs access to customers, technology, and other resources inside the company.

The benefits to this skunk works approach—such as independence and autonomy for team members—are outweighed by the demerits. As one manager put it, "In the past, we would innovate on the other side of the parking lot, and come back in two years if we had a real business. Management would then decide whether to keep it or spin it off. This never seemed to work." Indeed, externalizing innovation creates serious problems: The externalized project is quickly forgotten by colleagues working in the belly of the corporation—people whose help is sorely needed to leverage technologies and exploit existing channels and marketing relationships.

Externalizing development is also a bad idea from a human resource perspective. "Going over to the other side of the parking lot" is the last thing that many talented innovators want to do, especially those who aspire to a long and successful career with the company. Few people are eager to place themselves, their careers, and the financial well-being of their families at risk. In any case, the real risk takers will have left the corporation already—to start their own firms. To grow through internal means, a company must *retain* talented and effective managers and staff. It shouldn't hang them out on a limb or divest them along with the new applications they create.

The approach that has worked best for firms I studied can be described as "a company within the company," a colocated team that works in close proximity to key technological and marketing personnel to create new businesses. The team may be located next to a pilot line, or it might be located next to R&D. We saw that Honda's Element team shifted locations in each of the three key phases of our framework. During the prototype and business plan development phase, the team's work was based at the design center in California; for product and process development, it moved to the R&D facility in Ohio; and for scale and ramp-up, it moved to the assembly plant some five miles away. Other companies studied created specific new divisions to house new brand or business development that, at least in the beginning, draws heavily on the resources of the rest of the corporation.

Even when a team is kept on "this side of the parking lot," it needs a clear set of rules for engaging with the rest of the enterprise.

— Priority access to R&D. Even when a team has its own R&D staff, chances are that it will require access to more central groups for certain activities, such as integrating in current technologies or product platforms. If R&D does not give the fledging group attention, progress will grind to a halt. This also argues for the executive board in figure 12.1 having a current R&D executive as a member.

— Access to plants. If the firm has a pilot or scale-up plant to handle new product lines, its innovation teams have a tremendous advantage. A team requires "time on the line" to produce initial products for market testing and launch. In the companies I studied, this proved to be a serious and highly charged problem. The company must give the team product runs as needed or allow it to use a contract manufacturer.

— Access to key customers for concept development and test. A company's largest customers are often carefully protected from innovators, even if those customers are hungry for new products and services. A team needs access to such customers to test concepts, product positioning, and marketing strategies.

— The ability to set its own sales projections and other related numbers. The previous chapter described the hazards that befall a project when someone who is not a team member commandeers their revenue projections. The executive board must insist that its teams retain control of that important function.

These rules of engagement are best captured in a team charter, an example of which was described in the My M&M's case (figure 10.2). Signatories of such charters should include both the Board members and the CEO. The terms of the charter should provide autonomy for key decisions. Innovation projects falter when functional fiefdoms knowingly or unknowingly undermine their work. The CEO's signature on the team's charter says: "This is important to me and to the company." The team should frame its signed charter and display it prominently.

## Where to from Here?

The success of a new market application forces the Board to make one final decision: Should the successfully, market tested new product or service stand alone as a business unit, or should it be subsumed within an existing unit?

Most of the projects studied for this book did not qualify for new business unit status but fit comfortably within existing units. The software product lines developed by The MathWorks's innovation teams described in chapter 5 are a case in point. Once developed, these products found a natural fit within the company's operating business.

Those separated did so primarily because *their business models were unique.* The new software for manufacturing validation developed by Mentor Graphics (described in chapter 3) was given P&L center status because it targeted new users and had a different business model relative to the company's other software. Or consider My M&M's. Physically, the product was very much like standard M&M's candies—only the customized printing on one side set it apart. However, everything else about how the product was ordered, manufactured, packaged, priced, and distributed was different. Because of those differences, it made sense to place My M&M's in its own P&L center that reported directly to the president. In fact, putting the new product line under the thumb of the standard M&M's unit would have deprived it of the attention needed for further product and market development.

Each choice—to spin out or spin in—has pluses and minuses. These must be weighed carefully by the Board and the rest of the senior management team.

Executives have a key role in bringing successful new market applications to life. If your company already has a special process for handling new market applications, that's great. If not, or if that process is not producing results, it may be because of how executives participate and interact with teams.

The governing board and processes described in these pages are tuned to the needs of developing and growing new product lines and services. It ensures *active engagement* in new product line and service development. At the same time, that involvement must be appropriate. Armed with experience and insight, Board members must nonetheless try to resist making a team's key decisions. This is a very fine but clear line. Innovation teams must be encouraged to make their own market, business model, and technical decisions. It is all too easy for an executive to step in and say, "I'll have my marketing group create your product concept" or "I will decide where you will manufacture your product." Instead, the executive should be a coach who asks for the team's process in making its decisions, helps to improve it, and responds to team results. A team will work much harder if it knows that the decisions are its own and that it is responsible for them. The executive's role is to anticipate and secure the human and financial resources necessary for innovation teams to work well and work fast.

We now turn to team leaders and their staffs. If you are a new market applications team leader, or aspire to be one, how can you be most effective? The answer to that question is the subject of our next and final chapter.

## Notes

1. Robert D. Hisrich and Michael P. Peter, "Establishing a New Business Unit within a Firm," *Journal of Business Venturing*, 1986, 1, 307–22.

2. Henry Chesbrough, "Making Sense of Corporate Venture Capital," *Harvard Business Review*, 2002, 80(3): 4–11.

3. Mehrdad Baghai, Stephen Coley, and David White, *The Alchemy of Growth: Practical Insights for Building the Enduring Enterprise* (Cambridge, MA: Perseus, 1999).

4. Michael Tushman and Charles O'Reilly III, *Winning through Innovation* (Boston: Harvard Business School Press, 1997), 219.

5. Robert G. Cooper, *Winning at New Product: Accelerating the Process from Idea to Launch* (New York: Perseus, 2001).

6. Michael McGrath, *Product Strategy for High Technology Companies* (Chicago: McGraw-Hill, 2000).

# CHAPTER THIRTEEN

# Leading Teams to Growth

*Can you be a team leader?—Forming empowered teams—*
*Characteristics of the team leader—Staffing teams—*
*Organizational placement of innovation teams—The job of*
*the team leader—Keeping top management informed.*

Previous chapters have described a framework (see figure 2.2) for fueling enterprise growth by leveraging technologies to new market applications. That framework is applicable to all types of companies, as reflected by the research sample for this book.

If you are a manager—in R&D, marketing, manufacturing, business development, or some other key function—you are probably wondering, "This sounds great, but how can I put this approach to work in my company?" That's the right question to ask, because the answer begins with people just like you. The management framework and the templates that operationalize it are no more than a mental concept that, no matter how intellectually appealing, is totally useless until an individual with personal drive and organizational skill pulls together a capable team and implements it. If you are such a person, this chapter is written for you.

## Do You Have the Right Stuff to Lead?

After selecting its innovation and business development target, the Board described in the previous chapter must pick a project leader and then help build a winning team around that individual. Executives should know that their choice of team leader will make or break the effort, no matter how attractive the business and market opportunity.

So, are you that person? Do you have what it takes to work effectively on the activities described in our framework, to create new businesses and not just new products or technologies?

## No Magic Formula

When we look at a leader, many of us say to ourselves, "I would like to be like him." Well, you are never going to be exactly like that person—that's not possible. The real question is what were that leader's qualifications before being asked to lead the team, what skills did he or she demonstrate on the path toward success, and do *you* have the foundation of experience and skills you can use to venture forward?

The debate regarding who should lead enterprise growth often leads to a conventional discussion of background and affiliations: "Must have an MBA. Must have P&L experience. Must have been an entrepreneur. Must have sales experience." Be skeptical of formulas that dictate the characteristics of effective leaders, particularly when novel and integrative applications of company technologies are involved. Consider these examples of successful team leaders for new product lines and services observed in my studies:

— The leader of a new medical robotics team was a music major in college and had served as a product/market manager for the firm. In mid-career, he entered an evening MBA program.
— The leader of an insurance services development team had an operations background and was already a seasoned manager with years of health care industry experience.
— The leader of a new agricultural products team came out of product management but had deep technical knowledge. He was also a weekend farmer.
— The leader of The MathWorks financial services team had database experience and a deep understanding of the target domain.
— The leaders of the various Mars initiatives included mid-career professionals with strong backgrounds in process engineering, food science, and marketing.
— The large project leader for the original Element team was an expert in flexible seating design. The leader who followed for the next model was also a senior R&D manager. Their assistant large project leaders had backgrounds in sales, manufacturing, and R&D.

— The leader of a risk management information services team was an expert in risk management in a particular domain and had worked in consulting services with clients for many years.

— The head of the reinsurance innovation cited earlier was not only the head of underwriting but was also recognized as an exceptional salesperson and client manager.

## This Can Be You

So, what did these team leaders have in common? Here are four key traits that can be readily measured and three that cannot:

1. *A balanced view of the world where marketing, technology, and finance make equal contributions to enterprise growth.* In certain industries, a healthy respect for manufacturing and supply was also essential. "Our team leaders must understand the technology and how it can be applied to benefit customers," noted one executive. This can be objectively seen in a person's record of accomplishment. Have you ever defined, built, or marketed a commercial success? Have you ever worked outside a particular function, such as R&D? If you haven't, try to get an assignment that gives you that different perspective.

2. *Maturity and organizational credibility.* "We can't give these projects to freshly minted MBAs with little work experience. Those people might be good team members, but not leaders who can drive projects through the organization." You should have at least five years of work experience before seeking leadership of a new market application project.

3. *Customer experience.* Said one executive, "A team leader without direct customer experience, or R&D people who've never worked face-to-face with customers would be disastrous." If you have not had direct customer experience and want to become a team leader on enterprise growth projects, transfer to a position that will give you that exposure.

4. *Comfortable working with the numbers.* An innovation team must own its numbers, but it can't do that if its leader does not understand the basics of financial analysis. A leader with demonstrated competence in developing revenue and cost estimates will earn the respect of senior management and of the company's financial staff. Finance people appreciate anyone who can speak their language.

---

**How IBM Provides Its Managers with Fresh Perspectives**

---

IBM makes a deliberate practice of placing its managers into different functional and customer-interfacing roles and responsibilities. For example, the executive who helped me with the first chapter of this book leads the portfolio management team for the company's mainframe server hardware products. Over the past decade, he had been team leader for development of an early zSeries machine, manager of IBM's all-important Wal-Mart account, director of the manufacturability test group sitting between R&D and assembly plants, and also at one time the head of IBM's program management group. His career migration, while exceptional to those of us reading this book, is by no means exceptional within IBM's top management. Seeing the business from all sides is a necessary qualification for promotion—as well as for company survival.

---

Each of those four traits can be measured to some degree. Three other essential team leader traits cannot be measured as easily, but you'll know if you have them.

— *The ability to communicate.* Good leaders excel at getting the message across and giving it weight. They communicate both *what* must be done and *why* it is important to the audience. They deliver the message in a way that inspires confidence—among team members and sponsoring executives. These people also know that listening is an essential part of communicating.

— *A flexible outlook.* In every development project, some things inevitably go wrong. A prototype cannot be made to work correctly. A valuable team member leaves at midstream to take a job elsewhere. A market test produces disappointing results. An able team leader isn't paralyzed by such problems and, instead, brings people together, troubleshoots the situation, and gets people to develop an alternative course of action.

— *A passionate champion.* All things being equal, executives back individuals who demonstrate true passion. Passionate people are committed, which means that they are not easily discourage by small failures or diverted by other opportunities. They are "junk yard dogs" who will not let go. Equally important, their passion is infectious, which translates into a circle of equally committed and determined confederates.

## Building a Team

New product and service development is too big a task for any one person to handle, no matter how inspired or brilliant. No one can take this journey alone. If you aim to succeed, make sure that you get senior management to understand the importance of dedicated resources. Then, build a team.

What type of team do you need? What skills and talents should be included? The best way to answer these questions is to enumerate all the tasks and subtasks required to turn a raw idea into a budding business. Our growth framework (figure 2.1) can help you with that chore. By design, that framework encompasses all the challenging things a team must do to develop a new business: segment the market, conduct user research, design and test prototypes, put together a business case, design the product subsystems and interfaces, and so forth. Your team must include people who are either experienced in those activities or capable of handling them.

So make an inventory of the capabilities you need, and then start matching names to those necessary capabilities. Figure 13.1 contains a staff template you can use for this purpose. As you develop your team roster, keep the following ideas in mind.

You will have to go through the organization and recruit individuals who you feel are best suited for the tasks at hand. If they are good, most likely they will already be busy. Have your sales pitch ready. Talk just as much about the business that can emerge as the new products or services within it. Also, the issue of executive sponsorship will invariably come up, so be prepared to address it.

A team has two aspects: specific functional skills needed to do the work and personalities that lend themselves toward integration of those skills, such as team work.

### Build around a Solid Core

Because new market application developments require intense work, a solid core of full-time members is essential. For the first phase of the framework—concept, prototype, and business plan development—you will require dedicated resources for the user research and prototyping work and some committed part-time resources in the financial area. Then, as the project proceeds to more complete product line development and market testing, more staff will be needed. There is so much work to be done to execute strategies and plans that one or two dedicated team members would quickly feel isolated and underresourced. They would have to beg and borrow from across the organization to get anything done. Some team members, however, can and should be part-time;

| Market Research | |
|---|---|
| Joe | |
| Sarah | |
| | |

*Fill in these tables...*

**Team Leader**
*Name*    *Current Job*

| Steve | |
|---|---|
| | |

| Manufacturing, Production | |
|---|---|
| Karen | |
| Ralph | |
| | |

**Engineering, Development**

| Joyce | |
|---|---|
| Rob | |
| | |

**Sales, Channel Dev.**

| Scott | |
|---|---|
| | |
| | |

**Support Functions**
Legal, Finance, HR

| Lee | Finance |
|---|---|
| Tom | Legal |
| | |

FIGURE 13.1  The Team Template

just steer clear of individuals whose attention is fragmented by too many other duties. For the last phase of our framework, the ramp-up and scale of these new product lines and services can be appropriately determined to match the growth of the new business.

### The Membership Roster May Expand or Contract as the Project Moves Forward

The need for new skills will emerge as the effort proceeds. Jon Katzenbach and Douglas Smith have noted, "Most teams figure out the skills they will need *after* [my emphasis] they are formed."[1] The new skill might be the ability to understand a new channel or some new area of technology or science that emerges as a key enabler for the new product line or service. So be prepared to adjust the team to the shifting demands of the business.

### Use as Few People as Needed to Do the Job

More people translates into more coordination problems, more meetings, and more reports, each of which will consume energy. You do not have to accept an individual you know to be substandard. This will only slow you down. Resist!

---

**Four Screening Questions**

Four simple screening questions can help a team leader determine if a person has the right stuff to be on a new market applications development team:

1. In the area that you need filled, does this person know his or her "stuff"? Where is the proof? How much learning needs to be done, and does this person have the time to do that?
2. Has this person ever achieved concrete goals and delivered tangible results in a timely way? You require doers.
3. Has this individual ever done anything truly innovative—in product design, marketing, or business modeling? Someone who does not enjoy creativity or risk taking is not suited to this endeavor.
4. Does this person have a reputation as a good team player? This can be assessed with a few phone calls to colleagues in the corporation.

You can find answers to these questions during your first interview. Finish the interview by asking the individual to think about the business opportunity, visit some prospective users, and think about problems and solutions. *What frustrates our customers, and what can we do about it?* Regardless of function, each team member needs to be focused on markets and customers. A finance person, for example, who can help define user needs and solutions might prove to be one of your most powerful team members because he or she will be able to link the product or service concept to the business model and plan. Set up a second meeting with the prospective team member, perhaps at a customer site. After that meeting, and the diligence done before it, you will *know* if you have the right person for the job.

---

## Create the Right Work Environment

In the business of developing new market applications, real estate matters. Dedicated work space, co-location of key team members, and information persistence are the coins of the realm.

Even well-organized and wisely constituted teams will not optimize their performance if they don't have the right physical space in which to work, share information, and hold brainstorming sessions. Dedicated team space is needed. That type of space facilitates communications between team members from different functional area and imparts a unique sense of purpose.

---

**A Heavyweight Team in Action**

Honda (chapters 6 and 8) provides an example of what Steven Wheel-wright and Kim Clark called a heavyweight team, one supported by complementary resources.[2] Honda organizes new vehicle developments around teams that are explicitly multifunctional at the senior management level. Its organizing principle is the SED team: sales, engineering (i.e., manufacturing engineering), and development. The SED team leader has overall responsibility for completing development on time, on budget, and remaining true to the vision. Honda calls this person the "large project leader," or LPL.

Dedicated management personnel (assistant large project leaders or ALPLs) assist the LPL in controlling the project at the division level. Coming from sales, engineering, and R&D respectively, these ALPLs have strong working relationships with staff in their respective functions. Some 20 other senior engineers fill out the rest of the SED team. Called "project leaders," they manage specific activities with R&D or manufacturing. When work is needed for a particular subsystem, the ALPL and project leaders go into their functions to secure staff. The SED teams meet weekly from the point of business plan approval to launch.

As worked moves forward, the SED team grows in numbers to accommodate expertise in many different areas of vehicle development: interior packaging, seat performance, noise vibration, HVAC, vehicle dynamics and safety, reliability, and exterior design. Sales managers played an increasingly important role on the team as the project approached launch.

---

Figures 13.2 and 13.3 illustrate team space designs that have been effective for the companies observed in the study. Both of these physical arrangements provide a tangible home for the project and enhance a sense of membership among the individuals who, alone, are entitled to use it.

Figure 13.2 is a dedicated team room, where team members convene to work on joint activity. This space belongs exclusively to the team for the duration of the project, at least until the formal launch. It is not space that must be reserved in advance or vacated for others' use. It is always available to team members as a meeting space, a place to display prototypes and competing products, and a location where sketches, equations, and diagrams can be left on the whiteboard and revisited at a later date.

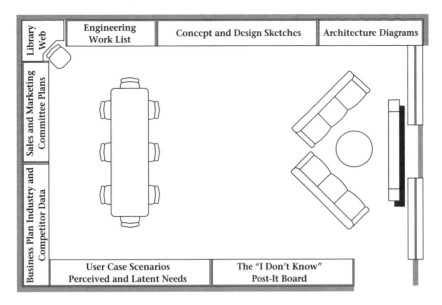

FIGURE 13.2 The Team Room

The second space is a clustering of team member desks and common space. This approach worked very well for several of the companies studied and is probably the better of the two arrangements. The cluster in figure 13.3 provides space for four workstations (perhaps for the project manager and three other full-time members), a conference table, and, like the other space arrangement, plenty of wall space for posting reports, schedules, diagrams, and so forth.

If you can get figure 13.3 for your project, take it! Figure 13.2 is powerful but second best. Of course, obtaining either may be difficult. Real estate is jealously guarded in mature corporations and is not easily freed up for new use. In more than one corporation I studied, dedicated space for new business development had to be carved out of spare storage space adjacent to a manufacturing facility.

Dedicated team rooms provide space where information and physical items, such as the disassembled products of competitors, can be displayed and shared. The use case scenarios and "personas" developed with the methods presented in our chapters on user-centered design clearly belong in the team room, as do design concepts and, if possible, the prototypes based on these concepts. Posters and whiteboards display sketches, user research results, and other information deemed essential for the integration design process. Key milestones and upcoming events should also be visibly posted. Engineers will want large whiteboards on which to draw and debate architectural choices. The team room should also have an "I Don't Know" area for posting unresolved questions.

FIGURE 13.3 The Team Office Cluster

For some of the companies studied, shared work spaces had a powerful effect on the interaction between development teams and the executives to whom they reported. Instead of passively listening to a team leader's progress report and sitting through a dull PowerPoint presentation, executives who entered the team room acquired a visceral sense of progress and future challenges. Videos put them in touch with the team's empathic observations of target users. They could see and manipulate prototypes and compare them with competitors' products.

This is why an innovation team should hold executive meetings in a team space whenever possible. Meetings held there create opportunities to show management prototypes, research data, progress along a graphic milestone map, and other displayed information. In fact, any excuse to lure a key executive into the team area is recommended. As one team leader put it, "We tried to catch certain executives in the cafeteria and bring them into our war room—that was our most effective strategy. We went through everything in those sessions and received great feedback, far deeper than what would come out in a formal review session where they were surrounded by their peers."

## Organizing Work during Those First Critical Months

It is obviously important to get a team off to a strong start. There is substantial uncertainty in the beginning, and a team can easily spin in circles without strong leadership and a structured process. The purpose of that process should be to develop

— Consensus on the target users, uses, and primary features of the new product line or service

### How One Successful Company Organizes Its Work Spaces

Continuum, a design powerhouse, has worked on many new market applications at the behest of large corporations. The rich and diverse results of its ethnographic user research, typically performed by an eclectic team of social scientists, engineers, and designers, are gathered into one of three design facilities (Boston, Milan, and Seoul). There, use case scenarios, photographs of the users' experiences, and concept sketches of products, packaging, and services are tacked onto massive display boards to create an information-intensive environment for brainstorming and concept integration. These work spaces can accommodate numerous fabricated prototypes. An example of a Continuum work space is shown in figure 13.4.

Thanks to its methods, creative people, and practical work spaces, this design firm has created a number of product breakthroughs for clients that include Procter and Gamble, BMW, Moen, and Reebok. Each of these breakthroughs (such as new Pampers and Swiffer) achieved an elegant blend of form and function.

FIGURE 13.4 An Information-Intensive Work Space
(Design Continuum, Inc. Reproduced with permission)

— The specific activities, month by month, needed to resolve market, technical, and financial uncertainty
— Accountability of team members assigned to do that work
— Continuous reintegration of that work into a unified whole, leading to not only products or services but also a business plan for launching and scaling them in the market. Every month, someone on your team (probably you as team leader) should spend a day revising the business plan to keep it current.
— Systematic feedback on that integrated whole from senior management. That feedback comes not only at the conclusion of the key decision gates identified in the previous chapters but more regularly to executives serving as board advisors.

This work must be controlled and managed to achieve a market test and subsequent full-scale launch. To facilitate that effort, I have developed a project status document, which is described here and available on www.fastpathmanagement.com as a downloadable template. That document reflects the practices of successful teams in the companies studied. The project status document identifies and integrates work across different functions (such as market research, R&D, manufacturing, marketing, and finance).

The document itself contains two summary pages and supporting pages of backup information.


### Page 1: Monthly Objectives and Meeting Times

The project status document provides a monthly statement of goals, challenges, and milestones.

— A list of key activities for the next 30 days. This information changes from month to month. The key activities list helps focus the team on what it must accomplish in the very near term.
— The times and locations of team meetings for the month.
— The when and where of pending senior management reviews.


### Page 2: Snapshot of the Emerging Business Plan

The second page provides an abstract of current agreements on key points of the business plan.

| | |
|---|---|
| Brand Name | New brand, subbrand |
| Target Buyers | By income, gender, location, etc. |

| Target Use | Highlight what's new or different |
| --- | --- |
| Price | Positioning, and any bundled or volume pricing |
| Product | Key features, including "good, better, best" |
| Channel | For launch, and then scale |
| Financials | Sales, gross margin, operating profit |

A team might wish to include lines for packaging and merchandizing strategies if its products go to the retail shelf. Summarizing this key information on a single page will encourage each team member and executive sponsor to refer to it often and use it as a guidepost. The fit of the different business dimensions on the single page should also be clear. In the beginning, many of these issues will be unresolved. That's acceptable. Simply listing them will remind people of choices that remain to be made.

## Page 3: Contact Sheet

The next section of the document is a contact sheet listing all official and ad hoc team members, the activities for which they are responsible, the roles they play, and how they can be reached. Email addresses, the URLs of Web-based team rooms, and so forth should be included. Include direct team members in one table and indirect or part-time team members on another. External suppliers should be listed in the second table.

## Page 4: Major Milestones by Calendar Date

A Gantt chart is useful here. Otherwise, a simple list of key milestones, month by month, leading up to launch, will suffice.

The remainder of the document breaks down each functional area into short-term tasks, task owners, and unresolved questions for each functional area. Each functional section should be kept to two pages of key bullet points.

Market Research
R&D
Supply
Logistics/Fulfillment
Distribution and Marketing Communications
Customer Implementation and Support
Business Planning and Financial Analysis

A systems or software project will have different functional areas, such as customer support and systems integration, than a consumer products company, which will have manufacturing and logistics. I also recommend that within the R&D section, explicit attention be paid to intellectual property tasks and outstanding questions as part of the prelaunch activity plan. Like a business plan, a project status document loses its value if it grows too large. Ten to 15 pages should be the limit.

## Dialogue with Senior Management

As team leader, you will interact with your executive board, which has responsibility for approving funding at key phases. These phases were the three "green lights" described in the previous chapter. Interactions with these executives should seek support for the *entire* plan and ward off micromanagement from executives who will look in on your venture perhaps once every six months or so.

### Dealing with the Executive Board for Major Phase Review Meetings

The executive board controls the purse strings, so be prepared to report to it at each major phase of the work. Your goal is to come away with a green light—and funding—for the next round of team activity.

To be effective in these meetings, a team leader must have the courage to *inform* executives on team decisions and results for that phase of development. This is much different than *asking* executives to make the team's decisions.

If executives are allowed to make product, process, pricing, and channel decisions, then two things are likely to happen. First, forward progress will be fatally linked to the executives' busy schedules. Your team will waste lots of time waiting and waiting for the decisions you need to move forward. Second, executive decisions in each functional area may be in conflict. For example, an executive may agree to your choice of target user but decide to market to that user through an existing distribution channel that is inconsistent with the best interests of the new business. It is far better to present a decision—such as an integrated plan for manufacturing—rather than ask executives where products should be manufactured.

Here is an example from a company I studied:

> We have decided to use a co-manufacturer for our initial runs because the volume projections cannot justify purchasing and installing our own production equipment at the outset. The intellectual property agreement with the co-manufacturer is very specific and, per our legal department, gives us solid protection. I have a copy of that agreement with me if you want to take a look at it.
>
> After the first 18 months, however, we can probably bring production in-house. I have provided you with our volume projections, related financial projections, our co-manufacturer agreement, and the estimated capital cost of doing our own manufacturing. Given these data, our team has decided that using a co-manufacturer makes the most sense. We need your support for that decision.

This is very different from going through a more traditional process where the vice president of manufacturing decides how to manufacture the product. That person will probably recommend a course of action that makes the most of current plant utilization—the manufacturing vice president's primary interest. Optimizing plant utilization may be best for a manufacturing department, but it might not be best for the new business, particularly if it burdens a fledgling P&L with manufacturing rates that are incredibly expensive for low-volume runs. In this and other critical areas, a team must jealously guard its decision-making authority and use its Board wisely for air cover.

Similarly, if a team defers to the vice president of sales on how to sell a new product line, it will almost surely be sold through the existing sales force and existing channels. That choice might suit the interests of the sales executive but may destroy a truly innovative new product line aimed at new users and uses. Often, a company's sales force knows how to sell only a certain type of product, whereas an innovation team has created something quite different, such as a system or a service. Or in a number of cases in my study, established sales forces had neither an incentive nor an interest in carrying low-volume new product lines.

Thus, you want the executive board to give its consent to a set of *integrated* decisions made by you and your team. Executives are certainly entitled to make refinements to your plan. In fact, I have personally witnessed executives tell teams, "Do more, go further, be bolder." However, avoid saying yes to one recommendation without first thinking through its implications for the new business as a whole. Rather, say, "That's a great idea. We'll come back next week with a reintegrated plan." The goal is to have the executive board confirm the entire plan, not its individual pieces.

At a more fundamental level, you must keep true ownership of your decision-making authority and your time—not pseudo-ownership. If you, as team leader, allow an executive to take over your project and, say, give it to corporate strategic planners for business plan development, the game will be lost. If management asks you to take on the project, but you do not get their agreement to have someone else take over your day-to-day responsibilities, allowing you to concentrate fully on the project, the game will be lost.

## Educate Executives on Users and Uses

To know the user is to know what to make and how to service customers. The innovation team will work long and hard developing that knowledge. Executives must share your understanding of users and uses. If they do not, each step of your journey will encounter cognitive turbulence. Executives who do not understand that new users are different than the company's current users will not understand or agree with your decisions with respect to pricing, marketing, and so forth. That understanding will be essential for you to sell your business plan to senior management, to drive through the choice of a new channel partner or price relative to established product lines, or the style and outlets for a marketing campaign. Decisions so obvious to you remain elusive to those executives who have yet to gain familiarity with the project. And it is they who hold the keys to the treasury.

Many of the teams studied made special efforts to educate their executives on the compelling needs of new target users and the business opportunities these suggested. Taking executives into the user's environment enhanced executive understanding and secured their support. Honda's weekend outing on San Onofre beach, as described in chapter 6, was the most striking example of bringing executives into the new users' world.

Enlightened executives understand the importance of understanding new customers and make such learning a regular part of their jobs. The Math-Works executives, for example, regularly interact with quantitative professionals in finance and the life sciences, not just engineers and scientists. IBM executives spend substantial amounts of time with lead customers, regardless of function. The more you can get executives to understand user frustrations and interests, the likelier they are to understand the value of your solution and provide support.

## Other Important Key Executive Advisors

Each team leader must identify and secure the advice and support of several key executives who might not be on the governing executive board for new market applications. Interaction with these executives is entirely different than the "informed consent" previously described. Here, the interaction is one of "I am thinking about bringing this person onto the team. What do you think?" or "What do you think are the pros and cons of working with a particular channel partner?" These are mentors and coaches with whom discussion safely turns to issues of personalities and politics. The team leader must nourish such relationships and remember to take specific steps to sustain them even as work accelerates. These advisor executives will help you make better decisions and become champions for your project among a broader executive audience.

## Is This for You?

Leading a new market application team is not for the faint of heart. It is also very different from leading a traditional functional unit. However, it can be one of the most professionally exciting and rewarding things any person can do. Whereas functional managers spend most of their time keeping operations running smoothly, innovation team leaders create something new. Instead of keeping the trains running on time, they extend the company's tracks into new and unexplored territory. That's a very different activity, and one that some people find mind-altering. "In this job," according to one IBM team leader, "you live your life to win. You have no time to take a breath. You're thrown curve balls every day. At some point, it gets in your veins and becomes like a drug. It would be hard to go back to a traditional job, where the challenges were straightforward."[3]

Leadership of new market applications development also holds many potential career rewards unavailable to others. Many managers linger in the shadows of their superiors, waiting for the boss to leave or move up so that they can be promoted. Their futures, in this sense, are tied to the fortunes of others over which they have little control. Leadership of a new market application project, in contrast, imparts substantial control over key market, technology, and financial decisions. The work can lead to ownership of a P&L and responsibility for the gestation, birth, and progress of a new business. This will bring you in direct and regular contact with top management, and this, in the truest sense, becomes your own fast path to growth.

My purpose in writing this book was twofold: to fuel the growth of companies and to accelerate individual careers. Both are closely aligned because companies grow only through the vision, commitment, and hard work of people like you.

Now that we are at the end of our journey, think for a moment about how your career might be different if you applied the new market application framework to your work and your company.

Whether your experience is in marketing, R&D, business development, or any other, taking a leadership role for a new product line or service development will change your working life. Yes, you will work harder than ever, but you will no longer be sitting on the sidelines like so many of your colleagues, waiting for a career break and frustrated that your ideas are going nowhere.

Do not expect opportunity to fall into your lap. You cannot sit back and wait for an executive to ask you to lead an enterprise growth initiative. You must *ask* for the job and secure your claim by sharing your vision for a new business possibility, and by demonstrating your commitment and *passion* for it.

Share your thoughts about what you perceive as new market opportunities and the potential to leverage competencies for growth. Find out where your idea fits within the executive's own vision for growth. Perhaps you can position your idea as a way to operationalize that executive's vision. And don't be afraid to share in a sincere way that burning desire to create a new stream of revenue.

Each new market application must have an evangelist who will champion the effort through thick and thin. We all take inspiration from others; mine often comes from students. The day before writing these final words, I watched a mid-level manager—whom we will call Bob—present a bold vision for a new market application for his company. Sitting before him was the executive team of his company. Bob had worked with colleagues on the concept for three days in an off-site, intensive innovation session. He presented the market opportunity, the user needs, and the "good, better, best" for newly proposed systems and services, as well as revenue estimations per target customer. Bob paused. Summing up his courage, he then stated in an impassioned and most heartfelt way, speaking directly to the president of his company, "Dave, *I must do this! We must do this*. It is a game-changing event for our business, and I will not rest until it is a success." The president had been waiting for this.

Bob got his charge to drop his day-to-day activity and focus instead on leading a team to seize the market opportunity. The next day—as I write these very words—he had begun to work toward 30-, 60-, and 90-day milestones to build prototypes, visit key accounts, and formalize the business plan. He had started building his legacy for the company. When we spoke, he said "If not now, Marc, when?" These are words for all of us to consider as we approach our jobs and our careers.

Do you have that level of passion? That level of commitment? If you do, you, too, can lead enterprise growth in your company.

## Notes

1. Jon R. Katzenbach and Douglas K. Smith, "The Wisdom of Teams," *Harvard Business Review*, 1993, March–April, 118.

2. Steven C. Wheelwright and Kim B. Clark, *Revolutionizing New Product Development* (New York: Free Press, 1992). See chapter 8.

3. David Garvin and Lynn Levesque, "Emerging Business Opportunities at IBM (A)," Case # 9-304-075 (Boston: Harvard Business School Publishing, 2005), 10.

# Underlying Technology Principles
# in IBM's Renewal

This appendix is provided for technology lovers interested in seeing more deeply how IBM managed its technology through the very difficult transitions described in chapter 1.

## R&D Strategies

These are strategies for the technological dimension of generational change. IBM uses these principles today as it looks toward the future.

### Platform Thinking

Platform thinking has been an essential part of IBM's renewal. As noted earlier, IBM bases each generation of a product line on a "reference architecture" that is clean-sheeted from generation to generation. While specific models are being produced based on current reference architecture, a new architecture is being designed by other staff to support the next generation of the product line. That next-generation design is driven by gathering fresh perspectives on evolving needs of major customers. This is how IBM continuously invests in its future. In each reference architecture are major subsystems and interfaces between the subsystems. IBM correctly views these subsystems and interfaces as its "product platforms." In this way, it is focused on sharing microprocessors, cache memory, I/O adapters, and electronics across multiple reference architectures—that is, different sizes and types of computers. This practice drives down cost of goods and cycle times for new model development.

A common error in thinking that I have seen at companies other than IBM, Honda, or Mars, is that managers persist in calling such reference architectures their platforms. This leads only to battles between competing divisions, each with its own product line architecture, as opposed to the sharing of modular subsystem platforms between product line architectures tuned to different applications. Before its near-death experience, IBM was the same way: S/390, AS400, and RS6000 were all different platforms, and there was very little reuse at the hardware level and absolutely none at the software level. Senior management at IBM does not let this happen anymore.

## Parallel Developments

One of the most impressive of all lessons came when senior management formed a task force—the ES2000 team—to plan the next-generation zSeries, just as the G2 was coming onto market and further developments on the G architecture were under way. In these days of relentless cost cutting, industry leaders must continue to invest in next-generation R&D, including the application of that R&D to new users and product uses. IBM is doing another ES2000 type of activity today, just as it is releasing new versions of its zSeries architecture. Parallel development is well understood across all functions within IBM—not just within R&D—for its business value.

## Microcode: A Safety Value for High-Risk Innovation

In the story told in chapter 1 IBM found a safety valve for high-risk developments on its most important product platform, the new CMOS microprocessors. That safety valve was (and remains) microcode, also known as firmware. Firmware is computer instructions that are permanently inserted into processor chips. These programmed chips can complement the general-purpose microprocessors within the computer. While the instruction set for the initial CMOS processors for G1, or the earliest zSeries, might not have had all the capabilities that the development teams desired, those features that could not be included in the general instruction set could still be delivered as microcode added later to the processors. Then, as the product line evolved, this special-purpose microcode could be replaced by engineering that functionality as part of the base general-purpose microprocessor. In the G1, for example, data compression and decimal-point operations were first implemented in microcode. The "real estate" or circuits on this first G series CMOS microprocessor were consumed by other core functions. By G4, that real estate had been expanded, and data compression and decimal-point operations became part of the core. Not all products across industry lend themselves as readily to a safety valve such as this, but if you can find one, use it!

## Binary Compatibility: Lessen the Customers' Pain across Generations of Technology

Also specific to the computer industry is IBM's strategy of preserving binary compatibility across multiple generations. A bank can run a decade-old S/390 database application (such as IMS) on its new, open systems, Linux-based System Z computers. Binary compatibility can be performed cleverly, but achieving it still requires focus and tremendous attention to detail.

## Balanced System Design

This is perhaps the most important technology learning from IBM. *Balanced system design* became a distinctive competency of the IBM server development team. IBM made sure that when it increased the MIPS of its microprocessors, it also increased the speed of its cache, the throughput of its I/O adapters, and so forth. In contrast, during the 1990s, the rest of the industry was focused primarily on adding more and more microprocessors to their respective systems. In high-volume applications, all this additional microprocessor computing capacity would choke the other important subsystems and, in worst-case volume spikes, cause system failure. IBM lives in the world of high volume. Balanced system design was the only way to ensure high reliability and consistent throughput in high-performance applications. Every product or system architecture, in any industry, can benefit from balanced system design.

## Focused R&D Effort

IBM carefully considers those subsystems it should continue to develop—such as microprocessors—and those subsystems it should buy from outside vendors—such as cooling fans or cabinetry. Over the past decade, the focusing of R&D activity has become a core part of IBM's strategy. The ability to create proprietary intellectual property is a key decision criterion. If IBM can see a worthy goal and develop patented or trade secret IP, it will invest; if it cannot see this prospect, management seeks an external supplier.

For example, in 2006 IBM announced the results of microprocessor research that will allow it to *triple* the performance of current lithography technology—the etching of circuits on silicon. In February 2006, IBM reported its breakthrough: Its scientists had created high-quality line patterns using deep-ultraviolet (DUV, 193 nm) optical lithography—the technology used to "print" circuits on chips—that were just 29.9 nm wide. The current width used in the industry at that time for circuit line patterns was 90 nanometers. This breakthrough was believed to give the industry at least another seven years for using photolithography for chip manufacturing and still keep pace with rapidly increasing performance requirements.

As a counterexample, the decision to source Linux was based on the appreciation that hundreds, if not thousands, of companies were already greatly skilled in core Linux operating system development. Also, Linux by its nature is open source software that shuns the creation of proprietary IP.

Although microprocessors and operating systems are equally important in the entire mainframe systems solution, IBM has chosen a different development strategy for each. When IBM invests, its goal is to create world-beating technology that can serve as the foundation for a major subsystem in one its product lines or services. The result is to more sharply define its R&D focus.

## The Product Line Architectures for Three Generations of IBM Mainframes

Figure A.1 shows the reference architecture for the H series. If you look closely, you can see a tight coupling of the central processors to the cache memory. Every processor had its own cache. (The subsequent generations would feature banks of shared cache.) Further, each central processor was accompanied by a coprocessor to assist scientific and numerically intensive workloads (termed "vector processing"), and other processors had hardware-based encryption. Each processing engine was placed in its own thermal cooling "package." The master processors controlling all operations in the H series—called "storage control units"—were also bipolar designs. These particular units had microcode that multiplexed data streams between processors and cache memory. This was referred to as *multipoint switching*, and it was marvel of systems engineering.[1] The old H series also had dedicated I/O processors to manage the movement of data from memory out to adapters feeding storage devices and other computers. This particular subsystem also had a separate processor design.

The G architecture came next. It was based on CMOS microprocessor technology. The new G architecture, shown in figure A.2, was a simpler design than

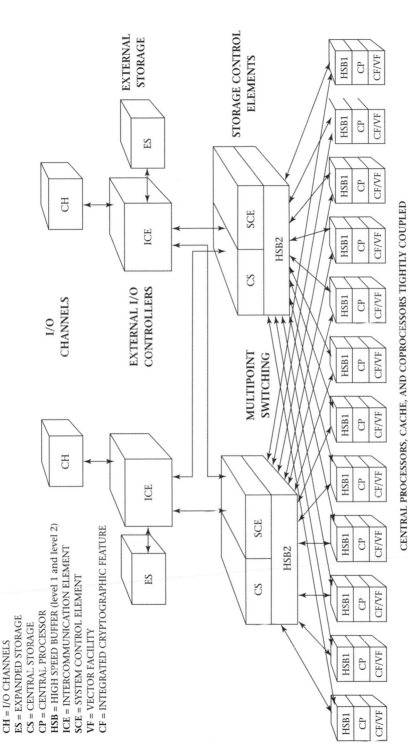

CH = I/O CHANNELS
ES = EXPANDED STORAGE
CS = CENTRAL STORAGE
CP = CENTRAL PROCESSOR
HSB = HIGH SPEED BUFFER (level 1 and level 2)
ICE = INTERCOMMUNICATION ELEMENT
SCE = SYSTEM CONTROL ELEMENT
VF = VECTOR FACILITY
CF = INTEGRATED CRYPTOGRAPHIC FEATURE

EXTERNAL
STORAGE

STORAGE CONTROL
ELEMENTS

I/O
CHANNELS

EXTERNAL I/O
CONTROLLERS

MULTIPOINT
SWITCHING

CENTRAL PROCESSORS, CACHE, AND COPROCESSORS TIGHTLY COUPLED

FIGURE A.1  The H Series Bipolar Mainframe Architecture
(IBM. Reproduced with permission)

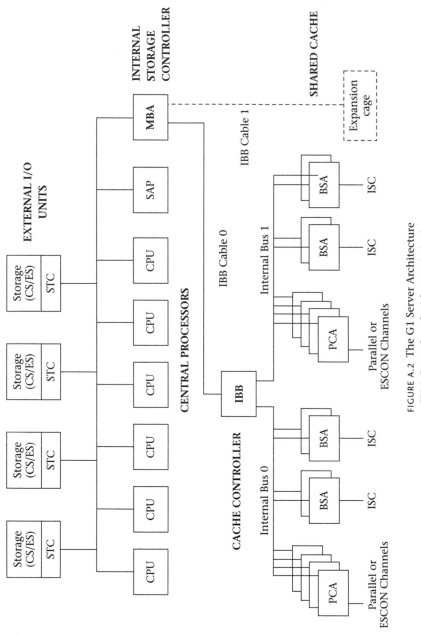

FIGURE A.2 The G1 Server Architecture (IBM. Reproduced with permission)

its older H series counterpart. Gone was the multipoint switching between processors, channels, and memory in the H series. The new architecture moved to a single-bus design where memory bus adapters (MBA in the block diagram), central processors (CPU), I/O processors (termed system assist processors or SAP), and storage controllers (STC) all accessed main storage through one electronic channel. This single bus passed data, address information, and controls between the various system elements. All the I/O adapters connected through an internal bus buffer (IBB) to the rest of the system. But most important was the fact that the unique, bipolar processor design of the H series was replaced with a new 31-bit CMOS processor (that's right, 31-bit, not the industry standard 32 bits—so that IBM's legacy software would function without significant change). This processor served as a common platform for all other processors in the G series. Then, microcode personalized the chips as either processors for computations or I/O. That common processor—a true product platform—was called "Picasso." Also, the new G architecture emphasized shared cache memory.[2]

In chapter 1, we described the incredible effort made to reimplement multipoint switching for the intelligent resource director in the zSeries. There were other major subsystem innovations. Figure A.3 shows the zSeries architecture. The intelligent resource director was contained on microcoded processors labeled as SCD chips in the center of the figure. The reader can also see two banks of PUs in the diagram. These are the processing units, up to 16 of which were used to run applications for the first zSeries machine, called the z900. Today, there can be many more. Other processor units in the diagram were used for I/O processing. All of these new microprocessors were 64-bit, RISC-based CMOS designs. Internal to IBM, these processors were called the Blueflame chip. The G series 31-bit processor could access only two gigabytes of random-access memory. Blueflame could access as much memory as IBM chose to place in the box. This would come in the form of banks of cache memory, as shown in figure A.3 In the z900, high-end configurations provided 64 gigabytes of internal cache. Like its predecessors, the zSeries architecture also featured arrays of cryptographic coprocessors. These cards are essentially tamperproof.

## Subsystem Evolution over Three Generations of Mainframe Architecture

These subsystem innovations are summarized in figure A.4. Although the table cannot do justice to the amount of work performed by IBM's engineers over the decade, it does provide a convenient summary of innovation within the mainframe product line.

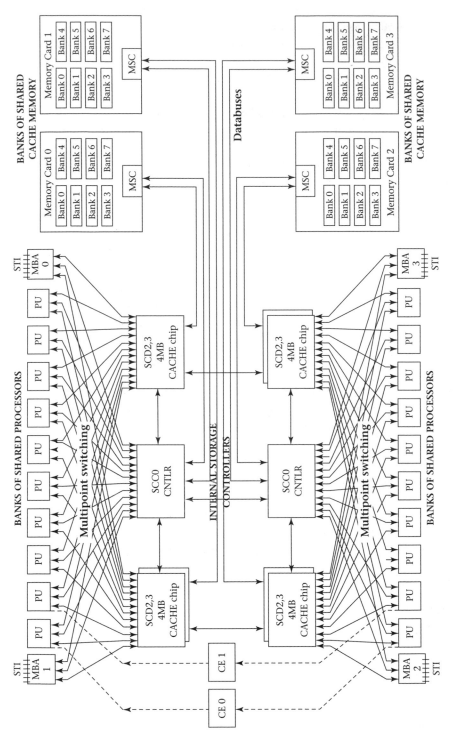

FIGURE A.3 The zSeries Architecture
(IBM. Reproduced with permission)

| Subsystem | H | G | Z |
|---|---|---|---|
| **Central Processors**<br>The circuits executing specific instructions | Bipolar circuits | CMOS circuits—31 bit | CMOS—64 bit. An entirely new design. |
| **Storage Controllers**<br>Switch data flows between different processors, cache memory, and I/O channels | Bipolar-based, with cross-point checking | CMOS-based 31 bit, starting with no cross-point checking | CMOS—64 bit, with cross-point checking. A complete overhaul. |
| **I/O Processors**<br>Coordinates the data flow on the I/O channel to networks and storage devices | Bipolar-based, with special microcode | CMOS-based 31 bit with new microcode | CMOS—64 bit with major revisions to microcode |
| **Cryptograpy Processors**<br>Encryption/security | Bipolar-based, also with special microcode with frequent security revisions | CMOS-based 31 bit with new microcode, also followed by frequent updates | CMOS—64 bit, with programmable encryption. |
| **Cache Memory**<br>Shared memory used by processors for executing instructions | L1, processor embedded high-speed cache, and banks of full shared L2 cache. | L1 cache and banks of independent L2 cache that was not fully shared | L1 cache and even larger banks of independent L2 cache. |
| **Input/Output Adapters**<br>Communication interfaces for various networking protocols | ESCON, parallel interfaces microcode in bipolar processors | ESCON, parallel interfaces on CMOS processors | Added IP, Token Ring, and Fiber Channel (Ficon). |
| **Power Supply**<br>Electronics | Massive, redundant chilled liquid cooling system, with direct feeds from the building facilities | Complete overhaul; mostly fans for air cooling with a small closed-loop cooling system | Incremental improvements. |
| **Housing**<br>Cabinetry, buttons, and switches | Large, approximately 800 square feet per machine | Reconfigured, and much smaller; about 50 square feet per machine. | Refreshed design. |
| **Service Processor**<br>Diagnostics and service communications | Dedicated "minicomputer" running VM, and microcoded applications | An IBM PC running OS/2, with applications developed in C | A Thinkpad, running OS/2 and moving to Linux, developed in C++. |

FIGURE A.4  Three Generations of Subsystem Innovation at IBM

Referring to figure A.4, the major subsystems in what IBM used to call its mainframes and now calls its high-end servers are as follows.

1. *Central processors* contained circuits designed to execute particular instructions. Each processor had thousands, and now millions, of logic circuits. Over time, these have switched from bipolar circuits to CMOS circuits and become denser in terms of circuits per square inch. By 2006, the basic 64-bit processor (code-named Blueflame, manufactured in Burlington, Vermont) in the Z machine combined 47 million transistors on a chip.

2. *Storage controllers* coordinate the activities of all the other processors. These storage controllers are really the master processors or brains of the computer, switching data flows between different processors, cache memory, and I/O channels. The transition of H to G was one of a complete redesign from bipolar to CMOS, equipped with different microcoded programs. The H was actually more sophisticated in terms of cross-pointing[1] checking between different elements in the architecture. This complexity was abandoned for the rapid new product introduction of the G, reintroduced at the tail of the G series, and taken to a new level of performance in the zSeries with 64-bit architecture. This was the focus of the major performance breakthrough for the zSeries. Called intelligent resource directors, these storage controllers dynamically switched capacity between different controllers and channels.

3. *I/O processors* coordinate the data flow on the I/O channel to networks and storage devices. These I/O processors also went through the complete redesign from a bipolar circuitry to CMOS. For the zSeries, the 64-bit Blueflame processor was the platform but with different microcoded programming.

4. *Cryptography processors*, special-purpose custom-designed chips, off-load functions from the general-purpose processor. These chips also moved from bipolar to CMOS. This is a fast-moving market. IBM has always excelled in this subsystem, using a variety of encryption standards including "triple data encryption standard" and double key message authentication. Traditionally a requirement for financial services OLTP, the Web introduces all sorts of new complexities and demands. IBM continues to increase the complexity of its encryption algorithms and has expanded the hardware platform to include hard-coded and programmable encryption algorithms.

5. *Cache memory* is random-access memory used by all types of processors. Over the H, G, and Z, these have become faster and denser. This will

continue, and IBM still manufacturers its own high-capacity chips in Burlington, Vermont.

6. *Internal bus to I/O*: A major design change with the internal bus that transmits data between the input-output adapters occurred when the move was made to the G series. Termed the "self-timed interface" (STI), this bus allowed different-speed processor subsystems to interface with the same I/O hardware structure. This allowed IBM in the G series to upgrade processor subsystem designs from one generation to another but not have to modify the existing I/O adapters, so design work was minimized. New adapters could be introduced to take advantage of bandwidth increases in this bus without driving redesigns of existing adapters. This technology was carried forward into the zSeries, albeit with greatly improved bandwidth—at 24 GB per second, it provides a threefold increase over the fastest G series machine.

7. *Input-output adapters* (to disks or networks): To go from H to G, engineers had to move the entire basic I/O infrastructure (IBM ESCON, parallel interfaces) from a bipolar implementation to a CMOS processor and microcode design. In G, designs had to be enhanced to include networking protocols such as Ethernet, ATM, FDDI, and Token ring. For the zSeries, adapter redesigns were required for 64-bit architecture inclusion, plus greater use of industry standard PCI (peripheral component interconnect) adapters to ensure that the platform can more quickly adopt performance or function improvements.

8. *Power supply subsystem*: There were many different individual power supplies in the H machines because of the bipolar technology. Each rack or cabinet frame typically had several processor boards, with each board surrounded by a thermal cooling unit. In the G and zSeries, the CMOS technology uses so much less power that simpler, more efficient power subsystems can used within the servers. Today, there are a combination of fans for air cooling and a closed-loop cooling system for the processors and cache (with an environmentally friendly equivalent to Freon) that enhances performance and reliability.

9. *The frame* is the cabinetry, which is obviously a lot less metal from H to G or the new zSeries.

10. *The service processor* performs the diagnostics and maintenance on the main element. In H, this was a small, general-purpose IBM office computer repackaged along with an identical computer (for redundancy purposes) packaged into a separate frame. It ran its own special VM-based operating system, with microcode software applications! This was obviously not the best environment for building flexible systems

management applications for IT managers. Under G, this was moved to an IBM PC running OS/2, and the applications were redeveloped in C. Today, the service processor is a nice-looking ThinkPad (again with a duplicate for redundancy) and downloadable software applications. It remains on an OS/2 base but is moving to Linux.

These data show that modularity and innovation at the level of major subsystems have clearly been key drivers in IBM's engineering success. Generational improvement in complex systems such as mainframes is most often driven—and most effectively managed—by step-order improvements to the major systems in the product line architecture. These are powerful, yet pragmatic, lessons for innovation and enterprise growth.

### Notes

1. Multipoint switching was dropped from the subsequent G series because of time cycle pressures but reintroduced later in the zSeries as the intelligent resource director. It is an important part of the "secret sauce" of IBM's new mainframe servers.

2. G. S. Rao, T. A. Price, C. L. Rao, and S. Repka, "IBM S/390 Parallel Enterprise Servers G3 and G4," *IBM Journal of Research and Development*, 1997, 41(4/5).

# Index